The Ghost City of San Luis Island

By Eileen M. Benitz Wagner

Based on the information I gathered during my research, to the best of my knowledge, I believe this book to be accurate.

Dedication

I would like dedicate this book to my family and friends who gave unending support to the assembly this book and to the saving of Texas history.

Eileen M. Benitz Wagner

Table of Contents

Preface

Having lived on San Luis Island in the Resort Community of Treasure Island for more than thirty years, coupled with the love I have of the history, some factual (and some maybe not so factual) stories of the area led me to compile this book.

Maps shows San Luis Island to be an 'island,' then part of a peninsula, then back to being an island many times over the past one hundred and fifty years are indicative of the very delicate shorelines depicted repeatedly throughout this book.

Finding the source of the information was of foremost importance to assure the facts are as accurate as possible. Untold stories from family bibles and letters bring new light to the importance of this barrier island to Texas history.

Author's Acknowledgments

Judge Robert Lowry for being the first to encourage me to write this book and sharing with me his stories and his collections of our early history. Judge Lowry was a Director of the Texas Historical Foundation, Historical Survey Committee. He was very excited that I might be able to capture the history of San Luis Pass.

Doug Lowry for the wonderful photos from his childhood gift of an 8 mm camera that saved the photos of our water tower and early photos of the Vacek Bridge being built.

Harry Bowles for gifting his personal records during his presidency of Treasure Island Municipal Utility District.

Caron Dobbs for sharing her collections of photos, postcard, and many hours of reading each new discovery I found.

Ken and Anne Nutt for gifting a copy of the original Treasure Island color brochure.

Keith Chunn for gifting a copy of the J. B. Cassidy color brochure and many stories of the early years.

Michael Bailey, Curator, and Jamie Murray, Information Services Coordinator, Brazoria County Historical Museum for their endless support, information, and so much encouragement. Michael Bailey for proof reading for accuracy.

Roger Brown for sharing the wonderful aerial photograph that was left in the home he purchased from Meyer and Francis Jacobson.

Evelyn Austermiller for her endless efforts to help me locate a photo of all past presidents of Treasure Island Municipal Utility District.

Welcome Wilson Sr., for sharing his photos and so much information concerning the late 1960s and early 1970s. Welcome Wilson, Sr., President of Jamaica Corporation, developed Tiki Island, Spanish Grant, Jamaica Beach, Sea Isle, Terramar Beach, as well as Treasure Island. At present, Welcome Wilson serves his second term as Chairman of the Board of Regents of the University of Houston. Wilson is also Chairman of the Board of GSL, a Welcome Corporation.

Mr. K. S. (Bud) Adams, for the wonderful photos and maps. Mr. Nat Hickey, for the unbelievable aerial photos.

I sincerely wish to thank Fannie Mae Follett Gilbert for her endless information, artwork, and support throughout this project. Fannie Mae is a joy to know and has an amazing memory for details regarding San Luis. I would never have been able to find so much information from our early years without Fannie Mae. Fannie Mae who has worked so closely with me while writing this book, turned ninety years young in April of this year, 2011. When she was eighty-three, Fannie Mae participated in a fashion show for evening gowns, thinking to herself, "This will no doubt be the last fashion show for me." Now, last week, May 2011, a month into her ninetieth year, Fannie Mae participated in another fine upscale evening gown fashion show! I say, "You go Girl!"

The Follett family loved San Luis and their adjoining Peninsula, and endured all the elements, both good and bad, for nearly half a century. Judy Willy Bielstein, a descendant of the Follett family, for sharing her wonderful stories.

A special thanks to Eleanor Stevens Vaughn for sharing her original 1940's newspaper article regarding the beached whale at Surfside and the fabulous effort she helped in acquiring the photo's of all three Stevens men that owned San Luis Island.

Ron Paul for the cover photo.

To all my other dear friends and neighbors who have stood by me over these many years of research and writing, and who promised to buy the book, no matter the cost."

Ronald D. Livingston for the original historical edit.

Judge John Willy, Pre-Reader

Judy Willy Bielstein, Pre-Reader

Mickie McCunn, Pre-Reader

One of the most important acknowledgements is to Harvey Gover. He received his Master's Degree in Library and Information Science from the University of Texas, at Austin. Harvey found time to edit this book in addition to his daily job as Assistant Campus Librarian for the Max E. Benitz Memorial Library, Washington State University Tri-Cities in Richland, Washington. Harvey was ably assisted in the final editing stages by Robert J. Stalberger, III, Benitz Library Working Scholar for 2011. Harvey took on my massively unorganized manuscript and created a manuscript dedicated to great detail—I salute you, Harvey!

Lindsey Backen, a novelist, playwright and freelancer, who collaborated to smooth the flow of text and ideas.

Patricia Newsom's input for the Geo Textile project and the Waste Treatment Plant are both vital to the history of Treasure Island.

Harry de Butts for providing clairvoyant interpretation and linguistic realignment to these many pages.

Lew Fincher - Pre-reader

Vice President/Founder Hurricane Consulting Inc.

Past President – The Houston Chapter of the American Meteo-
rological Society • Founder and Former Chairperson – The DuPont
Hurricane Roundtable & it's Coastal Severe Weather Alert Team •
Chairperson – The National Hurricane Conference's Private Industry
Committee • Awarded the National Hurricane Conference's "Out-
standing Achievement Award" • Awarded the National Weather Ser-
vice's Southern Region "Special Service Award" • Awarded the Du-
Pont "Safety Gold Cross" • Awarded the DuPont AG-Products Chem
Safety-Health-Environmental (SHE) Excellence Award • Member –
The American Association for the Advancement of Science • Associate
Member – The American Meteorological Society • Member – National
Weather Association • Member – Texas Gulf Coast Emergency Man-
agement Association • Member – Emergency Management Associa-
tion of Texas • Member – Galveston County Historical Commission

Dr. Cary J. Mock - Racers Storm Track Map

Dr. Cary Mock is a graduate of the University of Oregon (1994) and
is currently an associate professor at the University of South Carolina
in their Department of Geography. As a synoptic and paleoclimatologist, Dr. Mock's research links atmospheric patterns with climate variations (El Nino/Artic Oscillation in particular), and recently received a
grant from the National Science Foundation to study climatic extremes
during the 19th century. Featured in many professional publications, it
is our pleasure to have Dr. Cary Mock join the Southwest Pennsylvania
Chapter of the American Meteorology Society on Friday, November 3,
2006 in EST 110 at 2 p.m..

Stan Blazyk

Stan Blazyk is a weather expert and the author of A Century of Galveston Weather: 1900-1999 People and the Elements on a Barrier Island

Sincerely,
Eileen M. Benitz Wagner

Introduction

Just beyond the West End of Galveston Island, Texas, lies the barrier island of San Luis which is created by two passes, Big Pass & Little Pass. Big Pass, once known as Folletts Pass was renamed San Luis Pass. Little Pass opened and closed many times during the next 150 years of record keeping. Depending on hurricanes and tides, it is either a separate island or connected to Stephen F. Austin Peninsula, later renamed Follett's Island, as noted in Brazoria County Abstract 29. This expanse reaches westward to Old Velasco and the Brazos River. San Luis was once a major building block and a key link to the success of immigrant families looking for opportunities to build a new life in Texas in the mid 1800s. These were a special breed of people, described in the 1906 obituary of A.G. Follett as "the matchless heroism that distinguished this race of pioneers who blazed the path of progress and civilization and carved an empire out of the wilds of Texas."

The area was once inhabited by approximately 13 Native American Indian Tribes. It was home to the Karankawa Tribe. Known as a coastal tribe, they traveled the bays, estuaries and the coastline. The map "The Ancient Domain of the Karankawa Indians" indicates a settlement at San Luis. As early as 1855, wars and disease had taken their toll and no Indian Tribes remained.

Following Christopher Columbus, additional Spanish expeditions set out to explore the Western Hemisphere. Among them were a few names such as Coronado, Cassidy, De Soto and Moscosco. When Alvar Nunez Cabeza de Vaca shipwrecked at San Luis in 1528, he was credited giving it the name "la Isla de Malhado" (the island of Bad Luck). Historians still differ on whether he named Galveston Island or San Luis Island. De Vaca is also credited with the naming of the Brazos River "Los Brazos de Dios" or the Arms of God, because of the fresh water it provided for his shipwrecked crew.

Then in 1684, Robert Cavelier, Sieur de La Salle, with a crew of 280 men and colonists sailed past San Luis with his fleet of four ships. They were to found a French colony just to the South on Matagorda Bay. This colony failed. Mutineers murdered LaSalle and seven members of his crew in 1687. The year 1689, Spanish soldiers under Alonso De Leon, governor of Coahuila, New Spain, searched the region in vain to locate the French colony in Spanish territory.

A magnificent oil painting of the LaSalle voyage near the coastline of Louisiana would have looked quite similar to the coastline of Spanish Texas. Additional expeditions by Carlos de Sigtlenza y Go'ngora in 1689, and Joaquin de Orobio y Basterra in 1727 were sent to learn the truth regarding the French occupancy of this territory. Parts of the colony were finally located, quite by accident, in the late 1990s.

An early 1775s the Western Coast of Louisiana map shows San Luis to be an island. Here Galveston Bay was known as "Baye de St. Louis." The name of "Galveston Bay" was given in 1783 by Viceroy, Don Bernardo de Galvez. An 1803 water depth chart by Aaron Arrowsmith notes the opening to San Luis Pass as very shallow. Galveston Bay on this chart is also very shallow. "Isle St. Luis" is the name used here for "Galveston Island," while "San Francisco PT" is what we know today as Follett's Island. An 1805 Spanish map shows "Island of St Louis or Galvezton" to be alternative names for Galveston Island.

The charisma of a man known as "The Gentleman Pirate," Jean Lafitte used Galveston as his home base from 1817-1820. Many romantic stories have been told about him. He was tall, had pale skin, dark hair and hazel eyes. He was the son of a French father and Spanish mother. Though known as a "lover" not a "fighter," he truly was a smuggler and a privateer. During the storm of 1818, he gave his home, named Maison Rouge, to be used as a hospital for the French Colonist. Galvestonians loved Jean Lafitte. When he left Galveston in 1820, he burned his home. Rumor has it that he buried his treasures all along the coastline, maybe even at San Luis Island.

Another historical figure capitalized on the potential of what the land could yield, rather than what it could conceal. In 1821, Moses Austin received a land grant award of 200,000 acres to place 300 colonists, sparking the beginning of great change for the entire region. Known as an empresario or administrator, Moses died before his envisioned plans could be completed. Upon his sudden illness and death, his son Stephen F. Austin, fulfilled his father's dreams. Within this grant territory and part of that dream, the City of San Luis would soon spring up. This city would become very important link to the Import and Export market of the world. The thriving trade continued, even as storms began to shift the island's boundaries, joining it to the mainland and breaking it off again. The French map, "L'Amerique Septentrionale Alexandre Emile Lapie 1830," gives no indication that San Luis is an island.

Terrific narratives remain as testimony of nature's fury. Francis Rebecca Bouldin Spragins Brown Raine described the terrible 1832 storm after she and her family arrived in Texas for the first time. Her personal letter explains how the Brazos River Flood caught everyone by surprise. The worst part of this flood was that it spread cholera throughout the region and reduced the population to near nothing.

Along with natural disasters, the island saw more than its fair share of action during many wars. When General Santa Anna lost the Battle at San Jacinto in 1836, he and fellow prisoners received board by Isaac Coleman Hoskins, who owned a hotel at Velasco. A handwritten receipt show the costs charged per day from May 10 to June 1.

A new settlement offering 10 to 40 acre lots on the West End of Galveston Island in 1838 brought families with household goods, livestock and great plans for a wonderful future. Among them was John Bradbury Follett, a shipbuilder, who ended up playing a very important role in the success of the City of San Luis.

The City of San Luis begins in 1839. Both, strong men and women led the way to develop the City of San Luis. Key leaders were Matthew Hopkins, George Hammeken and Mary Austin Holley, cousin to Stephen F. Austin.

Matthew Hopkins purchased a League of Land and formed the San Luis Stock Company. As this history unfolds, forty homes were built, a post office was established, construction began for the Brazos and Galveston Railroad, and beginnings of a "hand dug" canal to the mainland were initiated. Even construction of a bridge to the mainland began. Two newspapers called San Luis home.

Industry prevailed. The island employed bridge builders, homebuilders, cattle and sheep ranchers, as well as fresh produce farmers. Hotels were built and two large warehouses. The finest wares were for sale at General Stores. The Navy once planned to move its homeport from Galveston to San Luis. By the early 1840s, the City of San Luis boasted of a population of 2,000 souls and became an exciting hub for shipping and receiving of goods. A new 1,000-foot wharf could dock up to ten tall ships and sailing vessels at one time. Manufactured goods were imported, while wooden barges, sloops, wagon teams of horse, mule and oxen transported fresh produce, livestock, sugar cane and cotton for export. A cotton gin produced 5000 bales for shipment at one time throughout the world. The climate was temperate, fertile prairies and rich loam river bottomlands could grow almost anything.

During each era, many people were important to the success of the City of San Luis. One family from the 1840s stands out; the John Bradbury Follett family. He received a contract to build the first steamship built in Texas. The well-known hotel, the "Halfway House" located on Peninsula Point, halfway between Velasco and Galveston, was owned and operated by his wife, Anne Louise Follett. Their son Alexander Glass Follett designed and received a patent for a "seawall" that he hoped to have built along Galveston's shore 14 years before the 1900 storm. Sadly, this was never built. He and his brother Alonzo Follett ran the very important ferry between Galveston Island to San Luis Island and San Luis Island to the Peninsula. Their "Uncle Joe" who was Captain of the schooner Lucille, recalled in a letter the forty to fifty foot swells at San Luis Pass during the 1900 storm. The strongest recorded hurricane in history devastated lives and lands, but even its influence was diminished by the arrival of war. During the Civil War, San Luis Island, Mud Island and Titlum Tatlum Bayou were an important stronghold for the Confederate Army.

You will feel the strength of character from those who experienced great heartbreak as they lost everything to the violent storms, and even worse yet, life and family from wars and disease. A combination of events led to the demise of the City of San Luis: Little Pass sanded in from storms and hurricanes. Low economic growth throughout the Republic stunted progress, while hardship and disease ran rampant. San Luis City became a ghost town. It remained a barren island for nearly a century. Then in the 1950s, developers saw a great future for a resort community. The economy in the United States was booming again and owning a second home was all the rage. Developers K.S. (Bud) Adams, Welcome Wilson, Sr., and J.B. Cassidy envisioned grandeur with hi-rise condos, yacht marinas, air strips shopping centers and more. Their vision of San Luis Island and the Follett's Island Peninsula was a place for fun in the sun not far from the major city, Houston.

Though cultures have risen and fallen on the island, one factor remains constant throughout the centuries. This entire book turns your attention to maps of this barrier island and how the shorelines are in continuous change. Tides, hurricanes and man continue to shape and erode this land. For every action man has instigated, it is accompanied by a reaction. Some reactions have not always been favorable. You will see how storms rule the very existence of those who call this home. The land then dictates how or even whether man can live there.

Ownership of San Luis Island

Spain, Moses Austin, Stephen F. Austin 1821- Dec. 27, 1836 (On the same year he died, the Republic of Texas was formed.)

William G. and Eliza M. Hill (Estate of Stephen F. Austin) 1836- July

19, 1839 -? Matthew Hopkins and Associates July 19, 1839 - (Railroad and Stock Company formed and later reverted to the Estate of Stephen F. (William G & Eliza Hill) at which point Pennell bought the land.) Stevens Family - 86 years- 1876 - 1962 Ownership of San Luis/Treasure Island San Luis Island Corporation - 1962 - 1967 Jamaica Corporation - 1967 - 1971 TIMUD - 1973 - (Sales were made through real estate brokers)

Introduction Map[1]
BCHM Accession Number 1863.052.0001 1910 Book -"Hammond's Handy Atlas of the World"

Chapter 1
Karankawa Indians, Early Explorers
to the Development of the City of San Luis

Dictated by violent tropical storms and epic hurricanes, San Luis Island has transformed itself from being a peninsula to an island and back to a peninsula again many times in just 150 years. It is known either as an island or part of a peninsula extending eastward from the mouth of the Brazos River, Texas. As a barrier island, it was created by two passes from the Back Bay which emptied into the Gulf of Mexico, San Luis Pass and Little Pass.

We can only speculate how many times in the past that this land has changed shapes.

It is difficult to note any impact to the island from storms during 1818, 1867 and 1875 when there were no residents living there.[2] Similar to the peninsula, the water passageways often change width and depth, enhancing or encumbering its explorers or inhabitants.

This small island's "Little Pass," located on the west side of the island was once thirty-four feet deep where its waters met the Gulf of Mexico. Little Pass has opened and closed many times during recorded history. A second "Little Pass" was mapped slightly to the west of the original pass. The fragile sandy bottom is in continuous change, as is its shoreline.

Despite its variance the island has long held an intrigue for people searching for a chance to explore and expand. San Luis was once a major building block and a key link to the successful migration of immigrant families looking for opportunities to build a new life in Texas in the mid 1800s.

Early explorers mapped and named San Luis and its tributaries according to their personal choice; some Spanish, some French, some British and some Mexican, finally keeping with the names in use today.

The ability to navigate from the Gulf of Mexico to the inland waters was definitely a positive factor. Brazoria County had numerous navigable openings to the gulf waters. Relative to San Luis Island were the Brazos River, Oyster Creek and San Luis Pass. Though Oyster Creek no

1

longer directly enters the Gulf, it was once used for navigation.

> *Oyster creek is a stream of seventy-five miles in length which enters the gulf seven miles west of San Luis Harbor. It has it source near the Brazos, in Fort Bend County and runs parallel with that stream.*

In the early years traveling over coastal land was cumbersome at best. Mule- and ox-drawn wagons would bog down easily in the marsh-like terrain and sandy shorelines. Navigating by water was by far the method of choice. The inhabitants of the island learned to accommodate their traveling and trading according to the current waterways.

The waters surrounding San Luis Island are its lifeline. The position and depth of these creeks, rivers and bay inlets dictate where commerce and recreation can exist.

One of the semi-permanent features is the Brazoria County peninsula, which was originally named "Stephen F. Austin Peninsula," and later was renamed Follett's Island. Stretching southwest of San Luis Island was Old Velasco and the Brazos River, approximately fourteen miles.

Other landmarks have disappeared altogether. What is known today, currently nonexistent, was Follett's Pass. Unlike what we see today, Follett's Pass entered the Gulf of Mexico between Peninsula Point and San Luis Island.

The portion of *Follett's Pass* which turned directly east on the northern shore of San Luis Island was once known as *Mud Island Pass* and emptied into *San Luis Pass*. The portion continuing to the Gulf was named *Little Pass*. Little Pass, which separated the east end of Follett's Island Peninsula and the west side of San Luis Island, flowed straight to the Gulf of Mexico, thus making San Luis an island. Little Pass has opened and closed many times over the 150 years of record keeping, sometimes creating a second opening to the Gulf of Mexico.

Later, Follett's Pass and Mud Island Pass were renamed Cold Pass. Some historians also reference other names, including Coal Pass and Cole Pass. Generally, "Cold Pass" is used. The origin of the name is unknown. San Luis Pass was at one time referred to as Big Pass by the locals. Cold Pass originates in *Christmas Bay, Brazoria County*. This bay held the name of *Oyster Bay* until some time in the 1970s when the construction of the Texas link of the Intracoastal Waterway was underway, at which time it became Christmas Bay. *Christmas Point* was once named *Christian's Point*. (See Follett's Island Map)

Two bayous figure largely into the equation, Bastrop Bayou feeds fresh water into Bastrop Bay; Titlum-Tatlum Bayou flows from Bastrop

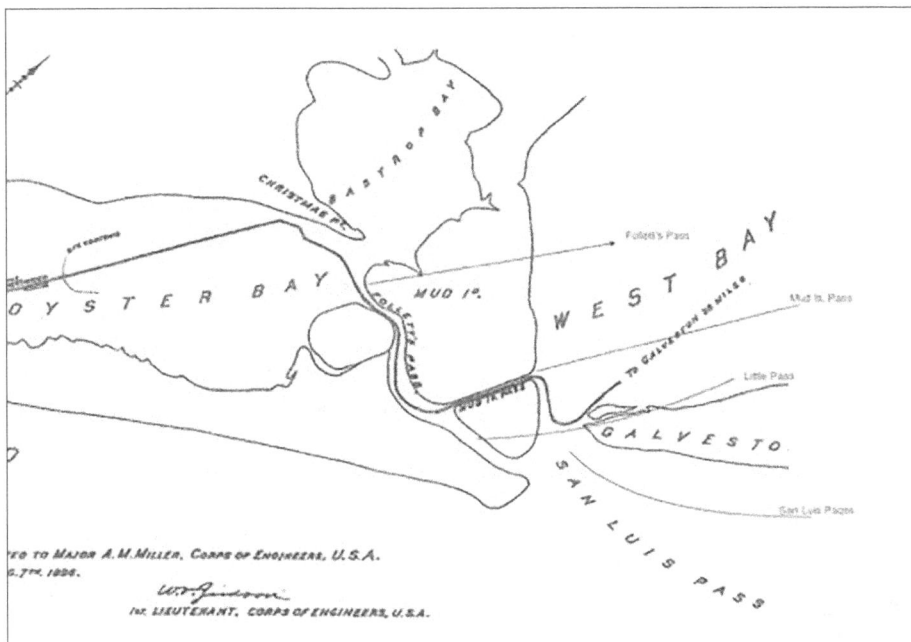

Follett's Pass Map[3]

Bay into the lower end of Cold Pass, just before Cold Pass flows into San Luis Pass. Titlum-Tatlum Bayou separates Mud Island to the south-southwest and Moody Island to the north-northeast.

Local legend gives us a glimpse into 19th century humor. The name, "Titlum-Tatlum" may be explained in the following manner;

> *that it was a literary reference in a poem (or book), and that the island was named by early settler James Follett Shannon because he just liked the sound of it---seems to be the most plausible story for the origin of the name Titlum-Tatlum.*[4]

Shannon was not the only settler to leave his mark on the map. The name "Bastrop" originated from the Barron de Bastrop. Phillip Hendrick Nering Bogel, a native of Holland, worked as a tax collector until he fled his country when he was charged with embezzlement. He changed his name to Barron de Bastrop and moved to San Antonio in 1806. In 1810, he was appointed second alcalde, (mayor of chief judicial official), of the Spanish town. In 1820, he met with Moses Austin, whose second request to bring Anglo-American settlers into Texas was rejected. Bogel used his influence to help Moses Austin and later son, Stephen F. Austin, obtain the grant to bring settlers to Texas. Without him, Texas may never have been settled by Anglo-Americans.

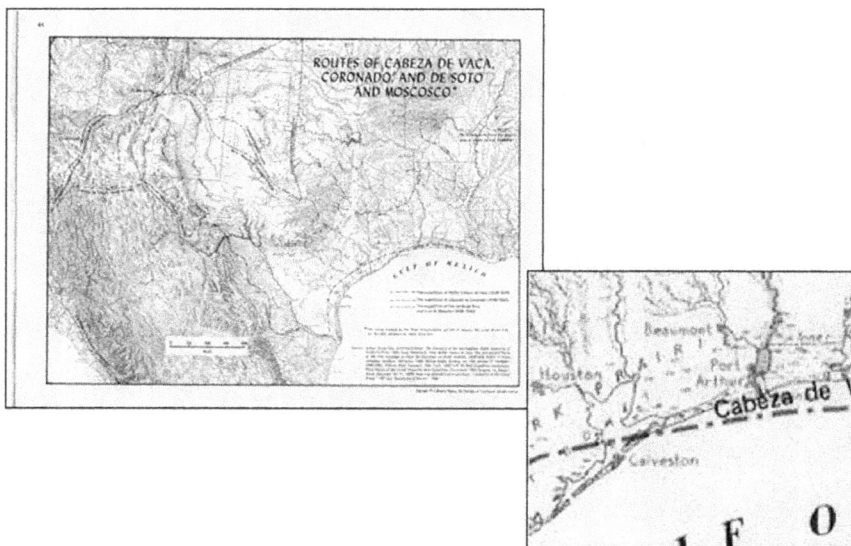

DeVaca Map[5]

As explorers first traveled through this region, a coastal tribe of Indians known as the Karankawa, lived in the bays, estuaries and along the coastline. A total of thirteen Native American tribes inhabited the local region of what would become the Brazoria County area. A map entitled "The Ancient Domain of the Karankawa Indians," indicates a settlement at San Luis. As early as 1855, wars and disease had taken their toll, and no Indian tribes remained. Conflicts and illnesses were one of many dangers hidden on the island. Turbulent waters threatened the lives and vessels of its inhabitants and explorers.

In November 1527, there is record of a storm sinking the poorly-anchored boat of Panfilade Narvaez off Galveston Island. Up to 200 lives were taken in this storm. This is the first record known of storms along the Texas coastline and also one of the most unusual because it struck during the month of November. Only one other hurricane—in 1839—has ever struck in November[6]

Following Christopher Columbus, additional Spanish expeditions set out to explore the Western Hemisphere. Alvar Nunez Cabeza de Vaca, the Spanish explorer shipwrecked on a sandbar at San Luis in 1528 and was credited giving it the name "la Isla de Malhado" (the island of Bad Luck). Historians still differ whether he named Galveston Island or San Luis Island. De Vaca is also credited with the naming of the Brazos River, calling it "Los Brazos de Dios" or the "Arms of God,"

4

because of the fresh water it provided for his shipwrecked crew.

Upon close examination, San Luis did not appear at this time to be an island on this "Routes of Cabeza De Vaca, Coronado, and De Soto and Moscosco" map. He is credited with writing two detailed works about the North American Indians. De Vaca's accounts provide a glimpse of an island that would remain undocumented for over 156 years. Although many explorers had visited this new region after 1528, not until 1684 did maps indicate travel near San Luis again. The French explorer, Robert Cavelier, Sieur de La Salle, set out on an expedition with a crew of 280 men and colonists. The fleet, consisting of four ships, sailed past San Luis on their journey to found a colony just to the south on Matagorda Bay. This colony failed. Mutineers murdered La Salle and seven members of his crew in 1687. In 1689, Spanish soldiers under Alonso De Leon, who was governor of Coahuila, New Spain, searched the region in vain to locate the French colony in Spanish territory. Despite the unsuccessful colonies and voyages, the doomed efforts left a lasting contribution by mapping the island in its various stages. According to these changes, San Luis will be noted as an island or connected to the peninsula many times throughout this book. In this 1685 French map,[7] San Luis appears to be an island.

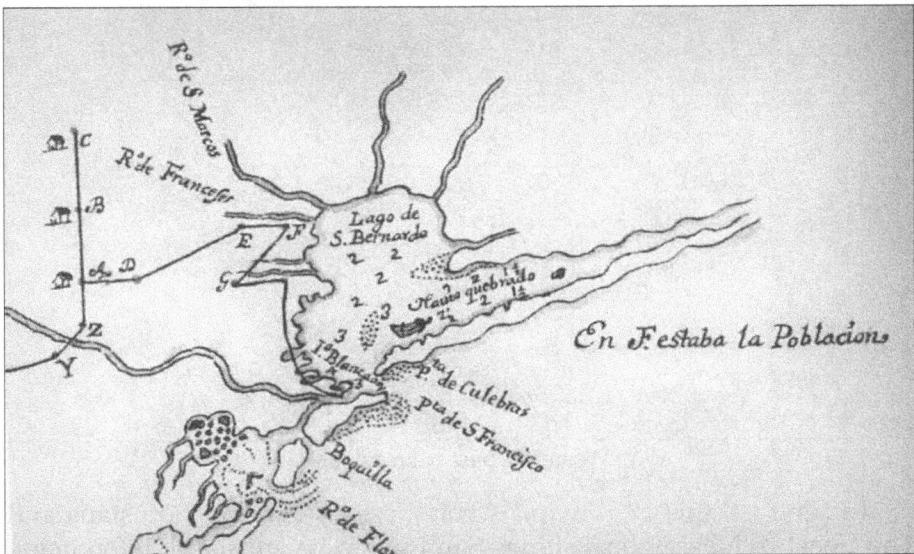

Carlos de Sigtlenza y Go'ngora created a map of Matagorda Bay,[8] which is labeled on this map as Lago de S. Bernardo and based on sketches from Alonso de Leon's 1689 expedition. Fort Saint Louis is marked as "F." This Spanish map depicts the *La Belle* shipwreck as *Navio quebrado* or "broken ship." San Luis appears to be part of the peninsula on this map.

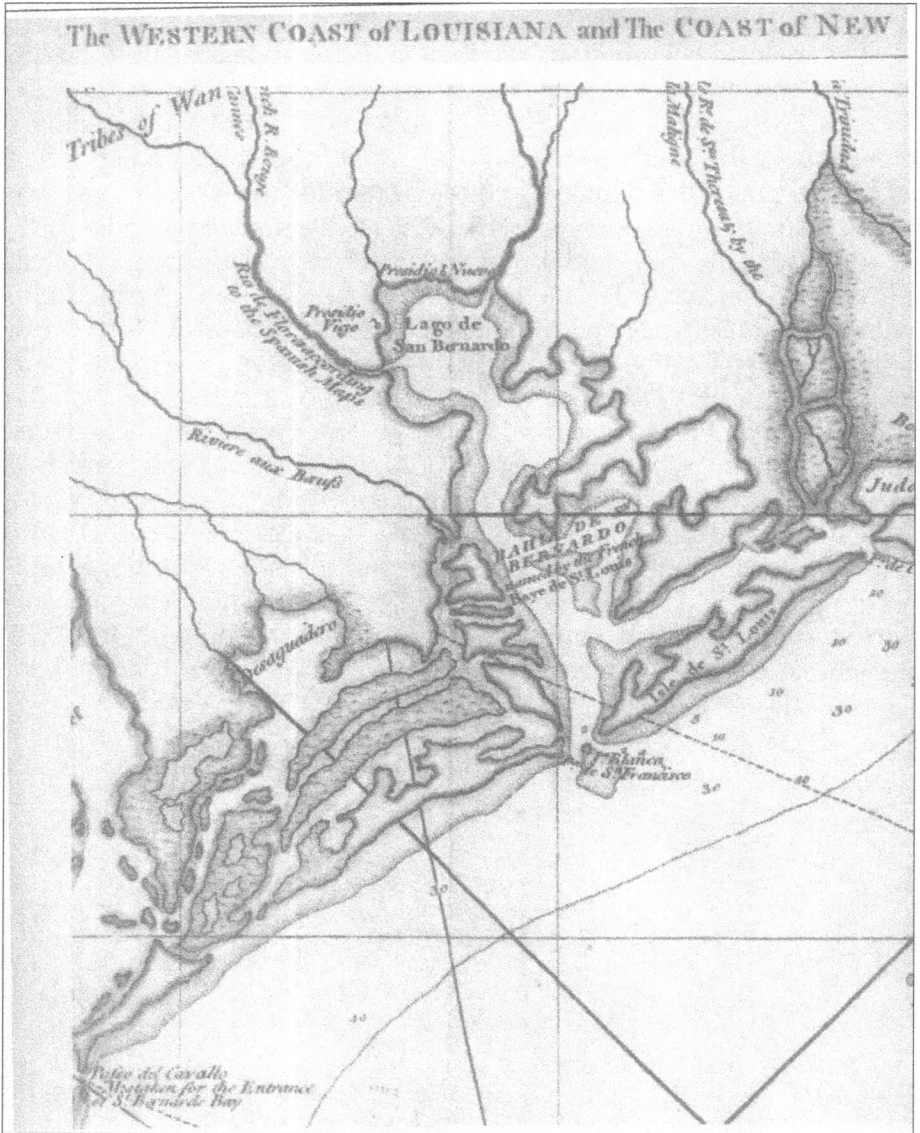

Western Coast of Louisiana

In contrast, this 1775 map,[9] "The Western Coast of Louisiana and The Coast of New Leon," shows San Luis to be an island, referencing Galveston Bay as "Baye de St. Louis." Vincroy, Don Bernardo de Galvez gave the name "Galveston Bay" in 1783. Galvez, a Spanish general who became governor of Louisiana, is attributed with the naming Galveston Island in his own honor.

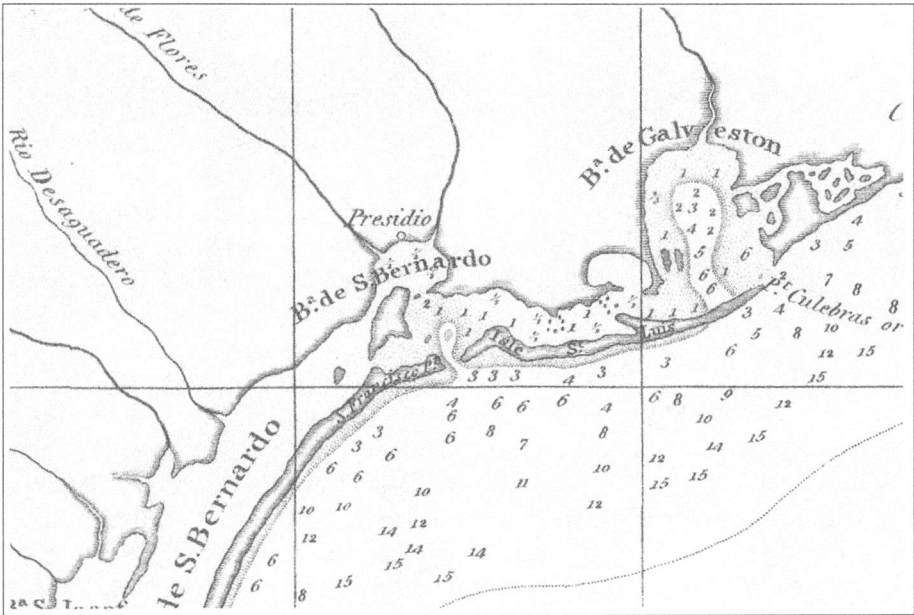

By Aaron Arrowsmith[10]

Offering additional details, an 1803 water depth chart by the well-known British geographer and cartographer, Aaron Arrowsmith, notes the opening to San Luis Pass as very shallow. Galveston Bay on this chart is also very shallow. As seen on the chart, "Isle St. Luis" is the name used here for "Galveston Island," while "San Francisco, PT" is what we know today as Follett's Island.

1805 Spanish map shows "Island of St Louis or Galvezton" to be alternative names for Galveston Island.

The 1805 Spanish Map[11]
This map shows San Luis to be an island.

http://tides.sfasu.edu:2006/cgi-bin/getimage.exe?CISROOT-Newton&CISOPTR-2719 (9/30/2007) *The Handbook of Texas Online* is a project of the Texas Site Historical Association

(http://www.tshaonline.org) Copyright ©, The Texas Historical Association, 1997-2002 Last Updated: January 18, 2008

Jean Lafitte, The Gentleman Pirate[12]

The charismatic man known as "The Gentleman Pirate," Jean Lafitte, used Galveston as his home base from 1817-1821. Though two different spellings have been ascribed to his name, written as Laffite or Lafitte, everyone agrees that he was quite the character. Many romantic stories have been told about him. He was tall, had pale skin, dark hair and hazel eyes. He was the son of a French father and a Spanish mother. Known as a "lover," not as "fighter," he truly was a smuggler and a privateer. During the storm of 1818, he gave his home, named Maison Rouge, to be used as a hospital for the French colonist. You might say he's as much myth as reality. A larger-than life figure in Galveston history. When he left Galveston Island in 1820, he burned his home to the ground. Rumor has it that he buried his treasures all along the Gulf coastline, and possibly even at San Luis Island. During the year 1987, the theme for Mr. George Mitchell's presentation of Mardi Gras was "Momus Sails the Caribbean." While the author served as chairman of the committee to bring entertaining "pirates" to the event, the following pen and ink drawing of the Pirate Jean Lafitte was a gift to me from the famous Blaine Kern Artists. Kern, from New Orleans, who was also known as "Mr. Mardi Gras." Momus was the Greek god of satire and mockery, or in more modern terms, the god of the clowns!

Another local legend was the man whose vision sparked the very foundation of Texas in 1820. Moses Austin was the first to try to establish an American colony in Coahuila, a province of Mexican Tejas. He traveled to San Antonio to petition for a land grant of 200,000 acres and 300 colonists. His second attempt for a grant was approved, but he died before completing his dream, passing the task to his son, Stephen F. Austin. Immediately, problems arose, because the newly independent Mexican government would not recognize his father's grant as approved under Spanish rule. Stephen then went to Mexico City and diplomatically secured a new law which permitted the right to establish the colony. He was given the title of empresario or administrator.

General Austin's Map of Texas with Parts of the Adjoining States-1840[13]

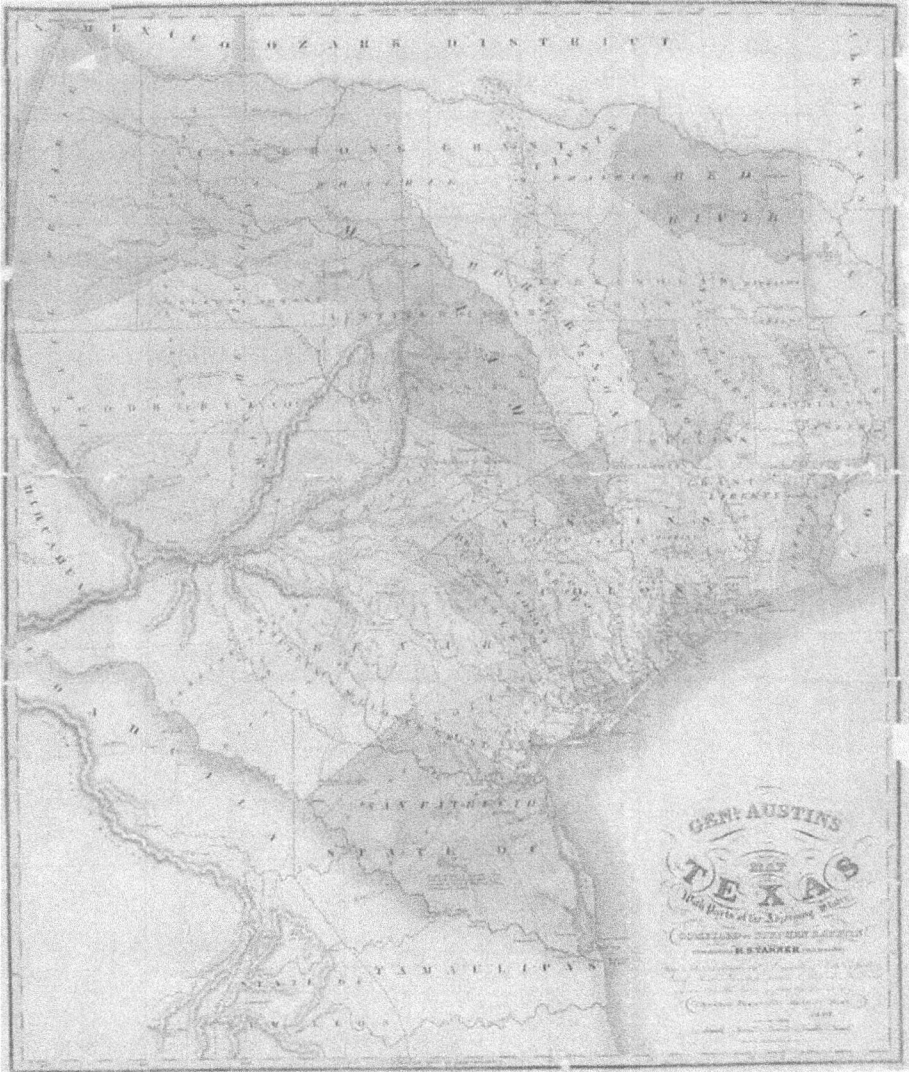

Stephen F. Austin[14]

Within this grant territory and part of his father's dream, the City of San Luis would soon be developed. This was the beginning of great change for the entire region. The city would become a very important link in the import and export markets of the world. These ports were instrumental in sustaining the settlers after Texas made a dramatic break from Mexico in 1836 and became the Republic of Texas.

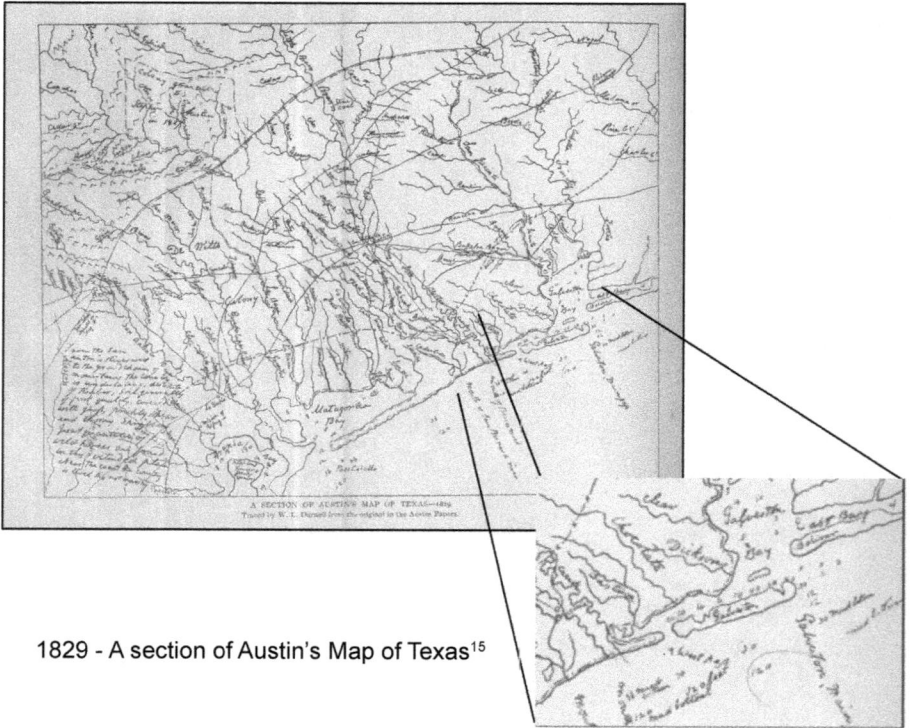

1829 - A section of Austin's Map of Texas[15]

From this tracing, San Luis does not appear to be an island. A handwritten note in the lower left corner reads:

From the San Antonio River west to the grand chain of mountains, the country is undulating, destitute of timber, soil generally of first quality, covered with grape, prickly pear and thorny shrubbery. Great quantities of wild horses are found in this extended plain. Near the coast the country is level tho not marshy.

The rivers are a dominant feature in this map based on the French explorations of the American coast. It shows Galveston Bay and West Bay were from ten to forty feet in depth to the first opening westward to the Gulf of Mexico. This became known as San Luis Pass, but also note that San Luis is part of the peninsula, which looks to be part of the mainland on this map.[16]

Elias R. Wightman, the first surveyor for the colony of Col. Stephen F. Austin, officially named "San Luis Bay" in 1829.

This enlargement of the 1829 Stephen F. Austin map, clearly shows Oyster Creek and the Brazos River parallel each other all the way to the Gulf of Mexico.

The first seeds of Texas Independence were no doubt sown with arrival of the first of Stephen F. Austin's authorized three hundred settlers in the state of Coahuila, Mexico, at the mouth of the Brazos River. According to the colonization agreement, Austin's colonists had to either be Roman Catholic or agree to become Roman Catholic. Under the Empresario land agent system, Austin successfully settled his colony, which became known as the "Old Three Hundred." Building on his success, Austin obtained three more contracts (land grants) and settled 900 additional families on his own, plus 800 more in partnership with Samuel Williams. Stephen F. Austin died from illness, on December 27, 1836, at the age of forty-three.

Brazoria County Judge, John Willy, is a descendent of Lydia Wilson Follett Hoskins, the daughter of Alexander Glass Follett who married John H. Hoskins. Willy noted:

There were not three hundred in Stephen F. Austin's 'Old 300' -- only 287. Split in two groups -- one group over land and one on the Schooner Lively. They were to meet at the mouth of the Colorado River (Matagorda County). The land group with Austin went to the Colorado River, but those on ship didn't show up -- so SFA began checking on them and found they had gone up the Brazos River by mistake and landed at Columbia (Bells Landing). They liked it there, so S. F. Austin brought the others to Columbia. Therefore, Brazoria County became the "Birthplace of Texas.

The history of land grants in Texas is a long and complex one. A "League of Land," or *sito*, represents 4,428.4 acres, intended for grazing, and a "Labor of Land" represents 177.1 acres for cropland. The new settlers were soon to become ranchers, raising both cattle and sheep. The first recorded land sale of Stephen F. Austin, Abstract No. 29, in Brazoria County tax records was for 4,428 acres.. Less than twenty people were owners of all this land. Both Mexican and Spanish land grants were made in Texas.

In 1823, after many delays in getting permits from the Mexican government, Stephen F. Austin was able to bring colonists to the Gulf Coast. A number of settlers from Illinois came to the west end of Galveston Island. The settlers came by boat, bringing cattle and large amounts of household goods to start their homes. The ground elevation of Galveston's west end is "Sea Level," as is San Luis Island, though little attention was paid to this very import fact! That fall a storm, possibly a major hurricane swept across the island, destroying their homes and killing all the people and livestock.

The Mexican government ordered the initiation of a plan for the first Port by order of the Mexican government through Alexander Thompson of the Mexican Navy in 1828. San Luis is an island on the following map. The end of Galveston Island has a very blunt shape. This shape changed many times throughout the history of the next 150 years. Though powerless against the natural forces of the island, men attempted to control the trading enterprises that the island offered.

Port of Galveston Map[18]

Decree - Order to Close San Luis Port in 1836[17]

The Mexican Government had a port at San Luis in 1836. On February 9, 1836, the Mexican Governor Cortina issued this decree to close the following ports:

President Interino (Jose' Justo Corro). [Decree promulgated February 9, 1836, by Jose' Maria Tornel, Secretary of War and Marine, closing until further notice ports of Matagorda, La Baca, San Luis, Goliad, Anahuac, Copano, and all Texas roadsteads, between longitudes 94°50' and

101°10′, commencing]: El C. Jose′ Gomez de la Cortina, Coronel del batallion del Comercio y Gobierno . . . Mexico City, February 11, 1836.

Just fourteen miles to the west of San Luis Island, settled by the mouth of the Brazos River at the end of the peninsula, was a small town named Velasco. After the Battle of San Jacinto, President David G. Burnet made the town the temporary capital of the Republic of Texas. This little town was an important connection of what was to become the City of San Luis. During the 1840s, people living in the City of San Luis regularly traveled to and from Velasco. Travel, however, was not always easy in this area. Heavy rains from the coast could swell rivers, causing them to overflow into pastures, farmlands and even towns.

Velasco 1825[19]

Francis Rebecca Bouldin Spragins Brown Raine was born May 22, 1816, in Halifax County. Frances Rebecca was the sister of Nancy Spragins Hoskins and the great-great-grandmother of Judith Willy Bielstein. In 1903, she wrote a letter to her granddaughter, recording a narrative of this terrible storm which struck shortly after she and her family arrived in Velasco

Her account is contained in *Reminiscences, 1816-1903*. Her personal papers collections can be obtained from the Virginia Historical Society, Call Number 21487.[20]

She describes a tropical storm which formed inland in 1832, causing the Brazos River to overflow her banks, flooding Brazoria, Columbia and Velasco. Crops were damaged beyond saving. Ships lay on their side. Devastation was far reaching. Flooding on this scale could not happen today because of dams placed along the Brazos River to control floodwaters from heavy rains inland. High water covered San Luis Island for three days from storms such as this one.

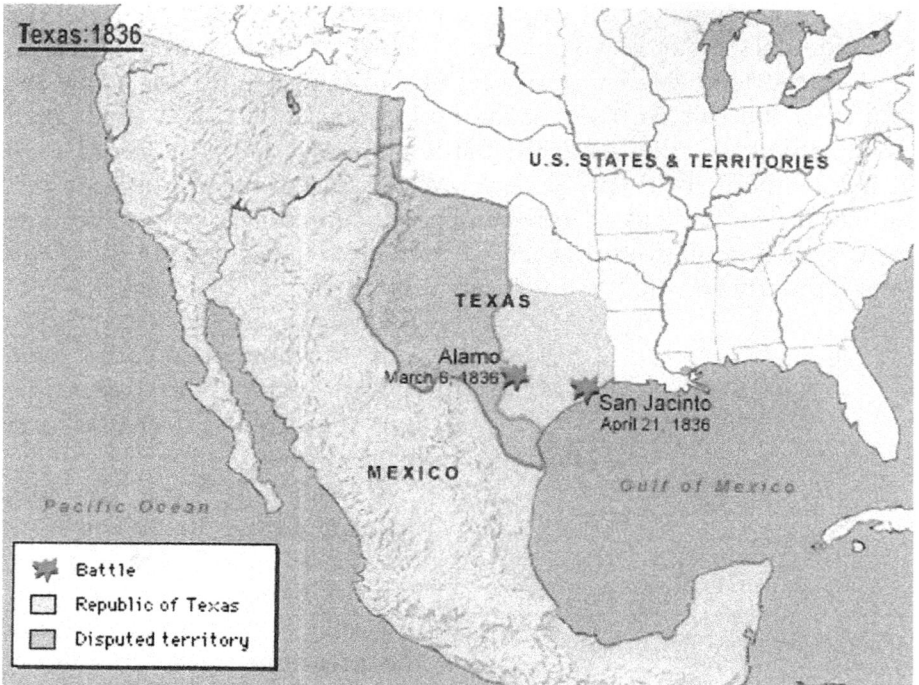

Texas:1836

U.S. STATES & TERRITORIES

TEXAS

Alamo
March 6, 1836

San Jacinto
April 21, 1836

MEXICO

Gulf of Mexico

Pacific Ocean

Battle
Republic of Texas
Disputed territory

Mexico, Republic of Texas, Disputed Territory and the United States and Territories[21]

Brazoria County was created on March 11, 1836 as one of the original twenty-three counties in Texas. This new county raised the question of which would claim San Luis Pass. An act was created to declare: "The better to define the boundaries of Galveston County, and to attach San Luis Island to the County of Brazoria.

> *Sec. 1. Be it enacted by the Senate and House of Representatives of the Republic of Texas, in Congress assembled, That the southern boundary of the county of Galveston hereafter shall be as follows, to wit: Beginning at the east side of the main pass, which enters the Bay of Galveston between the Island of Galveston and San Luis; to a point one mile north of San Luis Island; thence northwest till it strikes the main land, and thence as at present defined; and the territory south and west of the above line is hereby declared to be attached to the county of Brazoria.*
>
> DAVID S. KAUFMAN,
> *Speaker of the House of Representatives.*
> DAVID G. BURNET,
> *President of the Senate.*
> *Approved 16th December, 1839*
> MIRABEAU B. LAMAR

Laws of the Republic of Texas, in two volumes. Volume 01: The Portal to Texas History Brazoria County Historical Museum

The county's official beginning was December 20, 1836, though it was not until February 20, 1837, that Brazoria County became totally organized in its political jurisdiction.

Already well established, Velasco served as a stage for Texas history when it hosted General Santa Anna. Food was provided for him and his fellow prisoners by Isaac Coleman Hoskins, who owned a hotel there. A handwritten voucher for $182.75 records meals from May 10 to June 1, 1836.

Santa Ana[22]
REPUBLIC OF TEXAS &
        TO I.G. HOSKINS

1836
JUNE 1ST : To Boarding General Santa Ana and Suite from 10th May to
   1st June 22 days at 18.75 per day   *$191.50*
   Deduct one day Board -------   *8.75*
We do hereby certify that I. G. Hoskins of Velasco did furnish Board for
Gen. Santa Ana and Suite from 10th May to 1st June 1836
                          E. L. Junes Sr.
          TX   *Theodore S Lee*

Matthew Hopkins Land Scrip
County Surveyor's Field Notes[23]

Confusion and misconception about Spanish and Mexican land grants led to land speculators who took advantage of the situation by selling a "land script" as a permit to contract with the empresario. The General Land Office, newly formed in 1837, was ordered by the Republic of Texas to rule on the legality of land claims. Land totaling over one million acres were also sold for fifty cents per acre in the early years of the Republic. Applicants appeared before their county board of land commissioners and if they could produce sufficient evidence of eligibility were given certificates. The applicant then arranged with a surveyor to locate and survey the land from that available in public domain, usually giving the surveyor one-third of land as compensation.

Legal transactions were sluggish as Texas organized its new freedom. Matthew Hopkins, a land agent, took eight years to receive approval for his land script No. 385 (for 640 acres of land) application. The 1836 Brazoria County Surveyor's Field Notes name Matthew Hopkins for a parcel of land in Galveston's West Bay on "Navy Island," subsequently known as "Mud Island." It was signed by signed by Thomas

Toby to Samuel May Williams in New Orleans (on August. 6, 1836) had then been signed over to Matthew Hopkins (the assignee) by Samuel May Williams (who was the holder of the scrip, after having acquired it from Thomas Toby), the application was made at New Orleans on August 10, 1836.[24]

Curiosity about Texas's fledging country reached all the way to Europe. A newspaper from the time reports the arrival of the Her British Majesty's Brig of War, named *Racer.*

> *On the morning of the 12th ult Mr. Crawford arrived at Columbia accompanied by several of the officers of H.B.M. Brig of War, Racer, captain Hope. The object of this gentleman's visit to Texas, is we understand to investigate the civil and political condition of the country and report to the British government. We rejoice that the condition of Texas is now such that we have nothing to apprehend from the reports of the most fastidious and illiberal. To the report of Mr. Crawford, we shall look forward with pride, confident that the known candour and intelligence of this gentleman will promulgate truth alone at the court of St. James.*

Telegraph and Texas Register (Houston, Tex.),[25]
Vol. 2, No. 15, Ed. 1, Tuesday, May 2, 1837

After leaving the Brazos River in Brazoria County, the ship would spend a few short months back at sea before the *Racer* would encounter one of the worst storms recorded in the Gulf of Mexico. The *Racer* recorded in her log books that this viscous storm traveled nearly 2,000 miles, destroying almost everything in her path. The storm became known as 'Racer's Storm.' All storms that travel this route today are known as "Racer's type storms."

> *Telegraph and Texas Register (Houston, Tex.),*
> *Vol. 2, No. 41, Ed. 1,*
> *Wednesday, October 11, 1837*

Telegraph

Edited by Francis Moore, Jun.
HOUSTON, WEDNESDAY. OCT. 11, 1837

The late accounts from our sea board are of a most distressing character. A tremendous gale appears to have swept the whole line of our coast and destroyed an immense amount of property. It commenced on the lst and increased in violence until the 6th. At Velasco four house were blown down; the whole country for several miles around inundated, and all the vessels in the harbor, consisting of the brig Sam Houston, schooners De Kalb, Fannin, Texas and the Caldwell were driven ashore; this latter has since got off and cleared on Sunday last for New Orleans; the others will all be set afloat again without difficulty: at Galveston the waters were driven in with such violence that they rose six or seven feet higher than ordinary spring tides; they inundated a large portion of the east end of the Island, and compelled the soldiers of the garrison to desert their barracks and seek safety upon the elevated ground near the intended site of Galveston city. The large new warehouse of Mr. McKinney and the new custom house were completely destroyed and the goods are scattered over the Island. The brigs Perserverance, Jane, and Elbe were driven ashore and are complete wrecks, the Phoenix is also ashore, but slightly injured and may be easily set afloat again. The Schooners Select, Henry, Star, Lady of the Lake, and the prize schooner Correo are ashore, some of them high and dry. The Tom Toby is a wreck and the Brutus is considerably injured. The schooner Helen is the only vessel which has received no damage. So far as we have yet been able to ascertain only two individuals have perished.

The history of this country contains no records of any hurricane which has equalled this either in the violence of the storm or the extent of the devastation. There is reason to believe that the destructive influence of this gale has extended generally over the surface of the Gulf; we therefore apprehend that the next intelligence from the United States and from Mexico will be rife with accounts of disastrous shipwrecks, we sincerely trust however that either the calamities of our enemy or our friend have equaled our own.

After wrecking the entire Texas coast in early October, 1837, 'Racer's Storm' continued to Louisiana, Mississippi, Alabama, Florida and on to North Carolina where it exited into the Atlantic.

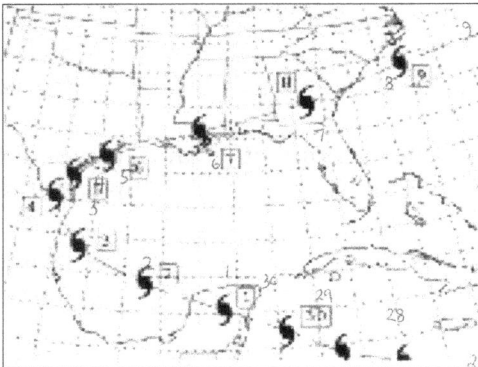

Map Provided by Dr. Cary Mock[26]

The damaged was similarly widespread. Near Cape Hatteras, North Carolina, a new paddle-wheel boat by the name of *Home* was demolished. With 130 passengers on board and only two life preservers, forty people swam to safety, leaving ninety to perish. One positive result from the horrific storm, occurred when Congress passed a law requiring all American vessels to carry a life preserver for each passenger. The storm left its mark, not only on the inhabitants of the island, but of the terrain itself.

Every map of Galveston Bay, West Bay and Christmas Bay, along with San Luis Pass and Little Pass show very shallow depths before Racer's Storm. My observation of the storms led me to wonder, "Could it be that Racer's Storm cut the very deep channels in the bays, San Luis Pass and Little Pass?"

Stan Blazyk, a weather blogger with the *Galveston Daily News*, commented:[27]

It certainly is possible. Accounts of the time talk about water pushing many miles inland, Galveston Island being completely covered with water and sunken ships from Matagorda north to Louisiana. Unfortunately, hard data is difficult to come by.

A second opinion confirmed the possibility when, on May 8, 2012, I acquired an e-mail response to Dr. Cary Mock.

According to M. Lewis Fincher, a hurricane consultant and historian.:

Please note that I would expect channels to be cut as well across the bays, as a full hurricane has been known to affect depths of 600' +.
Lew
M. Lewis Fincher[28]

The demographics of the map would mean very little without the hard work of those who settled on the island. The Senate and House of Representatives of the Republic of Texas, Second Session, March 12, 1837, put up a ten to forty acre tracts on West Galveston Island for auction.

Rumors about the exciting new developments near San Luis Pass spread everywhere. John Bradbury Follett heard about this great opportunity while working for the Pontchartrain Railroad Company in New Orleans. He had formally left his home in Canada to build a steam pile driver and a dredge boat for the Pontchartrain Railroad Company at New Orleans.

On May 1, 1838, intrigued by the possibilities offered by the new land, Follett moved to Texas and built a house for his family on the west end of Galveston Island. There he started a shipyard with his sons where they built and repaired small ocean-going vessels. He also ran a ferry to San Luis Island and Peninsula.

In 1840 Bradbury and his sons started building the *Lafitte*, which was the first steamboat ever built in Texas waters. It was built on the Brazos River near Quintana and Old Velasco.

The timbers were hewn from the finest cedars and live oaks. Other materials were brought by sailing vessels from Boston. She was described in the *Houston Morning Star*, October 5, 1841, "as being 138 tons burden and about 120 feet in length and having side wheels 18 feet in diameter, and as being equipped with the customary high pressure engine." She drew three feet of water, light, and five feet when loaded to capacity with 300 bales of cotton. She had no upper cabin but boasted 'a commodious cabin with staterooms aft'. Captain James E. Haviland was the first commander.

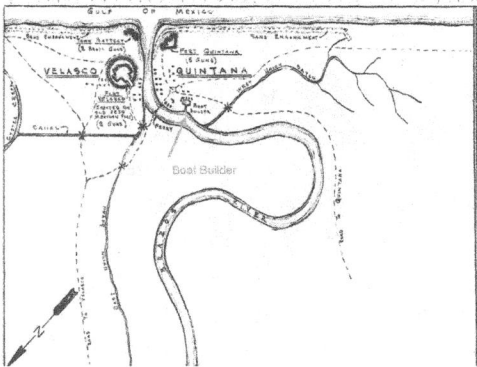

Boatbuilder Map[29]

A local reported boasting in his report, "The *Lafitte* and her maiden run was to Galveston where they were received in a manner commensurate with the importance of this achievement and occasion."[30]

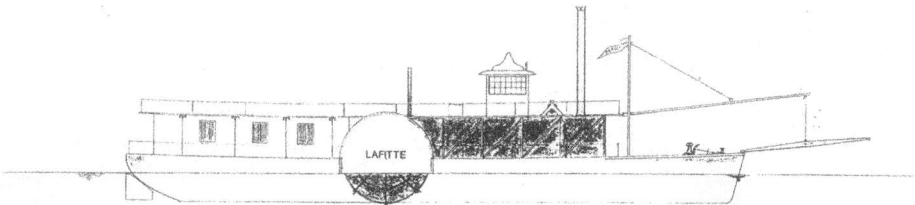

STEAMBOAT "LAFITTE"
FIRST STEAMBOAT CONSTRUCTED IN TEXAS
1840 AT VELASCO, TEXAS
120' LONG - 138 TON CAPACITY (300 BALES OF COTTON)
OWNERS: McKINNEY & WILLIAMS
SHIPBUILDER: JOHN BRADBURY FOLLETT
FROM FILES OF: PRESCOTT & FOLLETT
NEW ORLEANS, LA.
LETTERING BY: DEBORAH R. FOLLETT

As recorded in the Texas Census Books, Follett owned two lots in the new City of San Luis where he continued shipbuilding. Throughout the next sixty-two years, the Follett family became an intricate part of San Luis, Galveston and Follett's Peninsula. Its members witnessed the rise of a bustling city that began with the sale of the Island of San Luis and the Peninsula from the estate of Stephen F. Austin for $80,000, to Matthew Hopkins and Associates on July 19, 1839. The following documents[31] detail the beginning of the City:

Bernard July 19th, 1839

Mr. James F. Perry

Sir,

As attorney in fact as for record for my wife Eliza M. Hill, I hereby ratify and confirm the sale of San Louis Island and the Peninsula made by yourself & wife to Mathew Hopkins and his associates for the sum of eighty thousand dollars, in such payments as you may agree upon– In the event of the suit now pending, Wm G. Hill &

Wife V S James F. Perry and Wife terminating in my favor That the amount of cash & notes falling to me in that event be immediately refunded to me by you & wife without suit for the amount. The sale made by you & the passing of the deed to M. Hopkins be evidence of your consorts.

Very respectfully
& c
Wm G. Hill

(Addressed:)	*(Endorsed:)*
Mr. James F. Perry	*Wm. G. Hill & wife*
Gulf Prairie	*Power of Attorney*
Mr. Hopkins	*to sell San Luis*

The Sale
Perry Papers[32]

Memorandum of an agreement of Law made and entered into between Emily M. Perry wife of James F. Perry, by and with the consent of her husband of the one part and Matthew Hopkins of the other part witnesseth, that the said Emily Perry with the consent of our aid agrees to sell to the said Hopkins the Island of San Luis, at the west end of Galveston Island and the Peninsulas running from Oyster Creek to the said Island, except about four labors more or less, which are included in the Survey of a league of land granted to Branch T. Archer which peninsula & Island of San Luis make a league of land, less about four labors.

The price to be paid to said Hopkins for said land is the sum of eight thousand dollars one third of which is to be paid in the following manner: One half of the said third to be paid to her as to her order, in thirty days from this date in cash, and the other half of the said third to be paid in ample notes or acceptances, payable in eight months from this date in New Orleans. And the balance of the said eighty thousand dollars, to wit, the other two third parts, is to be secured to the satisfaction, of the vendor or her husband.

It being distinctly understood that if the said Hopkins shall fail to make the first payment in cash or otherwise to her satisfaction within thirty days from this time, then this agreement to sell, shall be absolutely null and void.

And if the said Hopkins shall make said payment and shall perform on his part the other terms of this agreement, then she engages to make a complete title to him or to whomsoever he may order.

In testimony of which, the said Emily Perry, James F. Perry her husband, and Matthew Hopkins, have hereto set their hands and seals, this 20th July 1839.

Witnesses
 Wm. Henry Austin

      Emily M. Perry (seal)
      James F. Perry (seal)
      (rubric)
      Matthew Hopkins (seal)

(Endorsed:)
Contract with
Matthew Hopkins

*With four thousand acres, more or less, Matthew Hopkins, Land Agent, formed
the San Luis Stock Company for the City of San Luis and the adjoining Peninsula. Whole land speculators sold lots on the west end of Galveston Island
and on the mainland across San Luis Pass. San Luis developers laid out a city
and sold lots, and soon forty houses were built on San Luis Island. In 1840,
Andrews & Hammeken were engaged as commission merchants at San Luis.
They built two large warehouses and an excellent wharf. In the winter of that
year they erected a cotton press capable of compressing seventy-five bales of
cotton in twelve hours. On one occasion, 5,000 bales of cotton were compressed
and shipped throughout the world. They planned to connect the port city with
the rich plantations of Brazoria and Matagorda counties by means of a railroad
and a canal.[33]*

Early accounts of the island show a booming growth in the trading
industry, offering what seemed to be ideal situation for the importing
and exporting of goods.

Another report is given by an early book on the Republic of Texas.[34]

*San Luis Harbour. — San Luis Harbour and Inlet are situated near the west end
of Galveston island, and derive their chief importance from their proximity to
the mouths of the Brazos River and Oyster Creek, the commerce of which with
foreign countries will perhaps be conducted through this medium of communication, in consequence of the obstructions to navigation at the confluence of
those rivers with the gulf. The harbour is formed by San Luis Island and a neck
of the mainland, which are said to afford effectual shelter in my weather. It is
connected with the bay of Galveston by a shallow sound of from four and a half
to six feet water. This harbour is pronounced by some authorities to be one of
the best upon the coast of Texas, and equal to any situated on the Mexican gulf.
It has been examined by officers of the Republic, as well as by private individuals, and the average depth of water is represented in these reports to exceed
twelve feet and a half. The harbour is described as perfectly safe--the channel
easy of entrance, and vessels drawing ten feet water may, it is stated, approach
within six feet of the shore, either on the island of San Luis, or the mainland.
Bastrop Creek, of which Fleus and Austin Bayous are branches, flow into San
Luis Harbour.*

Another section of the book reports:

*A company had purchased the island, with part of the mainland, including the
harbour, for the purpose of laying off a town, which they propose to connect
with the Brazos River by a railroad or canal, and thus obtain the shipments
of the produce of the great cotton region of Texas. It is proper to observe that
there is considerable difference of opinion (originating probably in conflicting
interests) as to the maritime advantages of San Luis.*

The success of the ports soon required that transportation of merchandise on land must be as efficient and productive as possible, bringing another modern improvement to the island: the railroad. George Louis Hammeken (? - 1881) was a key player in the Brazos and Galveston Railroad. He was a well-traveled businessman, possibly of New York, who met Stephen F. Austin in Mexico in 1833. Hammeken then came to Texas in October 1835, acting as the agent of English bankers to place loans with some planters, but the revolution interfered with these plans. It does not appear that Hammeken participated in the revolution. On March 12, 1839, President Lamar of the Republic of Texas, appointed Hammeken as secretary to Barnard E. Bee who was employed as a Texan agent to Mexico. Hammeken's travels included New Orleans, Mexico City, and New York.

His vast array of services and travels, recommended Hammeken as an ideal developer, and he soon became an integral part of Texas. Not only did he witness the birth and infancy of a new country, but he was also present to bade farewell to the man who planted the seeds of its development. Hammeken became a very close friend to General Stephen F. Austin and was at his side at the time of Austin's death. Hammeken was elected as both president of the Brazos and Galveston Railroad Company and a member of the San Luis Stockholders. Later he purchased several lots in the new City of San Luis.

The Brazos and Galveston Railroad Company was one of four railroads chartered by the Republic of Texas. The company, chartered on May 24, 1838, had the right to build turnpikes and railroads from the main channel of Galveston Bay to the Brazos River. Capital was set at $500,000, divided into 5,000 shares, and the office was at Austinia on Dollar Point. Subscription books for the capital stock were opened at Houston, where 2,000 shares were offered by W. G. Cooke and Asa Brigham.

Col. William G. Cooke, as young man of twenty-seven, came to Texas in 1835 with a company from New Orleans, and took a very active part in the storming of San Antonio de Bexar in December of that year. Asa Brigham was a signer of the Texas Declaration of Independence who served as state auditor under interim President David G. Burnet, as well as a state treasurer and under presidents Sam Houston and Mirabeau B. Lamar.

James F. Perry, who was the second husband of Stephen F. Austin's sister Emily, and George L. Hammeken had 1,500 shares available at Austinia. The remaining 1,500 shares were to be offered for sale at Brazoria under the direction of Edmund Andrews, who was a property owner, postmaster and successful businessman, and Frederick A. Sawyer of Velasco. Sawyer served as a lawyer and government official, serving President David G. Burnet of the Republic as secretary of war during the ad interim government. The company had permission to use boats, vehicles, wagons, or carriages of any nature, and to improve bays, rivers, and harbors. Recorded Stock Holders were from Texas, Baltimore, Mobile, New York, New Orleans and Mexico.

Congress reserved the right to regulate the rates charged, and in January of 1840, it amended the charter to substitute canals for turnpikes and to provide a maximum freight rate of 2 ½ cents a mile per 100 pounds. Men and munitions for the army and navy were to be transported free. In September 1839, the company announced that the route had been changed to run from San Luis Island to Velasco. Construction began on the new route; 860 feet of a 1,260-foot bridge from San Luis Island to the mainland had been piled by March, 1841. However, by September, the company had apparently gone out of the railroad business in favor of a canal connecting Bastrop and Buffalo bayous. In December 1843, Hammeken told Anson Jones, who was the fourth and last president of the Republic of Texas, that the company had spent about $3,000 and much labor on the canal project. The entire project failed shortly thereafter, and the railroad was never completed. As the settlers explored the possibilities offered by the land of the new Republic, information about the island was collected and revised as explorations uncovered and updated facts.

A very detailed description of Texas and Galveston Bay from 1838, was evidently flawed and was rewritten in 1839, as recorded in *The Colombian Navigator; or, Sailing Directory for the American Coasts and the West Indies.*

> S. Luis or Galveston Island is described as about 20 miles long, trending N.E. and S.W.; it is low, but may be known by three single trees about the middle of it: at the west end is a wide pass with a small island nearly in the middle of it, and at the back of it, about seven miles distant, is a long grove, called Oyster and Chocolate dye Wood." Chocolate bay is located to the north of West Galveston Bay. This may be the reason Chocolate Bay got its name.

Henry Stuart Foote reported in his book:

Texas has several ports with sufficient depth of water on the bar to admit vessels of commerce of considerable burthen; but no one will admit ships of war of the middle class. The best ports are those of Galveston and San Luis, which have from 13 to 15 feet of water at their entrance over bars of sand. Sabine Bay presents considerable less depth of water on its bar, but this is of soft mud. The mouth of the Brassos river is obstructed by a sandbar with from 5 to 8 feet of water, over which rolls a heavy surf. It appears to be the best opinion that the trade of the Brassos must be done through San Luis and Galveston. Farther west are the entrances to the bays of Matagorda, Aransas, and Corpus Christi, and near the Rio Grande is the Brassos Santiage. These are important to the commerce of Texas, but none of them afford a greater depth of water nor other facilities for vessels of war, superior to those of Galveston and San Luis.[35]

Looking to employ the full use of the ports to support Texas's newly gained independence, the Secretary of the Navy for the Republic of Texas once ordered the transfer of the Navy Yard from Galveston to the City of San Luis. Plans were made to build a wharf at the foot of Orange Street. The wharf was to be twenty feet wide with a pier head of seventy-by-twenty.

To complete the transition, it was important to establish to which district the island would belong and Congress chose Brazos, declaring:

Be it enacted by the Senate and House of Representatives of the Republic of Texas, in Congress assembled, that the port of San Luis be, and the same is hereby annexed to the district of Brazos, and that the northern boundary of said district, show be the same as that established for the northern boundary of the county of Brazoria, by an act passed the sixteenth day of December of the fourth session of Congress, and that all laws heretofore passed, which contravene in the provisions of this act be, and the same are hereby repealed.
David S. Kaufman, Speaker of the House of Representatives
David G. Burnet, President of the Senate
Approved December 10th, 1840.
Mirabeau B. Lamar

The Navy Yard added yet more growth to the small but thriving city. The picture below depicts a Port of San Luis with town site on the west end of Galveston Island.

Fannie Mae's artwork is derived from an old newspaper photo in the Brazoria County Historical Museum collection and her personal memories handed down through her family. Fannie Mae notes homes

Plan of City of San Luis/Port of San Luis Pass, 1839[36]

on the west end of Galveston Island. Mary Austin Holley, in August of 1840, marveled at a wharf a thousand feet long!

The earliest record located that indicates the size of San Luis Island was from a survey for Matthew Hopkins, October 26, 1836, which showed 360 acres. Four years later, W. C. Mitchell, commander of *Ironside*, of Liverpool, and Mr. Geo. Simpson, chief pilot, of *Galveston*, recorded San Luis Island to be 354 acres. Also, in 1840, Mary Austin Holley wrote in a letter that the island was three miles in circumference, while D. E. Shepherd of the Brazoria County Abstract Company, Inc.,

A pen and ink by
Fannie Mae Follett Gilbert
October 15, 2006

in his General Analysis of the Title for San Luis Island, estimated the "Ward" size of the 1841 Plat to be 434.51 acres.[37]

Despite the variances of reports of acreage, the enthusiasm of the settlers remained united, eager to both claim and tame the land.

Promissory Notes of 1839[38]

No 97

$80_____Twelve months after the _____
Thirteenth day of November 1839. We promise to pay
MATTHEW HOPKINS, Agent for the San Luis company, the sum
of Eighty_____Dollars and _____
Cents, payable in the City of San Luis, with interest there on
at the rate of ten per centum per annum maturity, for
value received.

Witness my hand this Twenty third day of November A.D.
1839, at Peach Point. Payable in the Promissory notes of the
Republic of Texas.

M. Austin Bryan

Wm J. Bryan

A promissory note stated: "Twelve months from the year of 1839 are available to be shared describing how they referenced payment." One note for $80.00 is signed by M. Austin Bryan, whose mother was a sister to Stephen F. Austin. Another is a promise to pay to Matthew Hopkins for the amount of $551.66. Under the control of the Republic, the land was a prime opportunity to draw a larger populace

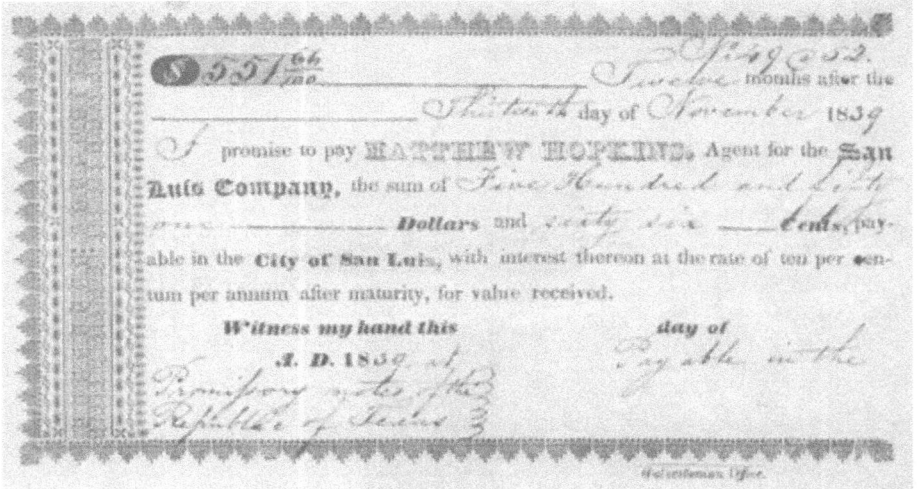

Promissory Note Receipt[39]

into the area. By 1840, the city of 2000 people was a huge rival to New Orleans and Galveston.

Advertisements about the new Texas appeared in many northern newspapers. This is a story of unconfirmed origin:

GLORIOUS CHANCE FOR GIRLS

It is well known that the Government of Texas, to encourage emigration from the United States, have offered a handsome bounty in land to any female who shall marry a citizen of Texas. A lady of Mobile, wishing to have a little more light on the subject, and to find out if possible what sort of an animal she would be required to wed, in order to obtain the land, addressed the editor of the Galvestonian for information. To all her questions, he gave straightforward answers. He said that on the reception of the letter, he called a meeting of bachelors, and there was not one of them but agrees, in case of importation should be sent out to take provide for at least one: and one chap went so far as to off to take six, if they could do no better. As to the comeatability and quality of the land, he says that it will not come to them, but they can go and find it as good as ever lay out of doors, and well adapted for raising soldiers, cabbages, lawyers, potatoes, pumpkins, cotton, sugar, dandies, ladies, babies, pigs, and chickens. Girls, Texas is the place. Pack up your duds, take your knitting work, and be off in the first boat.

Women were not the only group to receive unique offers in exchange for migrating to Texas.

Petition 11584001 Details –Legislative –Brazoria, Texas- October 19, 1840:
The Honorable The Senate & House of Representatives in Congress assembled.
"Residents of Brazoria County seek an exemption from the laws prohibiting
the residence of free persons of color in the Republic. Philadelphia-born James
Richardson, a free black man who operated an oyster house and rest stop
between Velasco and San Louis, is 'useful to the public in a situation suitable
to his class and at a locality where a white person equally serviceable could not
be expected to reside.' A man of 'industry, sobriety, and correct deportment,
Richardson served under John Bell during the War of Independence. In
addition, Richards is sixty years of age, and not likely to promote' any of the
'evils' contemplated by lawmakers when they enacted the prohibition laws.
Listing Petitioners: 5
Thomas P. Greer, L. C. Lyon, Reuben Potter, A. Underwood, D. R. Walker

The Steam Boat Constitution
Being purchased for the purpose, will now ply regularly between San Luis
and Columbia, touching at Valasco, Crosby's landing and Brazoria. The
Constitution has been fully over hauled and extensive repairs made in the
Engine department, her full is staunch and strong; being built of Locust and
offers a safe and speedy conveyance to the in habitants of the Brazos and to the
public —For engagements of Freight and Passage. —apply on board or to
JOHN NABB, & CO. San Luis.
Feb. 17th 1840.
OJ Charleston Courior, New Orleans Picayune and N.Y. Courier and Inquirer
will insert the above advertisement three times and forward the accounts to J.
Nabb & Co. San Luis, or this Office

Brazoria Courier Vol. 2 No 10, Ed.
1 April 21, 1840[40]

Chapter 2
The City of San Luis

The early 1840s witnessed a boom in the development of San Luis as a major port city along the Texas Gulf coast under the direction of Matthew Hopkins and Associates. The arrival of the first printing press at San Luis Island made possible the establishment of the first newspaper, the *San Luis Advocate*. The first and only post office was established and many new businesses were started in 1840. Among the projects contemplated or undertaken were a canal, a bridge, a cotton gin, port facilities, building houses, building business structures, shipbuilding, a hotel, and a railroad. The star of the chapter, however, is unquestionably Mary Austin Holley, cousin of Stephen F. Austin, and a great lady of her times, whose letters paint vivid, often enchanting, images of life on San Luis in this developmental era.

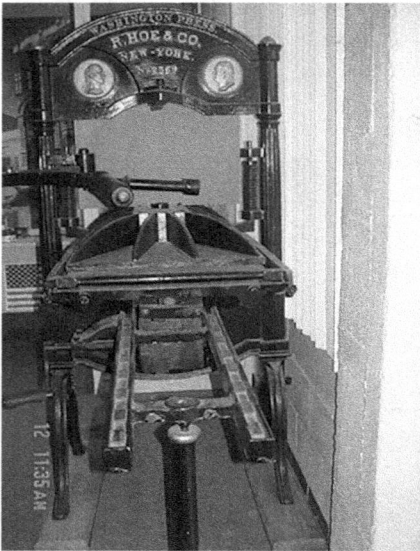

In a letter to James F. Perry of Galveston, dated February 14, 1840, Matthew Hopkins wrote that within a few days, a fine printing press would arrive at San Luis. Hopkins stated that he would leave for the Brazos the next day to pay the lumber bill and purchase timbers for the bridge and two warehouses. Hopkins then quoted the sale of twenty shares of San Luis stock at fifteen cents.

This is the Washington press that produced the *San Luis Advocate*. It is now located in the lobby of *The Daily*, Galveston's newspaper. *(Photos by Eileen M. Benitz Wagner)*

SAN LUIS ADVOCATE.

T. ROBINSON, & Co.   SAN LUIS, MONDAY, SEPTEMBER 14, 1840.   VOL. I.—NO. 3.

September 14, 1840 [1]

As fate would have it, February 14, 1840, San Luis became the four-teenth town in Texas to have a mechanized printing capability. A Washington Press was delivered to the new city, and in August, 1840, the first issue of a new newspaper came off the press. The first newspaper in the city of San Luis was located at the corner of Market and Liberty streets. S. J. Durnett printed and published the *San Luis Advocate*. T. Robinson & Co. was the owner. The newspaper was a weekly. The first issue appeared on September 1, 1840, and the last issue in 1841. Twenty-two copies are preserved on microfilm at the Dolph Briscoe Center for American History, University of Texas at Austin. Actual ads and stories from the *San Luis Advocate* range from the wars in Texas to poetry from Shakespeare. What a delight!

Later, as the city's economy was declining, Samuel J. Durnett sold the press to B. F. Neal of Galveston after less than two years of use in the City of San Luis and in 1841, the press was moved to Galveston. The first number of the *Galveston News* made its appearance, by Willard Richardson, who nicknamed it the "Old Sleepy." The reason is unclear why it got its name, but soon the newspaper became quite sought after by the citizens at San Luis. It was then renamed the *The Texas Times. Being a Continuation of The San Luis Advocate*. This was a weekly published by D. Davis with Ferdinand Pinckard serving as editor. The prospectus of *The Texas Times* on November 23, 1842, explained Pinckard's motives for moving the paper to Galveston. After the short lived *The Texas Times*; it came into the hands of Michael Cronican and Wilbur Cherry who used it print *The News*. The Washington hand press saw its last service after the storm of 1900 and 1915 when it was used to print handbills.[2]

Eleven numbers and forty-eight issues were to be published to fulfill their agreement and complete the last volume of the *San Luis Advocate*. Alexander G. Follett, brother Alonzo and Durnett were transporting the press from San Luis Island across San Luis Pass to Galveston, when Alexander's foot slipped and their ferry boat capsized. Nevertheless, the three managed to retrieve the press from the Pass and deliver it. In 1843, the Galveston newspaper changed its name again to the *Telegraph*.

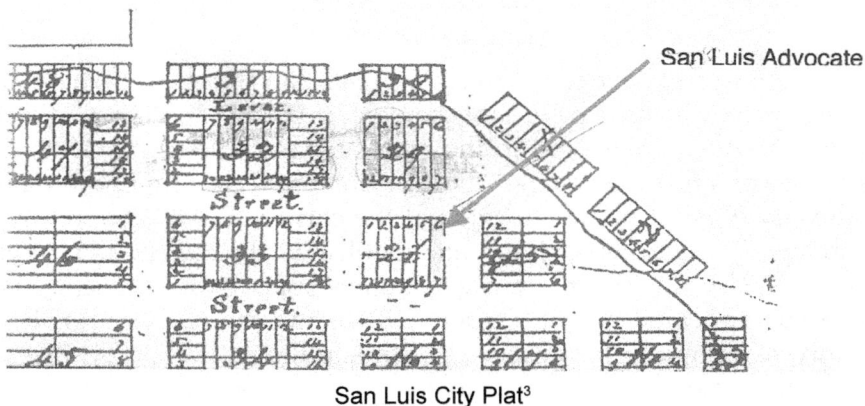

San Luis Advocate

San Luis City Plat[3]

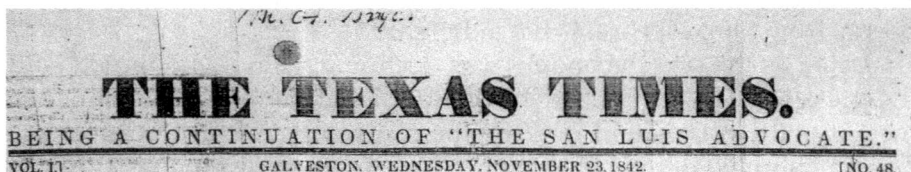

THE TEXAS TIMES.

BEING A CONTINUATION OF "THE SAN LUIS ADVOCATE."

VOL. 1.]   GALVESTON, WEDNESDAY, NOVEMBER 23, 1842.   [NO. 48.

The Texas Times masthead from November 23, 1842.[4]

PROSPECTUS
OF
THE TEXAS TIMES

P. PINKARD, EDITOR AND PROPRIETOR

The Proprietor is engaged in publishing in the city of Galveston, a weekly paper under the title of "THE TEXAS TIMES," the first number of which in connection with the "San Luis Advocate" is now completed.

The editorial department is under the control of the proprietor, and no effort shall be wanting on his part, to render the column of the Times useful and interesting to every class of readers. The aid of experienced and talented correspondents, in different sections of the county, has been secured, and readers may rely on being served with many rich treats, illustrating the habits, manners, topography,, mineral wealth, agricultural and all other resourced of the country, calculated to make known and ensure its interests.

The establishment has been removed from San Luis, mainly on account of facilities here afforded for communicating regularly with every section of the Republic, as well as foreign Nations; and with the hope of deserving and obtaining, a share of the business patronage of this commercial emporium of Texas.

Subscribers to the "San Luis Advocate" have had opportunities of judging of the mechanical skill used in the publication of the paper. An assurance is given to all, that the best materials only will be used, and unwearied attention given to avoid typographical and other errors.

The editorial departments: will be under the control of the proprietor, and no effort shall be wanted on his part, to render the columns of the Times useful and interesting to every class of readers. The aid of experienced and talented correspondents, in different sections moves with pecuniary aggrandizeinent, are ---amount with the proprietor, he is desirous of giving an extensive circulation to the Times as a general -- vehicle of intelligence, by reducing the ---price of Four Dollars in advance, or Five Dollars at the close of the succeeding volume.

This paper is established on a footing which, will ensure its permanent continuance.

On February 29, 1840, in a letter addressed to James F. Perry, Matthew Hopkins suggested that the lithographing of the city of San Luis should best be stopped until he could see the new plans—with consideration of extra expense. William Henry Austin surveyed and signed as accurate the first planned city, October 1, 1841. The plat states blocks were 30' X 150'; 30' X 75'; 42 6/7' X 85 5/7', and even some 25' X 150' feet. Streets were named for fruit trees. Levees were drawn around the entire city. To protect from high tides, North Levee, East Levee, South Levee and West Levee are visible on this plat. The map shows five districts with the levees, along with several parks.

In this undated analysis found at the Brazoria County Historical Museum, D. E. Shepherd's General Analysis of the Title of San Luis Island from Brazoria County Abstract Company Incorporated estimated the "Wards" as follows:

First Ward:	4,330,413	square feet
Second Ward:	4,797,550	square feet
Third Ward:	3,888,995	square feet
Fourth Ward:	2,965,200	square feet
Fifth Ward:	2,845,440	square feet
Total	18,827,598	square feet

or a total of 434.51 acres"

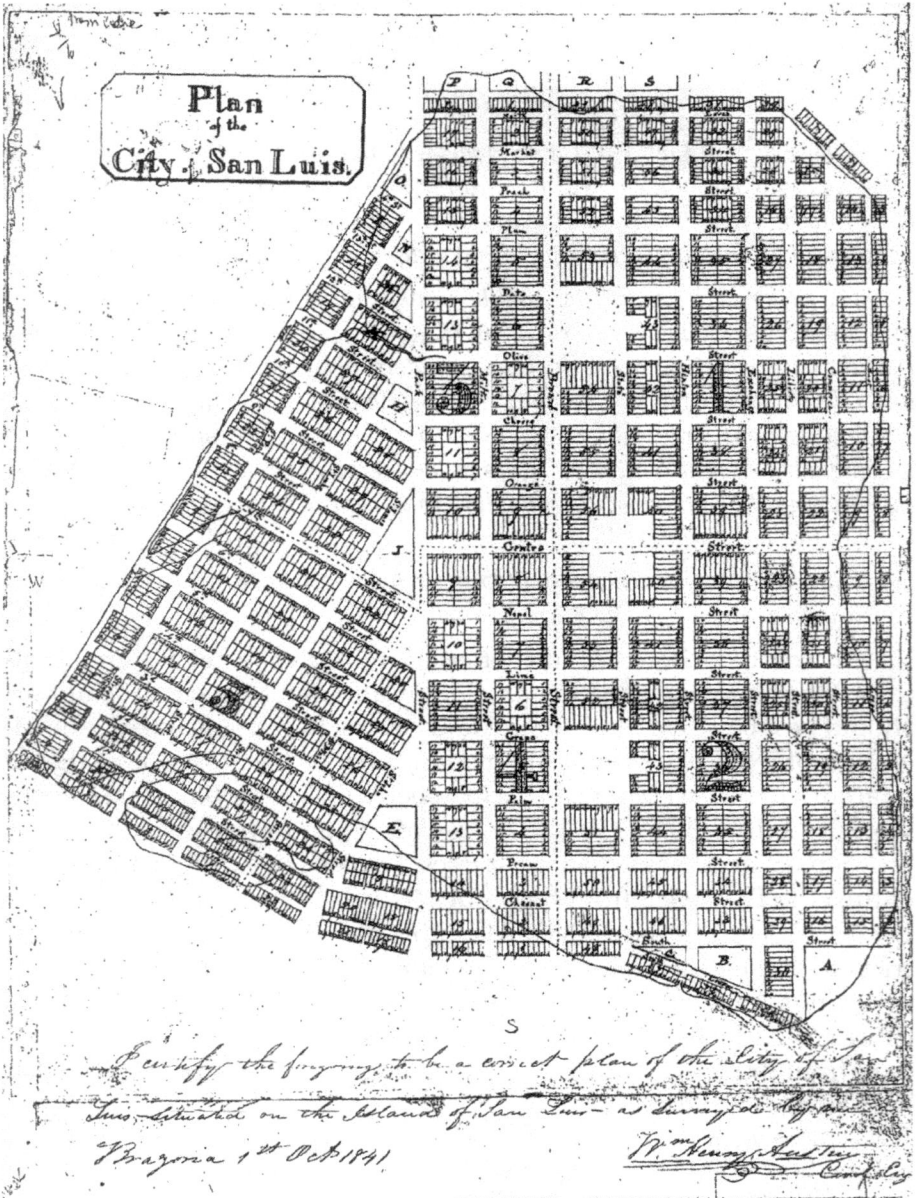

City Plat[5]

As the years pass, this acreage will continually decrease.

This original Certificate of Property[6] in the City of San Luis for Peter Gautier, signed by Matthew Hopkins, is located in the Rosenberg Library in Galveston, Texas. During several lean years the county seat for Brazoria was closed and important documents were moved to Galveston as a temporary location. This did not last long, but documents can still be found there.

Peter Gautier
Courtesy of Rosenberg Library

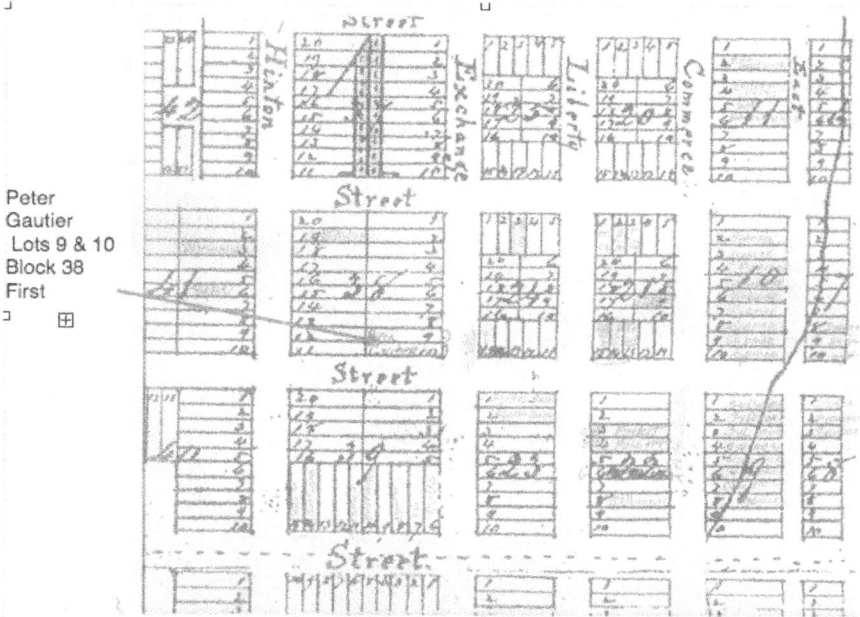

Peter
Gautier
Lots 9 & 10
Block 38
First

Peter Gautier lots 9 & 10[7]

As the sections of land were mapped and detailed, the venture paved the way for yet another step in establishing the city. The postal system of the Republic of Texas began in October 1835 when a special committee of the Permanent Council was appointed to establish a mail route. The Congress of the Republic of Texas created an act for a General Post Office as a division of the State Department on December 20, 1836. The San Luis post office was established on July 13, 1840, with the appointment of Edmund Andrews as Postmaster. A little later in this chapter, there is a photograph of an envelope marked with Edmond Andrews, Post Master. He served until the appointment of Augustus Burr on April 10, 1843. Burr was reappointed and remained in office from Annexation until the office was discontinued on August 16, 1848.

The Annexation of the Republic of Texas

AN ACT

Establishing a Mail Route therein named.

Section 1. Be it enacted by the Senate and House of Representatives of the Republic of Texas in Congress assembled. That there shall be a post route established between the city of Galveston and Matagorda, via: San Luis and Velasco, and shall be let out upon the same provisions as other mail routes of this Republic.

Approved, January 30th, 1845

Despite the official route, residents remained subject to the whims of both the island's conditions and the temperament of the deliverer. The mail was not always as important to the mail carrier as it was to the recipients. The *Daily Texian* tells of about how a mail carrier bought a new pistol and didn't deliver the mail for several days, as he needed to test it out.

A letter dated October 6, 1841, was written and signed by Edmund Andrews, Postmaster, San Luis. The letter is directed to Alfred Kelso, Sheriff of Gonzales County, at Gonzales. Edmund Andrews owned many leagues of Land in the Republic of Texas according to the tax records of 1841.

He discusses land that was advertised in the *Austin City Gazette* for taxes and tries to explain that he paid the taxes. The last statement, with great irony, reads, "I send you a copy of the receipt, because I do not like to trust the original by post."

Although the exact location of the post office is unknown, Edmond Andrews is recorded as the owner of the following, as well as several other lots in the City of San Luis.

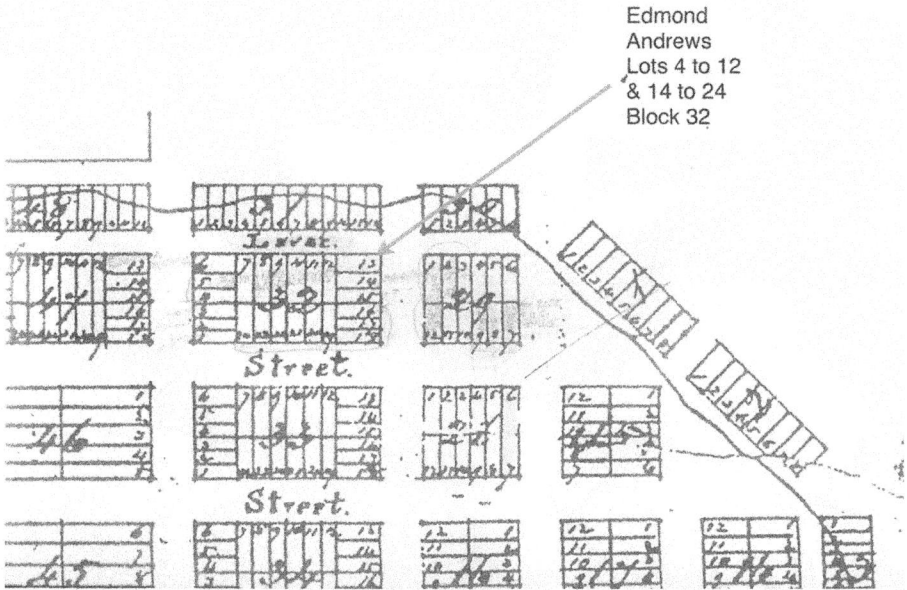

Edmond Andrews Lots[8]

For many years before and after the Civil War, in fact, until 1892, the mail between Galveston and points west was carried by the Beach Route. The mail was carried from Galveston, in a hack, along the beach. The mail was then taken across San Luis Pass to Old Velasco, which is now known as Surfside; finally along the beach to Matagorda. The Follett's carried this mail, from San Luis to Velasco the greatest part of the time.[9]

The following advertisement appeared in the *San Luis Advocate*.

BENNETT'S HOTEL
SAN LUIS, BRAZORIA CO.

The subscriber has opened his house for
the accommodation of Travelers and
Boarders.   CHARLES H. BNNETT
San Luis, August 26, 1841   1-tf

In a letter of August 9, 1840, from Matthew Hopkins to James F. Perry, Hopkins wrote that the Bennet's Hotel (also spelled Bennett's in the *San Luis Advocate*) was open and underway, with a plan for the first ball.

Goods for Sale[10]
JUST received, and for sale, --Five cases
fine Brogans,
3 cases Negro Brogans,
5 cases Hats,
10 dozen Umbrellas,
50 dozen mens Long Hose,
2 cases ready made Clothing
6 pieces Negro Cloth,
10 qr. casks superior Madeira & Port Wines
1 pipe Otard, Dupuy & Col Brandy
50 kegs Green Paint
30 cans Verdigris, a superior article,
50 Boxes Soap
2 1/2 dozen bottles writing Ink
10 cases Wafers.
August 26, 1840   J. F. WOODHULL

HAVANA SEGARS
20,000   *Havana Segars, just received*
and for sale by,
August 20, 1840 1-t F   J. F. WOODHULL

These were very exciting times; construction was everywhere. Businesses set up and opened for customers to buy the finest wares. J. F. Woodhull sold almost everything. Mr. Woodhull advertised in many issues of the *San Luis Advocate* that he had twenty thousand "Havana Segars" ready for sale. Here is one of J. F. Woodhull's ads for 20,000 Havana Segars, just received and for sale, August 26, 1840. He also met the transportation needs of his customers. Again these are copies of ads from the *San Luis Advocate* dated March 61 (16) 1841 Vol. 1 No 2.

The *Advocate* also had many ads from Andrews and Hammeken, offering various goods for sale. "Developer George L. Hammeken built a 1,000 foot wharf and two warehouses to handle the shipping," according to the *San Luis Advocate*, August, 1840.

Sale of goods and offers of services were not the only advertisements to make it into print. As the city expanded, the newspaper also served individuals seeking skilled labor. On August 26, 1840, the paper ran a dual advertisement seeking carpenters to build a house, while simultaneously piquing the interest of potential buyers. This advertisement gave the following specifications:

Was to be thirty by twenty feet on the ground, one and a half stories high, with a piazza in front eight feet wide...Crowned with a balcony and balustrade the roof... and a kitchen attached in the rear, fifteen feet square and in the neatest Grecian style...A dream about to come true for someone, this stately new home with the sun and the sea as your front and back yard. All the seafood you could eat with fresh produce garden from the very soil you own.

Despite the appeal of sunsets and waves, life on a thriving trading island did not come without risk, and measures were taken to avoid introducing any unwanted guest that might lurk among the imported goods. Yellow fever, cholera and other viruses were dreaded infectious diseases.

The quarantine laws, we are pleased to learn, are already in force, although every vessel as yet has on her arrival exhibited a clean bill of health. We have also the satisfaction of assuring our citizens and the public generally that the new city Hospital on the eastern end of the Island, will be completed in the course of five or six days. With all these precautionary measures taken, little danger may be apprehended of yellow fever in this city, this season.[11]

The inadvertent introduction of illnesses was not the only risk associated with those who chose to employ the sea for trade. Often cargo fell prey to the whims of wind and waves.

One vessel whose journey came to a violent end was the steamboat, *Rodney*. Regarding the loss, George Hammeken wrote on September 28, 1840:

Andrews is now at Quintana on board the Steam Boat Rodney that I have chartered to bring here Smith's cotton, destined to New York, Schooner Delaware now in port, & our live oak for a cotton press.

September 30, 1840, M. Austin Bryan writes to his parents—The Steam Boat Rodney was wrecked on the beach 4 miles this side of San

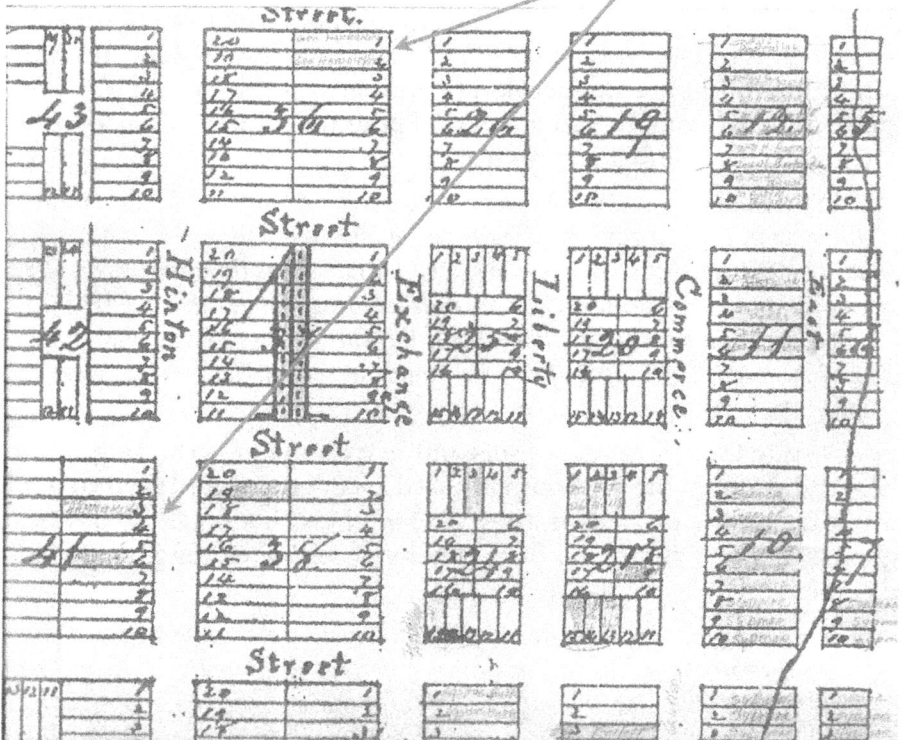

George Hammeken
Owned many lots
This is a few

George Hammeken[12]

Luis on the 22nd loaded with cotton for Smith & others at Columbia to be shipped from San Luis to N. York —Judge Andrews lost his live oak timbers for his press on her — she went all to pieces. Some of the cotton has been saved — The wreck of this boat is an unfortunate affair for San Luis in many respects.
Signed George Hammeken

Cotton from south central Texas was a common good often passing through the Gulf ports. A letter dated from September 30, 1840, from

Cotton Gin Ad[13]

M. Austin Bryan to his parents, boasts that Acock has upward of 140 thousand pounds of cotton, and estimates that the land would make nearly a bale to the acre.

Mrs. Mary Ann Burr Escher, granddaughter of Anne Louis Follett was a checker for cotton and other produce carried by riverboats from San Luis to Old Velasco.

Seizing the opportunity of supply and demand, J. F. Woodhull ordered a cotton gin, advertising in the *San Luis Advocate*,

I have just received an elegant Cotton Gin, sixty saws. Any person in need of such an article would do well to call and examine the Gin as it is a very superior make, and can be bought on very reasonable terms. J. F. Woodhull. San Luis August 26, 1840.

The advertisement worked, and several months later, Mary Austin Holley wrote a letter from San Luis that was published in the *San Luis Advocate* on January 26, 1840.

Dear Cousin: The Cotton Press is in operation here. It seems business-like.

With the growth of commerce, measures were taken to ensure that corruption did not follow. Maintaining law and order in this young territory was a great challenge. Anyone wanting the job advertised in the local newspaper, sometimes blatantly seeking to replace the existing sheriff.

San Luis Advocate Aug. 20, 1840 Hill announces:[14]

TO THE CITIZENS OF BRAZORIA COUNTY.

I take this method of presenting myself to you as a candidate for the office of sheriff of this county. I am induced to do so upon the following considerations:

1st. In all governments were the people select their agents to transact public business relation in office is a governing principle.

2nd. Where the people are oppressed and weighed down by the severity of the times -- where good money, as it is termed, is almost impossible to be had --- I hold it to be the duty of every officer of the Government to conform to the law, and require Texas money only in payment of their fees.

The second Congress passed a law requiring all officers to take Texas Promissory Notes and prohibiting them from demanding their fees in any other currency. The Sheriff of this county has demanded par money. I will take such money as the law authorizes me to charge. I have been a sufferer in common with my fellow citizens, and have determined to step in to the relief of both plaintiffs and defendants at law, with a determination to devote my best service to the county and country at large.
I beg leave to subscribe myself
Your obedient fellow citizen

August 20, 1840   WM. G. HILL

As the life on the island flourished, the islanders attempted to expand means of travel. The *San Luis Advocate* of March 23, 1841, discusses plans to build a bridge to connect the island of San Luis to the mainland. This was a huge undertaking. As recorded in the *San Luis Advocate* on Tuesday, Oct 13, 1840, Vol. 1, No 27:

In our paper of Feb. 23d we made a promise, without much reflection on the matter, to give, weekly an account of the progress of the Bridge, now being constructed; intended to connect our Island with the main land. During the week following the 23rd Feb. Hands were employed in preparing the Flat and Piling Machine.

Readers followed the weekly updates in the newspaper, and the editors took great care to report every detail on the progression.

We now give a description of the work finished at this time;--- As we stated before, the bridge when completed, will be 1260 feet in length of which 900 feet are made on piles, the balance on frame or tressel work.

The piles are at this time extended to 860 feet; the caps or cross-ties are placed on the piles for 540 feet—some of the workmen are now, engaged in placing the remaining caps on the piles—some occupied in driving more piles, and others are preparing the railing for the bridge.

Opinions raged as the bridge inched closer to the mainland, raising concern over lack of funding. Despite the fears, the newspaper remained optimistic.

We are thus particular in our description, as several of our friends have expressed doubts as to the construction of so costly a work at this time, but we are happy to state that the perseverance of those engaged is to be depending upon, and we feel certain that in a short time we shall be able to count another facility to those already possessed by this port.

Unfortunately, the hopeful forecast was wrong, and the bridge was never completed. It was not until 1966 that the dream became a reality.

Though commerce and construction soared on the island, other important services remained scarce. Compensating for the lack of doctors, medical publications were the lifesaving means on many occasions on San Luis Island and the Peninsula.

The October 20, 1840 issue of the *San Luis Advocate* carried an advertisement to the effect that Doctors Richardson and Smith proposed to edit a journal to be printed quarterly. The ad is as follows:

Doct's Richardson and Smith propose to edit a Medical and Surgical Journal, to be published in the Office of the San Luis Advocate, at the city of San Luis. It is intended to present to the reader, in a condensed Form not only the improvements in the science, but a faithful portrait of the prevailing endemicks of Texas, their treatment and medical topography. The first number will appear in January next. It will be published quarterly, and contain about sixty-four pages, octavo.

We are much gratified at this announcement. A publication of this kind will afford much valuable and interesting intelligence; and we venture the prediction, that it will be made the instrument of much good. The gentlemen, who are engaged to conduct the Journal, are men whose reputation will secure to it an auspicious surgery of its success. Dr. Smith has been long known to us as a gentleman of science and professional erudition. A work which he wrote, while in Paris, in 1832 on the Cholera Spasmodica, introduces him in a most favorable manner, as an author, to the professional public in France and the United States. Dr. Richardson is extensively known in this country as one of the most eminent and successful physicians of which the country can boast. The capacity of these two gentlemen, alone, will secure to the undertaking decided success, and may be relied on as a guaranty of the valuable character of the publication. Being the first Journal Wholly of a literary character, or devoted entirely to professional pursuits, which has been started in Texas, we feel much interest in its success, and commend the enterprise with our warmest advocacy.

The lack of medical care by no means indicated that the island lacked sophistication. Grand balls were held for many special occasions during this era, and frontier settlements were no exception. The *San Luis Advocate*, November 3, 1840 issue noted the first ball to be held in San Luis.

Well past requiring only practical services, San Luis began to offer opportunities for the finer points of life, including a portrait painter. J.J. Tucker ran this ad in the San Luis

J. J. TUCKER
PORTRAIT PAINTER

RESPECTFULLY informs the citizens of San Luis and Brazoria county generally, that he is prepared to paint Portraits for those who may favor him with their patronage.

N.B. Specimens can be seen at his room, nearly opposite Bennet's Hotel San Luis. Dec 10th, 1840 13-tf

With the city well situated in commerce and social opportunities, attention turned toward caring for the spiritual well-being of its inhabitants. No official church buildings were built yet, and this notice in the *Advocate* notes that services would be held in Bennet's Hotel.[15]

Another advancement took place when congress annexed the port of San Luis to the Collectoral District of the Brazos.

Be it enacted by the Senate and House of Representatives of the Republic of Texas, in Congress assembled, That the port of San Luis be, and the same is hereby annexed to the district of Brazos, and that the northern boundary of said district, show be the same as that established for the northern boundary of the county of Brazoria, by an act passed the sixteenth day of December of the fourth session of Congress, and that all laws heretofore passed, which contravene in the provisions of this act be, and the same are hereby repealed.

David S. Kaufman,   Speaker of the House of Representatives
David G. Burnet,   President of the Senate
Approved December 10th, 1840.
Mirabeau B. Lamar

No doubt there were many land agents, as indicated in the *San Luis Advocate*, December 10, 1840.

GENERAL LAND AGENCY

JAMES R. JENNINGS,
LAND AGENT, SAN LUIS
TEXAS,

*Will attend to the purchase and sale of lands,
lying in any portion of the Republic.*[16]

The city of San Luis provided a gathering point for those interested in developing the nearby land. The newspaper served as the connection between landowners ready to sell and potential buyers.

On the 25 and 26 days of December next there will be a large sale of Brazos, Bernard, Oyster Creek, Bastrop Bayou, and Chocolate Bayou Lands, at the city of San Luis, Texas. It is proposed that each holder of a league of land, on any of these streams, shall have surveyed off from the tract six hundred and forty or three hundred and twenty acres. The land to be sold on five years credit with interest at six per cent from the date of sale. The party purchasing to come under bond to improve upon and fence at least thirty acres, and erect a dwelling house on the land, Purchased within two years (from the date of sale. The purchaser to pay expenses of the survey, title, deed and sale, on delivery of the deed and on failure of contract forfeiture of the land. Not more than one tract will be sold from each league or part of league. The land holders are invited to forward to the subscriber as soon as practicable, a description of the tracts which they will offer at that time of sale, as it is important that bills of the lands shall be circulated as extensively and of as early a date as possible. Those who may offer their lands are expected to be prepared to give full warrantee titles.

San Luis, Oct 27, 9-31 MAT'W. HOPKINS[17]

SALE OF LANDS

*ON the 25 and 26 day's of DECEMBER next
there will be a large sale of BRAZOS, BERNARD,
OYSTER CREEK, BASTROP BAYOU and*

CHOCOLATE BAYOU Lands at the City of San Luis, Texas. It is proposed that each holder of a league of land, on may of these streams, shall have surveyed off from the tract six hundred and forty or three hundred and twenty acres. The land to be sold on five years credit with interest at six per cent from the date of sale. The party purchasing to come under bond to improve upon and fence at least thirty acres, and erect a dwelling house on the land purchased within two years from the date of sale. The purchaser to pay expenses of the survey, title, deed and sale, on delivery of the deed -- and on failure of con tract forfeiture of the land. Not more than one tract will be sold from each league or part of league. The land holders are invited to forward to the subscriber as soon as practicable, a description of the tracts which they will offer at that time for sale, as it is important that bills of the lands shall be circulated as extensively and of as early a date as possible. Those who may offer their lands are expected to be prepared to give full warrantee title.

San Luis, Oct 27, 9-31   MAT'W. HOPKINS.

Though the island's inhabitants fully utilized the opportunities offered by the surrounding waters, one man harnessed the power of another natural resource: the wind. As the new city's growth was moving forward very rapidly, Charles Bryant advertised for workmen to erect a "Wind Mill for the grinding of corn, &c." in the *San Luis Advocate*, December 10, 1840 issue.

Building the railroad assured that any labors who came for short term work had plenty of opportunity to find their next job.

George L. Hammeken's planned railroad took on a massive promotional program.

The directors of the Brazos and Galveston Rail Road Company, resolved that the installments remaining to be paid on the shares of the company's stock, were to be payable as follows:

"	*On the 1st October, 1840*	*Five per cent.*
"	*1st January, 1841*	*Five per cent.*
"	*1st April, "*	*Five per cent*
"	*1st October "*	*Ten per cent*
"	*1st January 1842*	*Ten per cent*
"	*1st April "*	*Ten per cent*

"	1st July	"	Ten per cent
"	1st October	"	Ten per cent
"	1st January	"	Ten per cent

Resolved, That the aforesaid installments shall be paid in the Company's office, at the city of San Luis, to the Treasurer of the company, who is hereby authorized to receipt for the same. And should any of the stockholders advance any installment prior to its becoming due, as per foregoing resolution, the treasurer is authorized to discount the same at the rate of ten per cent, per annum.

Resolved, That the President be, and he is hereby authorized to open new subscriptions for stock forfeited for non payment of the installments; and may re-donate the lots in the city of San Luis, corresponding to the shares forfeited.

Resolved, That these proceedings be published once a month in the Texas Sentinel, and in the New Orleans Bee.

GEO. L. HAMMEKEN, President.

By the order of the Board.

M. Austin Bryan, Secretary pro tem.

San Luis, June 3, 1840. 5-if

Eager for expansion, both in the town and in their personal wealth, the offer was noticed by investors from far beyond the island.

The *San Luis Advocate*, December 10, 1840, listed the stockholders, including many familar names in Texas history.

"Texas"	*James F. Perry*	*Arnold Thouvein*
David G. Burnet	*Lorenzo Zavalla*	*Asa Brigham*
Edmund Andrews	*Frederick A. Sawyer*	*John Chassaigne*
Frederick Lemsky	*Aguste Gosse*	*Lewis Helzie*
George Brisonneau	*Herman Holstein Kagen*	*John Prescot*
George Fisher	*William G. Cook*	*Casgrave*
Auguste A. Cardet	*Reinauff Desoto*	*George L. Hammeken*
Hamilton P. Bee,	*Miller*	*Conrad Franke*
Frederick Helmiller	*Jacob W. Cruger*	*Milburn & Underwood*
James Knight	*William T. Austin*	*Samuel Fuller*
Drosig	*Wilhelm Hennig*	*John. W. Cloud*
Joseph Mims	*M. Austin Bryan*	*William J. Bryan*
Matthew Hopkins	*William H. Austin*	*Tod Robinson*
William B Corbin	*"Baltimore"*	*James Smith*
"Mobile"	*D. Manson*	*F. Daniel*
"New York"	*Habert Meugens*	*Peter Cullen*

Peter J. Francia	"New Orleans"	Hypolite Thomas
Henry G. Hearu	Francois A. Tete	Dudougt & Tenlade
Auguste Tete	Francois Pougel	Joseph Matin
Louise E. Mace	Auguste Bonneroe	Charlotte Mexia
Henri Tete	Anjoine Isard	Charles H. Ogdn
Josephine Price	?	Charles A. Jacobs
Francois Jourdan	Bernabe C. Sanches	John A. Roberts
Jules Benit	John A. Roberts	William M. Goodrich
Christopher Adams, Jr.	Francois Lampre	Antone Delpeauch
Henry A. Mexia	Joan Garcie Negrete	Henry Boulet
"Captains of Vessels"	Capt. Brotus Burrows	Capt. James D. Boylan
Capt. Dodley Stark	Capt Joseph J. Henry	"Mexico"
Miguel Gignous	Maximillan M. Chabert	James Wright
Pierre Gautier	Joseh Prom	Martin F. Pezara
Robert F. Lapham	Jan Vifiba	

Navigating San Luis Pass

W. C. Mitchell, commander of the brig *Ironsides*, wrote the following detailed report for the navigation of San Luis Pass to the wharf at the City of San Luis.

Communications From the Commander of Ironside, 1840:
Communications on the Ports of Galveston and St. Luis, some Banks in the Mexican Sea, Salt Kay Bank, Bahamas, and St. Helena Sound in Carolina; 1840." The Colombian Navigator, vol. 1, 1839, ran the following article:
1.—Directions for proceeding to Galveston Bay, by Mr. W. C. Mitchell, Commander of the Ironside, of Liverpool, and Mr. Geo. Simpson, chief Pilot. of Galveston, 1840."The East end of the Island of Galveston lies in 29° 16' 37" N., and 94° 49' 41" W.* This has been deduced from numerous observations, as shown by Mr. Simpson**. The rise and fall of the tide on the bar is only from 2 to 3 feet. Variation of the compass, 9° E.

Vessels bound to this place, says Captain Mitchell, should endeavour to make the land about the Sabine River, or the meridian of 94° W. They may stand toward the land with the greatest confidence, always keeping the lead going; as there are 3 1/2 to 4 fathoms of water at 5 to 6 miles off the land to the eastward of Galveston Island; but, to the westward of the east end of that island they should never stand within the depth of 5 1/2 fathoms. The current always sets strongly to the S.W. at the rate of 2 to 2 1/2 miles in the hour, and the prevailing winds are from S.E. excepting during the winter months, when there are very heavy gales from North to N.W. With the latter, if you are any where near the land, or in 6 or 7 fathoms, it will be much better to anchor than to keep under way, pro-

vided you are near the port.

On approaching Galveston Bay the first objects seen will be the masts of vessels, and a little while after the houses will appear. The land may not be seen until about two miles from the anchorage without the bar.

The best anchorage off the Bar is in 5 1/2 to 6 fathoms, (mud) about one mile off, with the Flagstaff on Galveston Island bearing W. by S., and the pilot's house, which is the largest house on Bolivar Point (north shore) ...N.W. by W. The ground is good, and, with good ground tackle, there is no risk of driving. Within the bay, vessels are quite sheltered from all winds, and have good holding ground. At about twelve miles to the N.B. of the entrance of the port is a long range of bushes called Pepper Grove, and if you see these you may make sure that you are to windward of your port. To the westward of the port, near the centre of Galveston Island, are the three trees, ...and which may be seen, in clear weather, from three to four leagues off. They are the only original trees on the island.

Mariners ought to be very careful, when standing in for the land to the westward of Galveston Bay, during the night, as the soundings are very irregular; but in the day-time there is no danger, while keeping the lead going.

Mr. Simpson has observed that the port of Galveston was formerly difficult to make, the coast being so low; but there are now more than 3000 houses, and many so lofty that they may be seen, from a vessel's masthead, at the distance of 20 miles. Vessels of heavy draught should not approach the Bar nearer than in six fathoms, and then, by making signal for a pilot they will be promptly attended to. Those making the port by night will do well to come to an anchor until day-light. For the convenience of obtaining a pilot, those drawing 8 feet or less may approach to the depth of 4 fathoms.

If, on approaching from the eastward, the town comes in sight and a little to the southward of W.S.W., haul off immediately to 6 fathoms, and until it bears S.W. by W. when you will then be in a fair-way for the Bar. If approaching from the westward, run to the eastward until the town has the same bearing of S.W. by W.

2,—SAN LUIS, or the West Pass of Galveston. The following description and directions for this port were obligingly communicated by Mr. John Nabb, agent to the Charleston Insurance and Trust Company for Texas, and dated San Luis, Jan. 1st, 1840.

The little isle of San Luis, containing 354 acres, is situate at a mile and a half from the western end of Galveston Island. A town upon it is rising very fast. The Bar is only two miles from the island, and the port has the

best water known on the coast of Texas. The harbour is good, capacious,
1 and of easy access, and is expected, from its peculiar advantages, to
become the chief commercial port of the new Republic.

Those bound to San Luis should endeavor to make Galveston Island,
which may be known by the three trees in the middle of the island as
above mentioned. Then run down along shore in 5, 4, or 3, fathoms,
soundings regular, and thence to 5 fathoms. Keep in the last depth, steer-
ing S.W. until you bring a beacon on San Luis in a line with the build-
ing known as Polites House, bearing W.N.W.; with this mark on run for
it, which will lead you in over the bar, in ten feet at low water, until you
come within half a mile of San Luis Island; then haul up N.W. gradually
opening Polites House to the northward of the beacon, rounding a buoy,
close on board, which is placed on the shoal that stretches from Galves-
ton Island, leaving it on the starboard side, and after passing which you
may anchor at pleasure.

A flag half-mast on the beacon will indicate 10 feet on the bar; one ball,
11 feet; two balls, 12 feet; three balls, 13 feet; four balls, 14 feet; five balls,
15 feet; and the flag hoisted to the mast-head or Flagstaff, will indicate
high water. Spring-tides rise 5 feet, and neaps 3 feet.

Captain Mitchell has given it in Lat. 29° 18', and long. 94° 48'.

Mr. Simpson's Remarks were first given in the Nautical Magazine,
June, 1840.

Captain Mitchell says, I took observations, when lying at anchor, which
gave 29° 16' N. and 94° 44' VV. When I left, there was a pair of snares
erected over the wreck of the steamer Cuba, on the north breakers, inside
the Bar, and on the south breakers lay the wreck of the ship Virginia.
No vessel but of very easy draft should attempt to cross the Bar. My
vessel drew 8J, feet going and coming, fully laden, and a vessel of the
same draught, or a foot more, may always cross the Bar in safety. The
Virginia was said to draw 12 feet, and, in attempting to cross, became
a total wreck. There is now a first-rate pilot-boat constantly on look-out
for vessels nearing land; and it is expected that a light-vessel may be
stationed as a direction for the Bar.

London Printed for R. H. Laurie.

The *San Luis Advocate* , January 29, 1841, depicts a very active port.
There were numerous Customs House Collectors. The shipping news
section of the *San Luis Advocate* reported as many as eight to ten tall
ships from throughout the world, dropping anchor in the harbor at the
same time.

Ironsides[18]

Arrival of Ironsides.

The undersigned has received by the above vessel, direct from Liverpool, an assorted cargo of British Manufactures, which will be found on inspection to be suited to the taste and wants of this country, as well as the Mexican market, consisting of --

Printed Calicoes, Toweling, Hosiery, Domestics, flannels, Bagging, Irish Linens, Tickings, Bale-rope, Crenelias, Merinos, Linen-twill, Platilias, Muslins, Cutlery, Moleskins, Crossovers, Velveteens, Linseys, Broadcloth, Blankets, Sheeting, Fine Shirts, Plain & Colored Shirts, Tons of Iron, cut Nails, Crockery, Saddlery, Trace and Log Chains.

--ALSO--

Ready made Clothing, Over Coats, & e.; Negro Clothing, and other articles too numerous to mention, which will be sold cheap for cash or exchanged for hides or cotton.

The undersigned will also make advances in cash, or short date bills in New Orleans of New York, on cotton, to be shipped direct to Liverpool, or will buy at fair market rates.   *CHARLES POWER*
Galveston, Dec. 9 1840 -16tf

PORT OF SAN LUIS

ARRIVED

SEPT. 4	*Schr. Delaware, Brookfield, master, from N. Orleans*
5	*Sloop Brazoria, Lombart, master, from Galveston*
"	*Sloop San Domingo, Johnson, from Galveston*
6	*Sloop Barrows, Haskins, from Galveston*
7	*Tom Jack, Matison, from Columbia,*
"	*Steamer Rodney, Bogart, master, Galveston*
11	*Sloop Brazoria, Lombart, from the Brazos*
"	*Sloop Champion, Leetch, From Brazos*
12	*Sloop Tom Jack, Matison from Galveston*

CLEARED

SEPT 6	*Sloop Buirews, Velasco*
8	*San Domingo, Velasco*
8	*Tom Jack, Galveston*
8	*Sloop Brazoria, Velasco*
8	*Steamer Rodney, Columbia*

The *Advocate* noted on January 29, 1841 that the brig, *Ironsides*, direct from Liverpool, had docked at San Luis. The ship brought with her a cargo which included printed calicoes, toweling, hosiery, linen-twill, velveteen's, and plain and colored shirts. The advertisement stated that the cargo will "be suited to the taste and wants of this country, as well as the Mexican market." Also on board were tons of iron, cut nails, crockery and saddlery, to mention a few items.

The brig was not sent away empty, and Captain Brown returned with a ship holding 688 bales of cotton. The *San Luis Advocate*, March 16, 1841 announced: the clearance of *Ironsides*.

This notice ran in many issues.

Port of San Luis[19]

PORT OF SAN LUIS

ARRIVED

March 3	*Brig City of Perth, Captain Holliday, from London, in ballast.*
" 5	*Brig Magnet, Capt ---, From Galveston with 80,000 feet Lumber, consigned to Matthew Hopkins,*

CLEARED

March 2	*Brig Ironsides, Capt. Brown, for Liverpool with 688 bales cotton.*

As many as ten tall ships docked at the Port of San Luis at one time. The view may have looked very much like this when ten tall ships anchored at the thousand-foot wharf. I took this photo at Boston Harbor during the five hundredth birthday celebration of Christopher Columbus sail to America. This is no doubt what the wharf looked like at the Port of San Luis in 1841.

Not every ship served as a trading vessel. Smaller boats offered passengers travel among the local ports.

San Luis Advocate, January 29, 1841 ad reads:

BRAZORIA, VELASCO
SAN LUIS AND GALVESTON

The new and fast sailing Sloop BRAZORIA, T. Lambert, master, will run to and from Brazoria, Velasco, San Luis, and Galveston ports during the season. For freight or passage, apply on board, or to: John Butler, Brazoria; Juris Dockrill, Velasco; Sam'l J. Durnett, San Luis; Jones and Co., Galveston[20]

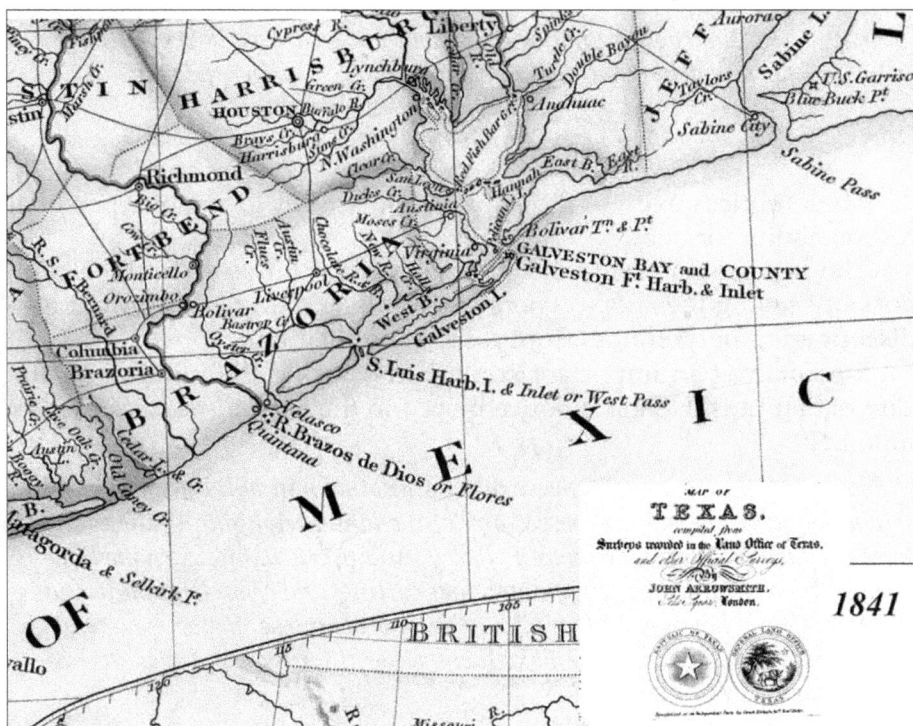

Arrowsmith Map[21]

Once again, San Luis appeared as an island in John Arrowsmith's magnificent copper engraved map. This map also shows Oyster Creek entering the Gulf of Mexico. At one time Oyster creek was seventy-five miles in length and entered the gulf seven miles west of San Luis Harbor. Its source was near the Brazos, in Fort Bend county and ran parallel to the Brazos. (Texas by Arthur Ikin) San Luis is an island on this map.

A Port City is a Port City! When sailors arrived from a long journey at sea, their captains would run notices to protect themselves from the actions of their men while in port.[22]

Notices

I hereby give notice that I will not be answerable
for any debts that my crew may contract during the stay
of the Brig City of Perth in this harbor.
JOHN HOLIDAY, Master
San Luis, March 9, 1841 23ids

———————

NOTICE
I hereby give notice that I will not be answerable
for any debts that my crew may contract during the stay
of the Brig Magnet in this harbor.
San Luis, March 16, 1841 2-1-ids

———————

These notices express the ship captains wish to remove personal responsibility for debt.

The newspaper continued to be an important asset to the island, not only saving the shop owners from potential unpaid debt, but also discouraging perpetrators from continuing their antics.

Timber was an important commodity during the building of the City of San Luis. Here is a notice placed in the *San Luis Advocate* issue, June 1840. :

Notice — All persons will please take notice, that suit will be commenced against any one who trespasses any of the lands belonging to the estate of Stephen F. Austin, or James F. Perry. And this is to forewarn particularly those who have been and are now cutting timber on Chocolate and Dickenson's Bayous, and on Clear Creek, that unless they cease operating, efforts will be made to make them account for their plunder.
M. Austin Bryan
Peach Point, June 30th, 1840

So many of the news articles in the *San Luis Advocate*, brought forth not only poetry, but also knowledge to its readers.

Number of Oaks Necessary to Build One Ship.--When we consider the number of trees that are required to build a single ship, and the length of time necessary to bring them to maturity, it becomes the duty of every landed proprietor to plant for the sake of posterity. 'An oak in good soil and situation,' says South, a practical planter, 'will, 75 years from the acorn, contain a ton of timber; or a load and a half of square timber.'

By a report of the commissioners of land revenue, respecting timber, printed by order of the House of Commons, it appears that a 74 gun ship contains about 2,000 tons, which, at the rate of a load and a half a ton, would give 3,000 loads of timer; and would consequently require 2,000 trees of 73 years growth. It has also been calculated that as not more than 40 oaks, containing a load and a half of timber in each, can stand upon an acre, 50 acres are required to produce the oaks necessary for a 74 gun ship.--London pa.[23]

Though the surrounding waters provided a livelihood, they could not sustain human life itself. To provide fresh water, rain that fell on the roofs of cotton sheds was diverted by gutters to a brick cistern, about seventy feet in diameter. The bricks were brought from Pennsylvania, and this cistern is now near waters' edge in Section I of Treasure Island, buried in the sand.

Although the account is incomplete, still what a wonderful find! The old newspaper was badly damaged with large holes, and thus, missing text. The *San Luis Advocate*, April 20, 1841, printed a very detailed article of how to get fresh water.:

----------------*Can store 2,500 bales of cotton protected from------------ A large new well manned and safe ferry that is for operation between this and the west end of Galveston Island and in a few days a smaller one will be in readiness to convey passengers from San Luis to the Peninsula which leads to Velasco. This channel is so narrow that a cable will be stretched across and used to facilitate the passage. Come, neighbors of Galveston, aid us in our endeavors to advance the interests of our common country, by recommending strangers to pursue this proper route to the heart of our beautiful and productive valleys; that they may return home like Sterne's cheerful traveler who had reported all he had seen as green and smiling – But continue to point out the broad and ocalent tract, and, like the jaundiced wayfarer, the weary and disappointed explorers will swear that all is yellow in Texas.*

The indefatigable Winney continues to run his stage from Galveston to Velasco, via San Luis (42 miles). We challenge the world to produce a road, of the same length, with such uninterrupted firmness and evenness of surface. And then the view of the boundless ocean—the glad breeze from the heaving bosom, and the perpetual music of the raging surf, laving the feet of your horses with its spray, charms three of your senses during the whole trip,-- the sheeps-head and red fish at San Luis gratifies a fourth and the fifth may revel in the sweets of some gardens we got in the Brazos valley.

The bridge now being constructed from San Luis to the main land spans a space of 500 yards; a sufficient number of strong cedar piles have already been driven the entire distance; caps or sills have been mortised to the same, to the distance of 325 yards. The bridge will afford us the mean of convenient access to lands on Bastrop Bayou, distant five miles – Chocolate 12 miles – oyster creek 16 miles and Brazos 25 miles. The soil on the different route is said to be sandy, and therefore capable of affording capital roads, during all seasons by proper ditching. If the planters' (who are to be principally benefited) would only act in concert and devote the labor of their forces during spare intervals, to the improvements, how soon could they complete them over ground unobstructed by trees or roots: what a bustle would we have in our embryo city next fall and how cheap could they get their cotton to market! Will some public spirited planter set this ball in motion!

This article was commenced on the head of improvements; let us not omit to place among the number of neat picket fences which already define so many boundaries, and are such proper appendages to lane houses.

A brick and cement cistern, capable of holding 8,000 gallons of water will receive contributions for the benefit of the thirsty, at the first meeting of the clouds.

Responding to an increasing demand for accommodations during the 1840s, several hotels advertised for business. Bennett's Hotel, was the first recorded hotel. The Central Hill Hotel operated by Mrs. Mathews. Her advertisement in the *San Luis Advocate*, Tuesday, March 6, 1842, Volume 24 as follows:

Mrs. Mathews respectfully informs the public that the above house of entertainment is now open for the accommodation of visitors. Appended to the establishment is a bathhouse, well fitted up, and supplied with fine soft water, certainly not best to the world. The temperature of the bath is regulated to suit the dialbesis of its subjects. No individual to Texas will regret a ride of the 12 to 15 miles, in addition to four bit fee for the luxury, net Mrs. Mathews would inform the public, that no extra charge will be made for the bath to those who patronize the house. Her house, stabling, bedding, etc., are well suited to accommodate the traveler, and her charges high in proportion and no discount made for length of time that ladies and gentlemen may choose to stay, yet there are now fitting up private boarding house, where the convalescent and he who seeks Hygeia may obtain prophylactics and an interview with the lovely goddess of Centre Hill, a place of resort during the sickly season. There are some three or four scientific and experience physician in active practice within

10 miles, on the Brazos and its tributaries.

Texas Planter, Brazoria, Texas, October 1, 1842, advertised the "Hotel San Luis." It was also called the San Luis Hotel. This 1842 advertisement regarding the hotel is as follows:

HOTEL.

SAN LUIS.

C, H. RHODES.

TRAVELLERS accommodated at the above establishment; Horses fed, &c., &c.

San Luis, Oct. 1. 1842.   tf.1

Streams, rivers, bayous, lakes and other water routes led to the rise of transportation by way of shallow sheltered waters. Barges and light-draft vessels could not withstand the harsh open seas but could be a dependable link to scattered coastal communities. The variety of waterways surrounding San Luis Island gave visions of grandeur: creating a need to build an inland canal from San Luis to the Brazos River. Engineers were sent to provide a survey and report by October, 1840. According to "The Perry Papers." George Hammeken wrote a letter to James F. Perry dated September 16, 1840. The letter as seen in the *Galveston Daily Courier* states, "Wm. H. Austin has returned – we left N. Orleans together on the 1st August - & has since been engaged in reconnoitering West & Bastrop Bay – the result of his investigation thus far is, that a canal will cost at least 3 times more than a rail road." Hammeken's first choice was a railroad, however, a canal was needed, and the officials heeded the people's petitions.

The Brazos Canal Company was chartered in 1841 by the Congress of the Republic. It was the effort of local landowners and was sometimes called "The Slave Ditch," because it was dug by bondsmen of the owners. The purpose was to connect the plantations to the shipping ports. The *Planter* of November 18, 1843 noted that Mr. Lemsky would carry out the project. Upon his death in October of 1849, Gail

Borden took the position as secretary of the Galveston-to-Brazos Canal Committee. He left that position in 1850. Only a small portion appears to have been excavated. This company failed, as a rival company was formed. Robert Mills, Brazoria County plantation owner and banker became the President of the Gal-veston and Brazos Navigation Company. Together with Gal-veston cotton brokers Robert and Joe Hensley the channel was excavated. The depth varied from three to six feet. Bondsman used Fresno Scrapers, also called a Slip Scraper for excavation. It was also called a Slip Scrapper with a flat cutting edge. Horse drawn scrapers were used in the Galveston grade raising after the 1900 storm.

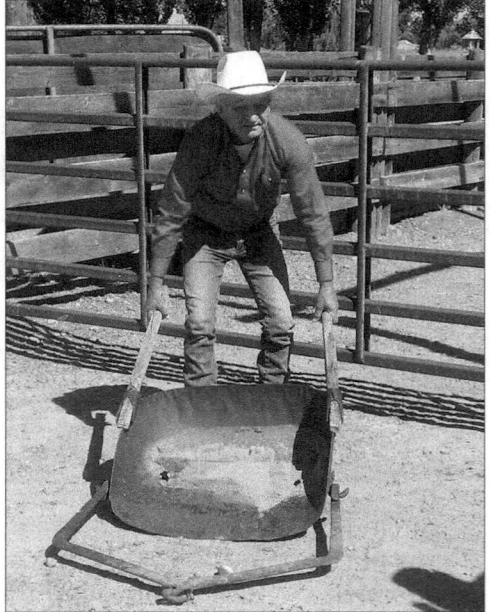

Max E. Benitz, Jr. shows how to hold a Fresno Scraper in the Rattlesnake Hills of Washing-ton State, in June of 2012.

Certainly the canal benefited those who utilized it, far more than the bonded laborers, but it was completed and began to bring in revenue.

The first toll collector was J. J. Hudgins and later his son,

Fresno Scraper
Art by Fannie Mae Follett Gilbert

58

William P Hudgins filled his job. Historians differ when it was completed, but 1854 seems to be the year most accepted. As the steamships left the canal at San Luis Pass, they would navigate the Galveston Bay waters to the Port of Galveston as best they could.

This canal project was an "On again - Off Again" project for many years.

The following are exerts from the August of 1880 the Chief of Engineers, United State Army;

SURVEY OF ROUTE FOR A CANAL TO CONNECT GALVESTON WITH THE BRAZOS RIVER, TEXAS.

The survey of the canal connecting Galveston and Brazos River, Texas, for which provision was made in the river and harbor act of 1879.
The total distance is 38 miles

GENERAL DESCRIPTION OF THE ROUTE

The canal will run for 22 miles through West Bay, thence through Mud Island Pass, Follett's Pass, Christmas Bay, and the old Galveston Brazos Canal, to the Brazos River, West Bay is from 2 ½ to 3 miles wide 3 to 7 feet deep, with occasional shoal reefs, and nearer the southwest end deeper channels making up from San Luis Pass.

The Bottom is principally mud and shells mixed, quicksand being found near San Luis Pass. Mud Island Pass is a narrow channel between Mud Island and San Luis.

Navigable Waters Report

The first segment in West Galveston Bay was improved by army engineers in 1859. It deteriorated drastically after the cyclone of 1875 and sustained more damage of the storm 1886. In 1892, Congress authorized a project for enlarging and straightening the channel to 3 to 3 ½ feet and widths of 100 to 200 feet.

Next attention shifted immediately southwestward to the canal of the Galveston and Brazos Navigation Company. This 11-mile-long represented the only obstruction to a federally improved, continuous channel between Galveston and the Brazos River. Tolls were levied on the river for steamboats carrying cotton to market, fishing schooners and other small craft using the canal made it ineligible for improvement by the federal government. Recognizing the value of this route as an alternative to the troublesome bar at the mouth of the Brazos River, Major Ernst had raised the possibility of acquiring the canal in 1887. Nine years later Maj. A. M. Miller recommended making the purchase. On February 11,1897 the navigation company offered the canal to the government for $50,000. Congress authorized the purchase at $30,000 and the transac-

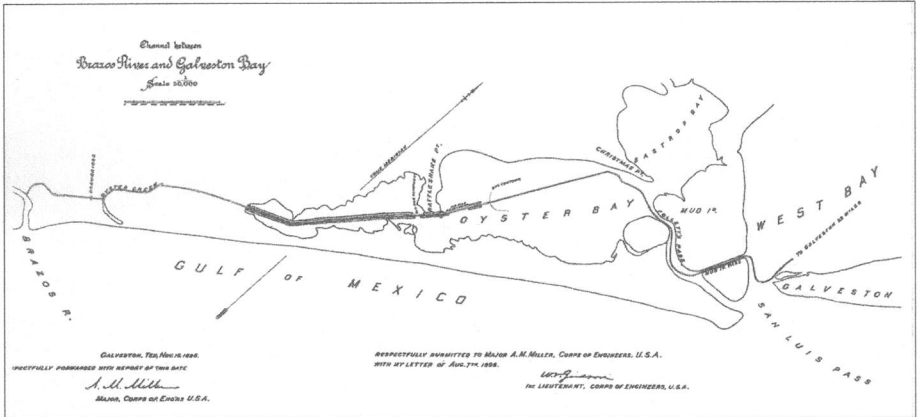

Brazos River & Galveston Bay Channel[24]
First channel between Brazos River and Galveston Bay included 11-mile canal of the Galveston and Brazos Navigation Company excavated through water of Oyster Bay and the mainland, and utilizing the bed and waters of Oyster Creek. Constructed in 1850, the navigation company's canal varied in depth from two to seven feet in 1896.

tion was completed in December 1902.

THE NATIONAL BOARD OF HEALTH BULLETIN, VOLUME 1, PUBLISHER

NATIONAL BOARD OF HEALTH, 1880, PAGE 97 TELL There is a steamboat (the Thomas) making weekly trips from Galveston though the bays and canal to Velasco, and landing on the Brazos as high up as Columbia.

A swing bridge was installed shortly after completion of an inland waterway from near the mouth of the Brazos River across land to West Galveston Bay near San Luis Pass in 1854. The canal provided three feet of water depth for stern-wheel steamers handling Brazos River to Galveston freight-hauling, and some passengers, thus avoiding the often shoaled river mouth and rough gulf waters. The canal project was jointly promoted, financed and executed by Brazoria County plantation owners and cotton brokers in Galveston. According to the memoirs of Addie Hudgins Follett, granddaughter of J. L. Hudgins, work began in June of 1851 and was completed in 1854. These memoirs and reports are surviving bits that tell the stories of these little bridges.

The 1900 storm destroyed the bridge. A pontoon bridge was then erected near the same site. Later storms disrupted the pontoon service and destroyed most of the immediate neighborhood homes. Several families gave up trying to buck the storms and moved inland. Another road was extended from "New Velasco" to a point on the canal nearer

This bridge was the first to be built almost exactly where the Surfside Bridge stands today. This photo was taken probably about 1885. Also shown are the dwelling and blacksmith buildings of the home site of John Longest Hudgins, the bridge-tender and canal-shipping toll-collector for at least the first thirty-some years of operation of the system. *Photo courtesy of Kathy Shaw*

its junction with the Brazos River, and a ferry crossing was installed where the present twelfth street ends at the canal in Surfside. With widening, deepening, and revising the old canal as part of the ambitious development of the Intracoastal Waterway, the ferry was finally replaced with a swing pontoon bridge. This service continued until the building of highway 332 and the opening, in 1954, of the high bridge over the canal.[25]

A small portion is still visible today near Christmas Bay. A Civil War-era map by Confederate engineer Tipton Walker (1864) depicted the canal that provided shipping access between the Brazos River and West Bay. The Canal became a strategic asset to Confederate Texas, which relied on cotton being transported through the Canal by blockade-runners. Later as more canals were dredged in Texas bays, it was merged and then named "The Big Canal." Once again the people of the City of San Luis were cornerstone building blocks to the nation. The original canal would become part of "The Great Connection" from Florida to Brownsville, Texas and what is known today as the Intracoastal Waterway.[26]

The island attracted many women, providing opportunities for both those born with a rugged sense of adventure and of savvy sophistication. Mary, a cousin to Stephen F. Austin, wrote the first English language history of Texas. She was also the first marketing expert for the City of San Luis.

Mary Austin Holley[27] describes her trip to Galveston and her first visit to the City of San Luis.

61

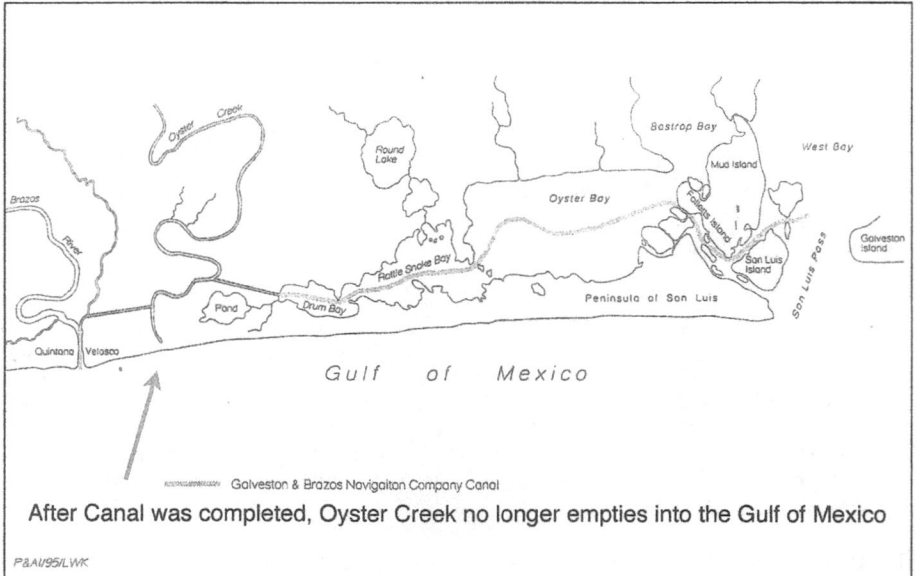

After Canal was completed, Oyster Creek no longer empties into the Gulf of Mexico

P&AI/95/LWK

Canal San Luis Pass to the Brazos River[28]
Map Galveston & Brazos Navigation Company

Mary Austin Holley, 1784-1846, author and teacher was the daughter of Elijah and Esther (Phelps) Austin. Born in New Haven, Connecticut. Mary attended New Haven schools and studied music and languages before her marriage to Horace Holley in 1805. Horace Holley died of yellow fever in 1827. In April, 1829, Mary became governess to the Hermogene Labranche family in Louisiana. After her brother Henry Austin settled in Texas, Mary communicated with him and Stephen F. Austin concerning possibilities which she had long considered gathering her family around her in Texas. The Empresario made arrangements to reserve lands for her on Galveston Bay, and in October 1831, she visited the Austin colony. As a result she wrote *Texas: Observations, Historical, Geographical and Descriptive, in a Series of Letters Written during a Visit to Austin's Colony, with a View to a Permanent Settlement in That Country in the Autumn of 1831*, her account was published in Baltimore in 1833. Mary also composed a *Brazos Boat Song*, illustrated with a vignette of Bolivar House, which was her Texas residence.

Back in Louisiana, Mary continued teaching while she made plans for a future in Texas. In 1833, Mary returned to Lexington, Kentucky to provide a home for Henry Austin's children and in 1835, Mary visited Texas for only a few months. Mary's manuscript diary of that trip, as with her charming family letters, is a valuable picture of the

In this silhouette, Mary Austin Holley stands with guitar in one hand, holding sheet music in the other.

Texas scene. Her writings were no doubt the first promotional pamphlets distributed to bring settlers to Texas. Mary continued to give good publicity for Texas and to arouse sympathy for the colony during the period of the Texas Revolution. Mary returned in 1837 and wrote letters to her daughter describing the changes made with the establishment of the Republic of Texas. Mary made the trip north in 1838-39, and then was back in Galveston in 1840. Her final trip was in 1843.[29] The following are two handwritten letters by Mary Austin Holley, which are now stored in the Dolph Briscoe Center for American History at the University of Texas in Austin. The first letter was an account of her trip to Galveston and the making of her plans to visit San Luis:

Galveston, Nov: 12, 1840

Here I am, dear Harriette, though my name is not Peter Parley: but I have as marvelous story to tell & wish I could tell you how beautiful it is & how easy I got here. As I write I look out from my window upon the sea—the beautifully blue sea. Ask Eliza how she felt when she first inhaled this life-giving breeze of the Cape she loves so much. So I feel, breathing health at every gasp. This is a perfect panorama. Whichever way you look there it is before you. A door of my chamber—second story—opens upon a gallery, there I walk every little while to enjoy the luxury. The weather is delicious—not hot—but just right. Never was sun or moon brighter, or air softer and sweeter.

As Holley continued to write, her prose showcased the beauty she saw in her travels. An adventurous soul with a touch of poetry, she relished both the adventure and luxury that Texas offered.

We left the levee at ½ past 10 Sunday morning and came down the 'Shining River' between shores of waving cane, (it is of soft pea green color like young corn)—glistening in the sunshine, then came the moon. It was glorious. When we approached the two light houses above and below the Balize I turned into my berth as if in the hands of Dr. Dudley & there I lay until next day noon in expectation, but no sickness came. I went on deck & looked out upon the ocean of waters the rest of the day with a sense of delight at being free from my old sea companion—that horrid nausea. I eat 4 meals a day with good appetite. They had such cooking on board as would have tempted the most frugal. Well, the next night before 12 we were at the Galveston Bar, but bright as the moon shone the Captain would not pass till day, & we played off & on. I could hardly dress before they were ready to land. We were but 32 hours. It seemed light magic--& the land truly fairy land. The boat is so beautiful I could think of nothing but Cleopatra as I lay in my luxurious couch of the finest & whitest—resting from the fatigue of running about N. Orleans. The cabin of the New York is on the upper deck like river boats, the whole of it of mahogany & maple polished like the finest pianos draper (where there is any) of blue satin damask dimity. The windows of painted glass representing the Texas Arms. The table china white, with a blue device in the center of each plate representing the New York at Sea with the Texas eagle hovering over her. Every article was made express for the boat—the ivory knives, polished to the highest degree, & the silver forks & spoons (not German Silver) have Steam boat N. York engraved on them. The lamps suspended & on the table, are richly painted. Into this dining room open the staterooms, completely furnished rooms—on both sides, the whole length. The light came from above. The chamber maid is a pretty white girl—all the time asking what she shall do for you & begging you to call on her & not mind giving her trouble &c &c. The waiters are curly-headed, rosey-cheeked Irish boys with white linen roundabout--&such waiters! It would do your heart good to see them— so neat & so subservient…Capt. Wright is the best of seamen, & his officers have been with him for years.—Could not be better. The boat is built for strength. They call it the finest work that ever came out of N. York…

With a keen eye for detail, Holley painted a vivid picture of the popular architecture of the local homes.

Col. Love met me on board and took me to his house while James got ashore the baggage. Mrs. Love and Mary received me kindly. They would have had me stay there but that Mrs. Davis occupies their only spare room. I came, then, to Crittenden's, who happened to have room. Hers is a two story square house—gallery above & below—back and front—4 rooms on a floor, no passage, 2 of the rooms being united for dining room, & having a stair case. It is very comfortable, not carpeted, except Mary's room which serves for parlour. They seem very happy—nothing could take them back to Kentucky. Parker & his family are here, but he goes soon to an upper county to start on his own book....

I found Hammeken here—the same obliging creatures as ever. He is negotiating with a young man who came in the N. York, with Negroes for some of my land I think he will take. We are all going down in a boat of Mr. Pinkard's (brother of Doctor & one of the proprietors) to San Luis in a few days. They say it is much pleasanter there—being higher. There are two or three respectable families & a good hotel. I shall get Chinn to survey my land and lay it off in small tracts to suit purchasers. It will be active employment for Horace when he comes. A schooner is expect from Baltimore. Hammeken sold his Dickson land for $2. I shall be able to do better here than elsewhere. Mr. Williams told me he has often opportunity to sell small tracts. All who arrive come to his store, & he engages to do his best for me. He is an excellent man & a gentleman.

James left today (13) for home. I hear brother has gone to the Colorado with a gentleman to look at his lands. All I know. Hope he will do something...I forgot to speak, in its place, of the whig procession the night we got to N. Orleans. We were on the balcony as it passed. It extended either way as far as the eye could reach. They had bands of music at intervals--& banners with devices, & log cabins illuminated, elevated on poles with pretty effect at night. They often chased the ladies, & gave of wrecks, too, are interspersed among them. 'Un gouverpail, de matsetdescordagessonteescartecaet lasurle sable.' I saw a large flat embedded in the sand, & a tall mast with some remaining cords at the top, some distance in the water, firm & unshaken by the surf that beat against it. Whence came they? We arrived at the west end long before the flowing sun sank into the bosom of water, hoister our signal—like your liberty pole—a flag with the one star floating on high. The ferryman was soon over, & we on the deep water of the channel, a mile & a half wide. The scene was beautiful & I enjoyed it all. It seems like the Brooklyn ferry, N. York, but wider.

As her travel continued, Holley continued to record her observations of island life, further committing San Luis Island to the pages of history.

I did not find in San Luis Calypso & her nymphs, but I am instantly reminded of Telemaque—especially in the town of Idomeneus, where they were all happy because so busy. It is a lovely spot by nature, & the houses about 20 of them, are in various stages of progression, from the skeleton frame to the neatly finished edifice. Carpenters, surveyors, wharf-builders & boatman are all active. There are no idlers here. The chief directors of affairs happens to be away on business of the company. Some of these are accomplished young men who have figured, of yore, in N. Orleans. One of them, Mr. Jennings, is as handsome as was John Hunt—that is very elegant. Hammeken has also returned for a few days to Galveston. He left me in charge of distant cousin of ours, by the name of Austin, one of the aforesaid Surveyors, & Mr. Bennet, keeper of the Hotel, who with his family is from the North & very respectable people. I am lodged & entertained as well as I would wish to be. The house is very large & spacious—my room is in the second story--has four windows all looking on the sea. I sit with them open that I may drink in the delicious view & soft fresh air. It is well furnished—excellent bedding--& the bedstead, table, wash-stand & arm chairs, with hair bottoms, are all of mahogany. The table is well served, first with a clean damask table cloth, on which is spread, morning, noon & night, more delicious venison that I can eat in Kentucky. The steaks are well cooked, hot, tender, swimming in good gravy, for breakfast & Supper, at dinner it is roasted, with ducks & geese roasted or stewed as happens. The sweet potatoes, so large you have to cut them in two or three pieces, are so sweet & juicy you would think they were done in sugar. They are sticky to the touch as if they had been in molasses. Great dishes of these come on three times a day. How I wish I could hand some over to your son William! They agree with me perfectly as does every thing. I have a ravenous appetite from the sea air, as have all here. I must grow fat if good living could do it. I have not got to go fishing yet as everybody is so busy. What sport it would be to William & Mr. Bakewell! the danger is of being pulled into the water instead of pulling the fish out, they are so large. All the points of land jutting out into the water & all shallow places are covered with birds. I can see long line of them as I sit at my window rioting in undisturbed profusion. There are geese, & ducks, snipes, large & small, & Kerlew, deer on the mainland plenty.

The best idea I can give of this beautiful little Island is to compare it to Nahautrazend (a place in Mexico). It is not so high by a good deal. It is, however, more verdant & the verdure is mixed with beautiful flowers. I have gathered seeds of some like the coriopsis, except the petals are common, tipped with yellow; & a flower like the evening primrose. Like Nahut the Island is studded with small houses, but not so pretty, & large hotel, as yet they have not wasted paint. Every thing with one or two exceptions inside & out is the color of the wood, new & neat. My room is well plastered & white washed—no carpets. Here is the same view of the ever glorious sea—the white surf as it breaks on the shore—the sea *gulls skimming in all directions—now & then they sail in the distance exciting curiosity, and little pilot & packet boats, & the feeling of health & enjoyment. I am alone, but I have books when I am tired of looking & knitting. Don Quixote & Gil Blas in the originals. Irwin's Conquest of Florida, British Poets, & more than I can use. Mr. Hammeken had his piano brought into the parlour below & last evening we had a little concert, of the household, around it. He and I performed, with the vocal aid of Mr. Allen, a Methodist preacher from Shelby, Virg., a very good, practical man by the bye. He has been in Texas 2 or 3 years, & knows how to manage. He preached in the long dining-room twice Sunday. I heard his evening sermon. We are to have another tonight. Holley was among those who eagerly followed the progress of the bridge, dreaming of the day it would offer easy access to the mainland.*

2 OR 3 piers of the bridge to connect the Island to the main done. When the whole is completed & the causeway, there will be a good prairie road to Brazoria, Columbia and Bolivar, each about 15 miles. Were money a little more plenty this would be soon effected & the place be all that its important position destines it be. All the cotton of Brazos would then pour in here.

Holley's eye for business ventures enabled her to own and negotiate sales of her own land to perspective buyers. She also portrayed a keen interest in the hunting ventures of the men in her company.

I intend to stay a week from the time I came. I am cogitating various plans & am expecting Horace, Brother Henry, Mrs. Perry's carriage & my young man to look at the land. An Alabama man came to day to look out for residence, & seems pleased here & wants a farm in the neighborhood. I gave him a description of mine. Said he had money to pay down. I think Horace will be suited here. Brother has a house on a neighboring Bayou. If I can get it brought here I will. He has a point of high land opposite that would be excellent for Edward & James to cultivate. The Island is three miles in circumference. We drink rainwater.

Monday 28. We are eating today Buffalo meat taken 8 miles off. It is very tender & fat, white looking like the best meat, but tighter texture. I suppose it was. It is excellent. They have just brought in two deer taken this morning across the pass. Some of the herd swam to the Island to escape the hunters, one of whom is our preacher.

I must close as there is a chance to send my letter.

Sincerely
Mother.

I am longing to hear from you & hope to get a letter tomorrow. Love to all — hope you continue well.

This is a fine place for hogs & hens & turkeys & they feed on the shell & other fish on the beach.

(Addressed) To,

Mrs. W. M. Brand

Lexington,
Kentucky."[30]

In spite of all that Hammeken had told her, Mary could hardly believe her eyes when she saw the wharf of San Luis---it was a thousand feet long, and there were six or eight vessels tied up there.

Often these ships brought amusements as well as supplies. Local society was greatly enlivened during the few weeks that two British brigs rode at anchor in the bay, the *Ironsides* and the *Milton*. Their officers were gallant and well-bred, and returned the town's hospitality with promptness. One mild sunshiny afternoon, the *Ironsides* captain-invited a party, including Mrs. Holley, to go on a rowing excursion in his official gig. They landed over on the mainland, disturbing clouds of birds as the boat was beached, and then they rambled a little distance along the shore. Afterward, the gig circumnavigated San Luis Island and got back to the wharf just as the brilliant sunset faded.

Mary had meant to spend only ten days or so on San Luis, but it was several months before she left. The happy interlude on the little island had been like a brief return to the days of her youth, and her goodbye in the *Advocate* to her friends was in the familiar romantic pattern.

Adieu To San Luis
Adieu! sunny island; adieu! verdant glade;
Adieu! sea-girt shore, where so long I have strayed;

Adieu! idlescribblings, that many a day,
Beguiled of its ennui, by innocent play;
Which ambling, or trotting, lame-footed or blind
In mad prose or dull verse, would an Advocate find;
Thanks, thanks for indulgence, though poorly deserved,

In memory's casket 'twill long be preserved.
San Luis, March 25, 1841 M.13

Mary Austin Holley
A Biography by Rebecca Smith Lee University of Texas Press, Austin

This is a personal photo taken by Eileen M. Benitz Wagner during Sail Boston 1992.

Chapter 3
Texas and San Luis Under Five Flags

During this era, Texas was under five of its six flags. First, Texas was under the flag of Spain from 1519 to 1821, then Mexico from 1821 to 1836. Next, it became a nation for nine years. On December 29, 1845, Texans said farewell to the Republic, when Texas was admitted as the twenty-eighth State of the United States of America. Texas remained a state until February 1, 1861, when it seceded from the Union, becoming part of the Confederate States of America on March 2, 1861. After the Civil War, due in part to its involvement in battle even after the surrender at Appomattox, Texas was not fully readmitted to the United States until March 30, 1870.

Texans have long been known for their grit, a trait that enabled their young state to survive, but their determination is often balanced with a keen sense of humor.

The Texas Times, Galveston, February 25, 1843, sought to add a little amusement into the day:

> *A FITTING PRAYER -- A clergyman recently, after exhausting all his zeal and eloquence upon his auditory, finding them still continuing obdurate, concluded his prayers as follows 'And, O Lord! Make the hearts of these sinners as soft as their ears.*

In spite of frequently shifting political affiliations, these were developmental years for the new port city of San Luis. During this early dynamic period, the City of San Luis continued growth. One additional interesting item was the initiation of ferry service.

Ferry Rates
West Pass, Galveston and San Luis Ferry

The following advertisement ran in many issues of the *San Luis Advocate*. These quotes are from October 20, 1840.[1]

The cost From: San Luis to Peninsula		From San Luis to Galveston	
Per Man	0.37	Per Man	0.62 ½
Per Man, do and horse	0.62½	Per Man do and horse	1.37 ½
Per Man a do and a wagon	1.25	Per Man do and do and wagon	2.00
Per Man do double do and wagon	1.75	Per Man do double do and do	3.00
		Cattle per head	1.50
		San Luis Oct. 20	

Son of John Bradbury Follett, Captain Alonzo B. Follett and brother Alexander Glass Follett ran the Ferry between San Luis Island and Galveston's west end and San Luis Island to Peninsula Point for many years.[2]

71

Docking for the San Luis Ferry
Courtesy of Fannie Mae Follett Gilbert

Tucked neatly into a family photo album belonging to John Alexander Follett, a descendant of Alexander Glass Follett, is this photo of the San Luis Ferry. Written on the back of this old photo: "St Luis Island Ferry before Island was cut off by storms." The photo date is unknown.

If a passenger wished to travel without a horse or wagon, he could rely on public transportation. A regular stagecoach to and from San Luis accommodated mail carriers and others who crossed by ferry from Galveston to Brazoria County. The ferry was a stout, sailing sloop with a minute-by-minute account of its coming and goings.[3]

The County Commissioners Court issued licenses for operating a ferry. An old newspaper article tells of Alonzo B. Follett being issued a license to operate a ferry as recorded in the Brazoria County minute books records dating back to 1857.

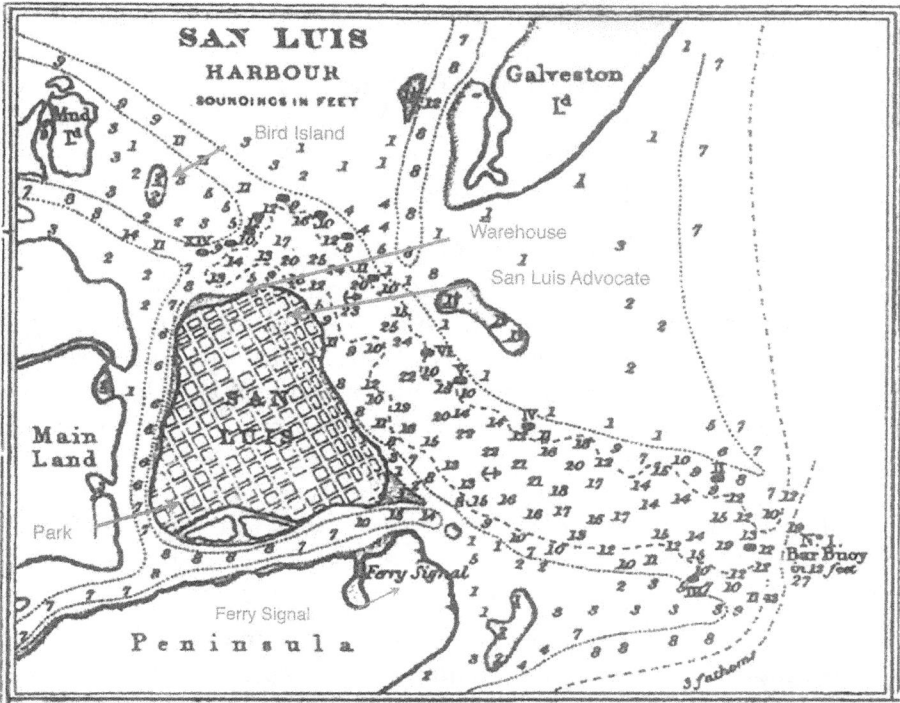

The Coast of Texas, From Documents Furnished by W. Kennedy, Esq.,
H.M. Consul at Galveston

London: Published according to Act of Parliament at the Hydrographic Office of the Admiralty, August 20th, 1844. J. & C. Walker, Sculpt. Huge engraved map, 40 x 26 inches, on fine thick paper in near-mint condition. Streeter Texas 1500, citing the British Museum copy as the only known copy. The map is superlative in every respect, with fine coastal detail and large insets of Matagorda (6x10 inches), Galveston (6x8 inches), Sabine Pass (5x8 inches), and San Luis Island (4x4 inches). The maps of Matagorda and Galveston are attributed to Commodore Edward W. Moore of the Texas Navy. St. Joseph's Island is shown in excellent detail. Streeter mistakenly called the sculptor Wallace instead of Walker.

San Luis Island Map with the Plat of the city was an insert into an 1844 Galveston map. It shows a tremendous potential for growth of the city of San Luis.

1844 Insert -- British Map of San Luis 'Harbour'[4]

As transportation increased, measures were taken to improve the safety of the ships that navigated the island's passes. Little Pass was thirty-four feet deep at the entrance from the Gulf of Mexico. The depth remained at least eight feet down, all the way around San Luis Island, where it joined San Luis Pass. Although maps were available and usually charted by sea captains, the sand bars near shore were not included.

Following the initiation of the ferry service, attention again swung to the need for a bridge and a canal to connect the island to Galveston and Oyster bays. A project on a much larger scale than the Hand Dug Canal was undertaken on the national level. Early groundwork was initiated for roads and canals in 1819 by Secretary of War, John C. Calhoun responded to urgent need for improvements to transportation including waterways. There was a proposal for "a coastal canal from Brownsville, Texas, to the Okeechobee waterway at Fort Myers, Florida." The Texas portion of the canal system was to extend 426 miles, from Sabine Pass to the mouth of the Brownsville Ship Channel at Port Isabel.

1906 Status of the Inland Waterway[5]

Continuously being expanded and maintained, the Gulf Intracoastal Waterway was financed and constructed by the federal government through the Army Corps of Engineers. The 1975 Texas legislature enacted the Texas Coastal Waterway Act, by which the State assumed sponsorship of the main channel of the Texas portion of the Waterway. Today, a safe journey can be had by both commercial and recreational boats.

The waters of San Luis were not the only provision the island offered to its inhabitants. When protected from the salt sea breeze, farming in San Luis/South East Texas was successful due to the rich soil and natural rainfall.

Tobacco[6]

HOME PRODUCTION

Some days ago we were presented with a few leaves
of Tobacco raised on San Luis Island. We are told
that the plants were large and flourishing, and ma-
tured very early. We had cigars made of the sample
sent to us, and found them remarkably well flavored.
The manufacturer says that she never handled leaves
so soft and pliant, and free from fibers.

This tobacco was raised from a stock of seeds found

some years ago in an Indian village taken by the Texians under Gen. Somervell. The friend who sent the tobacco will do us a kindness by furnishing some of the seeds procured from the plants. We believe that the soil and climate of Texas are peculiarly adapted to the successful culture of the best tobacco, and wish to draw attention to the subject. Any information from those who have experimented will be thankfully received.

Tobacco proved to be a lucrative crop, sold in local stores as well as exported. The *Columbia Planter* tells of Peter Gautier's new store which opened in February, 1843;

Gautier will sell sugar, coffee, flour, salt, tobacco, tea, Navy Bread, Lard, Hams, Molasses, Whiskey, Sperm Candles, Soap, Starch, Havana Segars, Dupont's Rifle Powder, Lead, Letter Paper, Brogans, Buckets, Brooms, &c, &c.

The above will be sold very low for cash, or in exchange for hides. San Luis, Feb 20, 1843.

Though the preserved newspapers offer much of the information known about the island today, receipts from the era give a second peek into everyday transactions.

A handwritten bill of sale[7] dated February 10, 1843, issued to Pierre Gautier. It reveals that he paid the sum of $75.00 for a lot in the City of San Luis;

Lot 6, Block 22 in the First Ward together with houses, fences and buildings and improvements thereon." The Wards were separated by sand berms to protect from high rising water.
Signed by Auguste Gosse, Seth Burr, and Geo. L. Hammeken.[7]

The bill of sale describes a lot with home and furnishings in the City of San Luis. This must have been near the end of the boomtown for this property to be sold for so little money.

The expansion of the island's influence demanded an increase in its communication network.

AN ACT
Establishing a Mail Route therein named.
Section 1. Be it enacted by the Senate and House of Representatives of the Republic of Texas in Congress assembled. That there shall be a post route established between the city of Galveston and Matagorda, via: San Luis and Velasco, and shall be let out upon the same provisions as other mail routes of this Republic.
Approved, January 30th, 1845[8]

Republic of Texas Communities and Roads[9]

Thus, along with development of a waterway and stagecoach transportation network, the mail service was initiated.

Settlements and connecting roads developed across the Texas Gulf coastal lands with Indian Territory looming to the North. The Republic of Texas was on the eve of becoming a state of the United States.

Though men had channeled, harnessed and redirected the course of the water, they would never be able to fully master it. An article from *The Texas Times* told of the Brazos River flood of 1843. "The Brazos River is higher than it has been known since 1833; it has overflowed its lower banks and done considerable injury, by floating off cotton and other property. The current is so rapid that the steamer Mustang is unable to...." additional information was missing.

Though swollen rivers could swamp farmland and destroy crops, their damage was miniscule compared to the storms that brewed over the water, spewing torrential rain and high wind onto everything in its path.

Mrs. Emma Follett King writes in her unpublished book, *Meg and Emma*;

> In 1846, our Grandmother, three of her children and a slave nurse, with Lydia Follett Wilson and her three children had gone to San Luis to visit our great grandmother. As they were returning on the steamer, New York, they were caught between New Orleans and Galveston in one of these terrible September hurricanes. The Captain of the boat lashed Grandmother Follett to a stateroom door. She held the youngest child in her arms; but, in spite of all she could do to prevent it, the baby was washed out of her grasp. The other two children and the slave were drowned along with Mrs. Wilson and her three children. Grandmother Follett was saved but for days they despaired of her life, so great was the shock of the loss of her three children.

For more than half a century, members of the Follett family made significant contributions to the development of San Luis and the Peninsula, which now bears their name, Follett's Island. Indeed, the Folletts were influential in the entire region surrounding San Luis, including Galveston Island. Much of this history was passed down through family letters. Dates and descriptions varied throughout the research.

John Bradbury Follett, whom we first encountered briefly in Chapter One, was born in Epping, New Hampshire, November 17, 1795. His bride to be, Anne Louise Fownes, was born January 9, 1794, in St. Johns, New Brunswick, Canada. They were married April 17, 1816. John was in the shipbuilding industry with his father-in-law, William Fownes, known as "William the Loyalist." John and Anne had ten children, four

The Follett Family

John Bradbury Follett   **Anne Louise Fownes Follett**

Photos Courtesy of Fannie Mae Follett Gilbert

girls and six boys. Their son, Bradbury, died shortly after birth from yellow fever as did his fifteen-year-old brother Hyram G. Sons Alonzo Beckford and Alexander Glass, as noted earlier, worked with their father John as shipbuilders. John also ran a ferry to San Luis Island and Peninsula. Then there were Joseph B., and John F. Follett. John F. may have died very early.

Three of the Follett daughters married local men: Lydia Wilson Follett to John Hoskins; Isabella to Augustus Burr; and Charlotte to A. F. Shannon. Julianne E. Follett was a fourth daughter.

John Bradbury left New Brunswick in 1838, with a pile driver to work on building the bridge on Lake Pontchartrain, Louisiana. When John learned of the new exciting city of San Luis, Texas, he made a trip to look for himself. It was ideal. In 1839, John built a home on the West end of Galveston Island, then sent for his family and, with his sons, began a shipbuilding and repair company.

Shortly thereafter, John moved his family to the City of San Luis, on San Luis Island. The Republic of Texas Tax Records of Brazoria County show two lots owned by Bradbury Follett from July 22,1841 through 1845. An unsigned letter shows, "Lots 3 & 4 in Block 22, First Ward," in the city of San Luis, as belonging to Follett, and are the same Lots on which his house is situated.[10]

The valuation for the two lots was $800. The *Planter* (one of the newspapers) reported the opening of Bradbury's Home of Entertainment, in 1845.

At fifty-one years of age, John Bradbury died in January of 1846. The tax records thereafter listed Mrs. Follett and Alexander and Alonzo Follett.

The Federal Census for Brazoria County[11] for October 12, 1850, recorded Dwelling Number 131, Anne Follett, as Hotel. This must have been located in the City of San Luis. Research indicates that, after her husband John died, Anne Follett, truly a heroine of her era, opened her home as a hotel in order to help support herself and her family. Later Anne and her sons built Halfway House on Peninsula Point, then known as Velasco Peninsula. As already noted, the peninsula later became known as Follett's Island.

Follett's Ferry

The first tax record of the Follett family owning property on the Peninsula is to be found in the 1851 Republic of Texas tax records. This is the beginning of what would become the famous Halfway House. Mrs. Anne Louise Follett with her sons Alonzo, Joseph, and Alexander Glass Follett, and daughters, built Halfway House at Peninsula Point

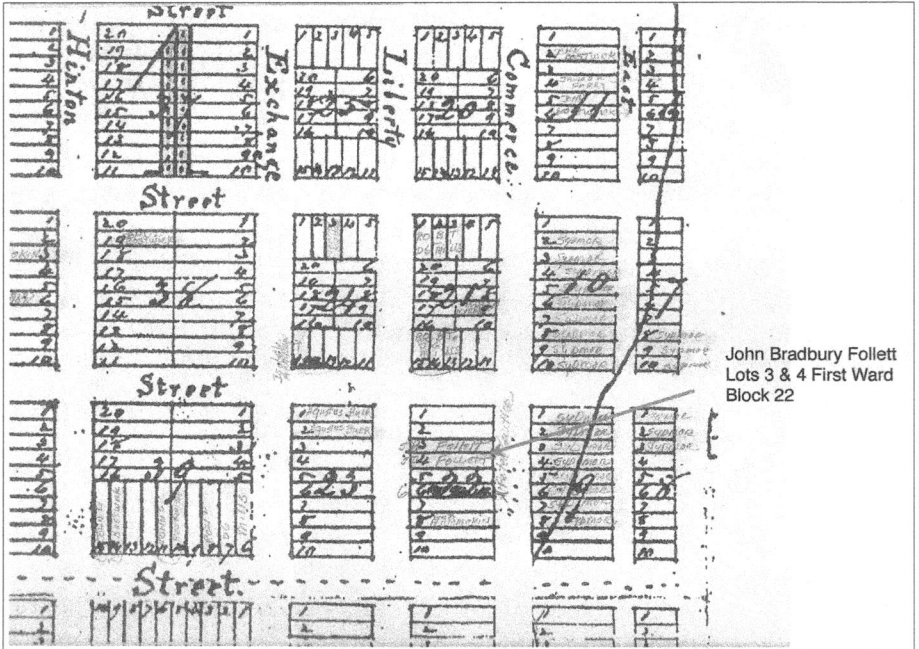

John Bradbury Follett
Lots 3 & 4 First Ward
Block 22

Plat with John Bradbury Follett Lots marked.[12]

Halfway House, 1851 to 1900
Halfway House on Peninsula Point
1994 Water Color by Fannie Mae Follett Gilbert
Please notice the pilings and chimneys are made of red brick.
Limited Edition Print Number One
Photo by Eileen M. Wagner

just above the west bank of what was later to become known as Little Pass.[13] Anne Ayers Lide McCurdy described Halfway House as "a co-lonial style building, two and half stories high with fifteen rooms and open galleries on each floor. Oleanders surrounded the house and they grew as high as the third floor."[14] Mrs. Follett served meals to promi-nent plantation owners and many weary travelers coming and going to and from Galveston Island. There were many family get-togethers at Halfway House. The Follett's ferry boats carried travelers, goods, and livestock across Little Pass and Big Pass. Anne Louise Follett's son Alonzo never married, and lived with his mother to help with Half-way House. Sons-in-law Alonzo Shannon and Augustus Burr married Follett daughters, and became closely associated with the family in the ferry business, livestock raising, and vegetable farming. At one time, Shannon, Burr, and the Folletts had 160 head of cattle at San Luis, and grazed 600 sheep on a prairie farm near Bastrop Bayou. The tax roll

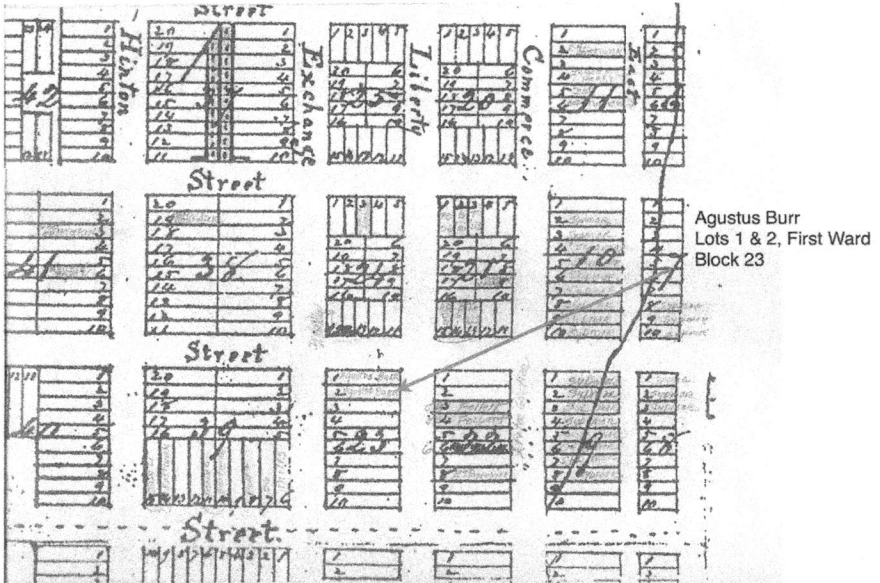

Plat with Burr's Lot marked.[14]

gives a value of the 160 cattle at $160.00. Alonzo Follett owned twenty oxen, as listed on the 1851 tax roll. Alexander Follett is shown owning schooners beginning with the 1852 tax roll. The valuation of the two lots fell from $800 to $100 by 1851. Alonzo Shannon was shown to have had two sailboats, *Valley* and *Nina*, which were used to ship the produce to market.

The magnolia trees around Halfway House were imported, as were the majority of the trees on the island, as settlers recreated the landscape to suit their needs. Early area residents planted salt cedar trees, now found all across South Texas, to protect their home and gardens from the salt sea breeze. Thirty of the first settlers were gardeners, whose products would find a ready market in the city. They found the soil on a large portion of the island to be very good, consisting of a rich black mould which was from a foot to a foot and a half in depth. The under layer was a stratum of sand and shell. With proper fertilization, they could grow every kind of vegetable, berries, grapes, and other small fruits such as figs, lemons, oranges and peaches. Additional fruits could be grown profitably, if shielded from the salt sea breeze.[15]

Halfway House was built like a ship. A story was told that after one hurricane, part of the roof came off and the interior filled with a great deal of water. The house no doubt shifted on it pilings, and the floors may not have been level, but the walls stayed firmly in place, requiring the family to drill holes in the floor to drain the water.

The Follet family sought to provide the same quality in their services as they had when building their establishment. A local advertisement reads:

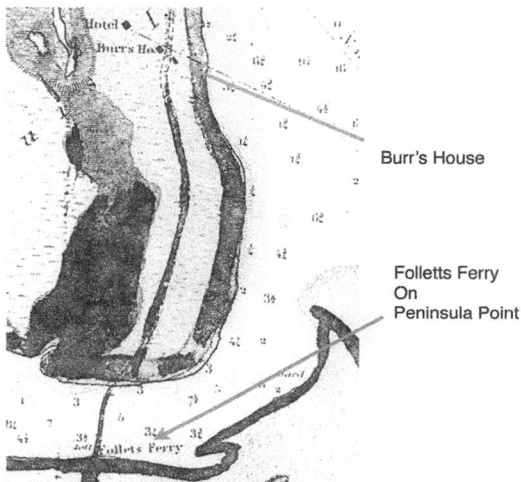

Burr's House

Folletts Ferry
On
Peninsula Point

Map indicates Burr's House, Hotel and Follett's Ferry.[16]

SAN LUIS:
The subscriber has opened an establishment for the entertainment of travelers at the West.

Anne Louise Follett's surviving letter offers a firsthand account of family life

Sept 19th
Since writing the above I have recv'd your letter dated Aug 9 land in answer, if I could have my wish whether I could come on a visit I will tell you, nothing would afford me greater pleasure than to go and see you. But my hand being lame, I had to go to Galveston to a physician and what little money I come by, I was compelled to use. So you see, it wouldn't be the best time & bill of expense to you to have me come now and the Ferry business isn't that great too, Since Charlotte left, I must have a servant. I have a servant belonging to Captain Hamilton, their slave and son. But he leaves in a couple weeks and will take her with him. If however if I come for a visit any month, I think it is likely to may possibly go, but I will not promise. If I do go, you must promise to let me have the Native.

Answer this as soon as you receive it and tell Mr. Wilson I want to hear from him very much and that I trust this land of his will be waiting from then. The family sends their love and also to you and give my love to Mrs. W. and accept the same of self.

Affection
Mother

The second portion of this letter states:

THE ISLAND'S NOW ENTIRELY UNDER WATER FOR THIRTY-SIX HOURS.
This is a poor place for cattle and with no feed, I will have them crafted off the island on the Schooner 'Lone Star,' belonging to Hendly and Co. I hope they would bring one hundred dollars or so. 'Schooner Gen., Hamilton now on her way from Galveston to Bastrop Bayou with fifteen hundred bushels of corn.

They have just built a new light for the Hamilton. And there is prospect for having plenty to do this winter.

The Follett family's establishment was one of many lodgings offered on the island.

The Federal census for Brazoria County, October 12, 1850, notes additional hotels:

Dwelling No. 129 James B Spann, Hotel
Dwelling No. 131 Anne Follett, Hotel
Dwelling No. 135, H. C. Wilgers, Hotel

Also noted:
Dwelling No. 132 Augustus Burr, Ferry Man
Charlotte (Shannon)
Alonzo Ship Carpenter (Follett)
Alexander Ship Carpenter (Follett)

Though the hotels catered primarily to travelers, they could be employed for lodging, as indicated when the Texas Census for Brazoria County, October 12, 1850, further noted that at Dwelling No 135, Hotel, resided Desriff Florers, Gun Smith, twenty-eight years old.

The hotels also provided shelter whenever the island was inflicted with a natural disaster. The September 17-19 hurricane of 1854 devastated the city of San Luis. The storm ravaged the coast from Matagoda to Galveston. Follett's Halfway House was damaged, but was quickly rebuilt and back in business.

Chapter 4
Brazoria County
During the Antebellum Plantation Era

Many developmental changes came to Brazoria County during this era, including the first bridge at Surfside, the first lighthouse, a fort, and numerous plantations. It was a time of prosperity for Brazoria County as foundations were laid for future developments. Though the road to prosperity was disrupted by both a major storm and the Civil War, Brazoria County stood resilient.

An 1853 survey shows San Luis Pass to be eighteen feet deep, large enough to accommodate full-sized ships. Also shown are Follett's Ferry on Peninsula Point, Burr's House Hotel, and the Warehouse with West End Ferry and Station on Galveston Island.

The survey records landmarks, water depths and vital information that a captain would need to ensure that his vessel safely arrived at harbor.

San Luis is known by the five houses on the Island, and the Ferry House on the West end of Galveston I. (Island) end by Follett's Ferry House on Peninsula. The Bar is one of the best in Texas, and has 8 feet water on it, at ordinary low tides...To enter the Pass. Bring the S.W. corner of the Hotel to bear W.N.W. 3/4 W.(N. 66° W.) in range with the N.E. Corner of Burr's house, and cross the Bar on this range...At the entrance of the narrow channel between South and South Breakers, there are 20 and 23 feet water.

When Follett's Ferry House is open with Peninsula Pt. steer N.W 1/2 W.(N. 41° W.) to the anchorage, in 34 fins water, between the Hotel and warehouse.... Vessels drawing 8 or 9 feet water will find the best anchorage off the warehouse... Note. The Courses and Bearings without the brackets are Magnetic, those within are true and the Distances are in Nautical miles. The Soundings are expressed in feet to 18 feet, or within the dotted lines, beyond them in fathoms, and show the depth at mean low water, the plane of reference.

"The dotted lines beyond low water mark represent the bottom within the respective depths of 6, 12 and 18 feet: thus -----------for 6 feet---------for 12 feet-------for 18 feet.

The characteristic soundings only are given on the Map. They are selected from the numerous soundings taken in the survey, so as to represent the figure of the bottom.

TIDAL REMARKS

The Rise and Fall of the tide is usually small. The time and height of high and low water are irregular and much influenced by the direction and force of the wind…From observations in April 1853 the average Rise and Fall was 1.2 feet. The Rise of highest tide above mean low water---------------------------1.9 Feet The Fall of lowest tide below--- 0.8 There is generally but one high and one low water in 24 hours expect when the moon's dec is nearly nothing when there are two small tides a day. The Rise and Fall is greatest when the moon's dec.n is greatest.

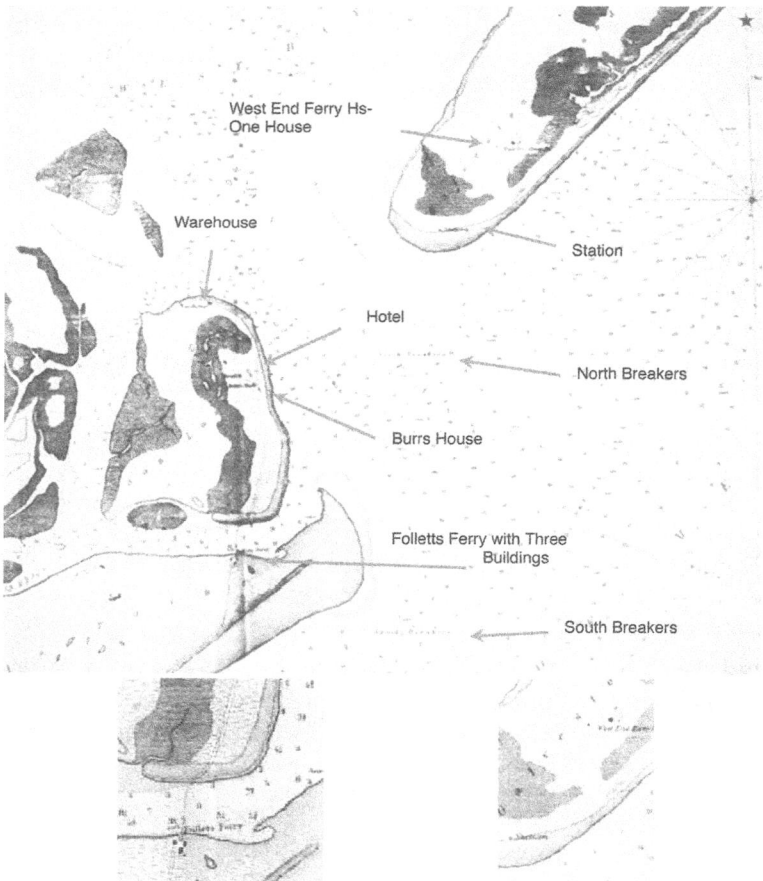

1853 Survey of San Luis Island[1]

Augustus Burr's house was used as a marker for ships to navigate San Luis Pass. The 1853 tax record from the Republic of Texas recorded Augustus Burr owning two lots on San Luis.

As winter approached, residents looked forward to the cooler weather. The respite from the grueling temperatures offered both comfort and a form of protection. The *Texas Planter* newspaper from Brazoria speculated that a white frost, the first of the season, would hopefully kill the remaining seeds of yellow fever. The article also noted the fatal outbreak of cholera in New Orleans. Reports of disease spattered every newspaper in the region, nestled between other tidbits of news concerning local residents.

S. J. Durnett, was well known in the publishing world of that era. The *San Luis Advocate* was one of his publications. Notices inform readers that J. M. Conrad and Durnett had taken the place of Mr. Furguson, as owners of the *Civilian* and *Galveston Gazette*. Offering more details about the change of hands, the *Galveston Daily News* advertised that the *Matagorda Tribune* was for sale, due to the ill health of the proprietor, Mr. Gilbert.

Other articles reported more drastic cases:

> *Dr. J. B. Miller and Judge C. C. Dyer, two of the oldest and most prominent citizens of Fort Bend County, are among the deaths from yellow fever at Richmond. So far, upwards of forty deaths in that place.[2]*

Among the reports of the illness, ads indicated that life could continue as normal. Mrs. Anne Louise Follett ran many advertisements for her hotel, promising horse feed and entertainment to travelers at West Pass. The *Texas Planter* ran many of these ads.

September 20, 1864 brought another sort of danger. The *Texas Planter* in Brazoria recoded this severe storm.

> *One of the severest Storms that we recollect of ever having witnessed, has prevailed here for the last two or three days. The wind commenced blowing from the North on Sunday evening, and continued increasing in violence up to Tuesday morning, when it veered around to the South, and blew with so much force that scarcely anything was able to withstand it. House, fences and trees were leveled to the ground in its course. During all this time it rained incessantly. We have no means of ascertaining the quantity of rain that has fallen since Sunday night, but there has certainly more fallen since then than we ever saw in the same length of time. Considerable damage has been done in the town by the wind. The Kitchen and Stable belonging to the Hotel of Mrs. Leonard were blown down on Tuesday morning. Mr. Dargan's Tin-Pan Alley, Mr. Brown's Black-Smith Shop, Mrs. Stanger's Dwelling House, a portion of the new Jail, but not enough to do it any serious damage. Several other buildings were con-*

siderably damaged; but fortunately no one was hurt, although some were in imminent danger for a time. Almost all of the Shade Trees in the town were blown down, and a great many of the fences were forced away by the great force of the storm. The storm continued up to this morning, but considerably abated in its fury. The wind is blowing now from the North, and we are threatened, with another storm of rain. We have been unable to hear from the country this morning, but we fear that when we do, we shall hear of nothing but disasters. The Cotton planters have been very unfortunate this year, on account of the wet weather, and the appearance of the worm among their crops but we fear that the wind and the rain for the last two or three days has blown all the bolls from the stalks, and in fact nearly ruined the entire crops. The Sugar Cane has certainly been blown flat to the ground, and we much fear that it is so late in the season that it will be unable to right itself.

One week later on September 27, 1854, the *Texas Planter* continued its account on the aftermath of the storm:

In our issue of last week, we made mention of the severe Storm that prevailed here on the 18th and 19th last, and noticed the damage that was caused by it in this place. Since that time we have been unable to gain many additional particulars concerning it, but from those portions of the County that we have heard from, it appears to have been more destructive that we had at first supposed. It was certainly the severest storm that has prevailed in this section of the county for a number of years, and it will be a long time before the country will recover from its effects. We have not heard from Galveston since the storm, but we greatly fear that when we do, it will be great losses both in life and property. In our own County the greatest loss will fall upon the planters. They have been unfortunate both, this year and last, but they should not be discouraged. It is true that the losses they have sustained will be adversely felt, but if they manage to get along through the next year, we think they will be able to regain all they have lost. It is very seldom indeed that such losses as they have sustained occur more than two years in succession. We sincerely hope that they may be more fortunate another year.

Since our notice of last week, we have obtained the following particulars of the damage occasioned by the storm. The Purgury (this is where the molasses is drained off of the sugar) of the Sugar House belonging to Jno. G. McNeal was blown down, a part of P.13, McNeel's Cane Shed was also blown down, the Purguries of the Sugar House of Mrs. Mims and J. P. Caldwell, a portion of the Sugar House of S. P. Winston, a portion of the Sugar House of R. & D. G. Mills, both on their upper and lower plantations; and all of A. Winston's Sugar House have been blown down. In addition to the above we hear of many negro cabins, corn cribs, fences &c, entirely leveled with the ground. The destruction of the timber has been immense. It is impossible to compute what portion of the forest trees have been blown down, but they have so blocked up the roads that they are almost impassable.

In regard to the crops, from the best information we are able to get, we do not think the Sugar will be more than one-third or one-half a crop, and the Cotton will not greatly, if any, exceed one-fourth the crop that would otherwise have been made.

We hear from the Island of San Luis that the house of Mrs. Shannon was blown down and washed out to Sea; a part of Mrs. Follett's house was also blown down, and about one hundred head of cattle washed away.

Since the above was in type, we have heard from Matagorda. The storm seems to have been much severer there than here. All the houses in the town, with the exception of twelve, have been blown down. All the Stores are down and the Goods have been greatly damaged. There were five persons killed by the falling of the houses, two American and three Germans, but we have been unable to learn their names. Dr. Terry's wife had her arm broken. The house of Col. Lewis, on the Peninsula, opposite Matagorda, was also blown down. The Livery Stable in Matagorda was blown down and all the Horses killed. From Caney, we learn that the Purguries belonging to the Sugar House of Col. Jones and Mr. Gibson, and the wall of Col. Warren's Sugar House were blown down. Col. Hawkin's Dwelling House was blown down and the thigh of one of his negroes broken. A new Schooner which he had just brought out to take off his crop was wrecked. There is a report in circulation that in Houston, the Old Capitol and a number of other houses have blown down and that fourteen persons were killed and thirty or forty wounded from the falling of the houses. It is also stated that the steamer Nick Hill was lost in Galveston Bay, and that General Harrison, her Captain, and all on board, with the exception of two, were drowned.

It is interesting how history is recorded differently. The reports of the storm circulated throughout the county. As noted in the *Texas Hurricane History*.

September 17th - 19th, 1854
Hurricane hit Matagorda/Galveston. The main impact of the storm was around Matagorda and Lavaca Bays. The town of Matagorda was leveled. Saluria suffered $20,000 in damage. Merchants on the Strand and Market Streets in Galveston suffered much water damage from the storm surge. Brazoria also encountered strong winds from the storm. Crops of sugar cane and cotton were ruined. Every wharf in Matagorda Bay was carried away. The storm surge went through with such force that the channel was straightened and deepened by two feet. Many small vessels capsized. The steamer Nick Hill went down near Dollar Point, in Galveston Bay. The steamer Kate Ward and her crew proved a total loss. The system then moved northwest over Columbus, and in its dissipating stage became a widespread rainstorm over the Western and Central Gulf Coast causing 5.55" of rain at Baton Rouge between the 17th and 21st with rain falling as far east as Pensacola. Four lives were lost in the town of Matagorda.[3]

Christmas and New Year's Holidays proved to be a time of rest and romance for all. The Star Hotel hosted a ball in Brazoria. The *Texas Planter* recorded the event stating:

> *The Ball came off at the "Star Hotel" on New-Year's night, as was announced. From various causes, such as the short notice given, very bad roads, and a prospect of rain on that day, the attendance was not as large as was anticipated; yet there was a sufficient number present to make the Ball a very pleasant one indeed. We do not recollect ever seeing a party of ladies and gentlemen of the same number appear to enjoy themselves more than the company did on Monday evening. An elegant sumptuous Supper was served up about 11 o'clock which certainly showed the skill and taste of the landlady, Mrs. Leouard, and to which ample justice was done by all present. The dancing continued until three in the morning, when the company separated highly pleased with their evening amusement.*

Alexander Glass Follett[4]

As noted in Mrs. Georgia Shannon's memories, this photo was taken when Alexander attended the unveiling of the Texas Heroes Monument, commissioned by Henry Rosenberg (25th Street and Broadway in Galveston) on April 21, 1900. He attended many conventions in Galveston.

Alexander Glass Follett was the third son of John Bradbury Follett. Alexander was born in New Brunswick, Canada, on April 13, 1823. His birth was registered in Boston, Massachusetts. He moved to Texas with his father to the west end of Galveston Island in 1838, where he worked with his father as a shipwright. Alexander later built a home for his family on Peninsula Point. Four miles from San Luis Pass to the west, lay the sunken *Acadia* which was directly in front of his home. Alexander was the father of ten children, several of whom died in infancy. A historian, engineer, writer, poet, architect, inventor, and medical advisor, Alexander was an influential man of many interests and abilities. He was

Alexander Glass Follett
1823 - 1908

a highly esteemed citizen and very much a part of San Luis, Velasco, and Galveston, as the history of Texas was in the making.

Alexander was a veteran of many wars. As a boy of eighteen, his first service was in a campaign against the Indians of Linnville River, and later the campaign against the Waco Indians. In 1842, Alexander was a soldier in the San Antonio expeditions under command of General Somervell in the war for Texas independence. In 1846, Alexander was a volunteer in the U. S. Army led by General Zachary (Old Rough and Ready) Taylor, in the war between the United States and Mexico.

According to the 1840 Republic of Texas Census based on land grants by Gifford White, Alexander Follett received three 320-acre land grants in Galveston on the November 17, 1845 for service to his country. They were located in Gulf Prairie and the Peninsula.

Alexander's desire for improvement ventured much farther than his own homestead. As an engineer, Alexander received a patent in 1881 as inventor of a 'Breakwater,' for protecting harbors and roadsteads, and keeping open channels through bars at the entrance of harbors, the mouth of rivers, and in other places, and which shall not be liable to be destroyed by the marine worm.

Eager for the safety of the islanders, Alexander mailed two letters on November 6, 1886, one to Judge William Ballinger, and one to R. W. Franklin, Esq. of Galveston, referencing his engineering ideas and plans on how to build a seawall at Galveston based on his 1881 patent. These two letters were sent fourteen years prior to Galveston's devastating 1900 Storm. Had the officials taken heed of Alexander's designs, they could have saved many of the thousands of lives and much of the property which were lost. These two letters are preserved at the famed Rosenberg Library in Galveston, Texas.

Though not a trained physician, early in his married life Alexander Glass Follett bought a volume called *Dr. Gunn's Medical Advisor.* Doctors were few and far away, so whenever anyone needed a doctor, neighbor Follett and his medical book were summoned. "Doctor" Follett treated fevers, set broken bones, sewed up bad cuts, stopped bleeding, attended births, and always took his book along with him, so he could look up the proper treatment and discuss it with the family.

Alexander was a great reader and writer and as such, a great contributor to the *Galveston News* and *Galveston Tribune.* Much to the loss of later generations, Alexander's writings of history and his poetry were tragically destroyed in the Storm of 1915.[5]

Alexander Glass Follett and brother Alonzo ran the ferry with Alexander's sons for many years, advertising their services in ads in the

(No Model.)

A. G. FOLLETT.
BREAKWATER.

No. 245,473.   Patented Aug. 9, 1881.

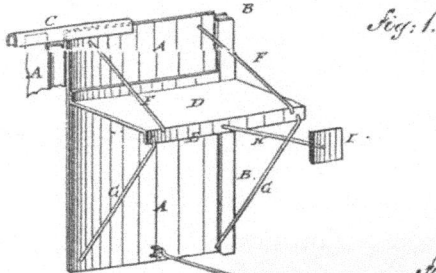

Fig: 1.

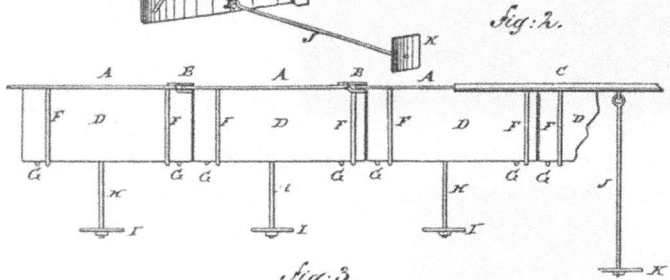

Fig: 2.

Fig: 3.

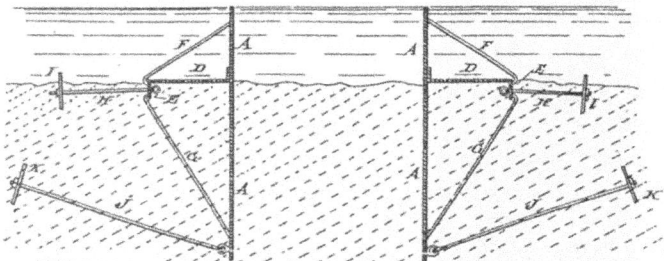

WITNESSES: INVENTOR:
Chas. Nida.   *A. G. Follett*
C. Sedgwick   BY *Munn & Co.*
                                              ATTORNEYS.

Follett Patent
Courtey of Fannie Mae Follett Gilbert

Columbia, Texas, *Democrat and Planter,* 1859.

Traveling over land was very dangerous and many times the Follett brothers would ride "shotgun" to assure a safe journey for their passengers. Full of ingenuity, kindness and honor, Alexander Follett embodied many of the best traits of the island's founders.

Anne Ayers Lide McCurdy describes;

he was a jolly man with a wonderful sense of humor and a ready sit. He had deep blue eyes, good features, and a short now-white beard and all his forty-seven grandchildren adored him. During the summer we all spent a month at his huge white home four miles from San Luis Pass on the mainland across from Galveston Island -- that month each year was pure joy for us for we were free as birds! He owned all the land in sight -- and more, where great herds of cattle, horses, sheep, and goats roamed. He raised all the food except flour, coffee, and sugar and his household had food fit for a King. His barnyard was alive with chickens, guineas, ducks, and turkeys; he raised his own pork also. The Gulf was not more than half a block from his front steps and two huge sand hills hollowed out and planked in contained his sweet and Irish potatoes the year round. He dried beans and fish, made his own syrup, he ground his own cornmeal. The watermelons he fed the hogs would sell for 41.50 easily now. He also fed them gallons of milk--no wonder his hams and sausage were luscious![6]

Another advertisement, this time in the *Democrat and Planter* published in Columbia, appeared on August 11, 1959.

The author's journey to uncover the clues about San Luis followed

---

NOTICE TO TRAVELERS

"Persons traveling the Beach Route to Galveston from Brazoria or adjoining counties can always find buggies to carry them to Galveston from the West End, at Galveston Rates."

A. G. Follett

---

a scattered trail throughout two counties. During economically hard times, the Brazoria County records were moved to Galveston. That did not last long, as prominent Brazoria County citizens succeeded in securing the partial return of these records. However, many of the records for Brazoria County are still found in Galveston with many in the Rosenberg Library.

The records, include information from the San Luis Pass Cemetery, concerning the Follett family, who were buried on the island they loved:

```
             S F AUSTIN 1 LEAGUE ABSTRACT NO.      2 9
                        4428 acres

          All interests in this survey undivided, except those conveyances
          which recite "500 acres West End" and "300 acres, San Louis Island"

0/327     A B Follett     20 acres                              11/5/1873
          O F Shannon     20 acres                                   1908
          H Stevens     2685 acres                                   1877
          J H Sheppard    no acres shown                             1877
                          -----------------------

          J H Shepherd              to  H Stevens 1/2 of 300 acs  1895
          H Stevens                 to  S W Stevens1/2 of 300 acs 1929
          J H Shepherd              to  S W Stevens1/2 of 300 acs 1908
212/351   S W Stevens 1/2 of 300acs to  F K Stevens Tr.        2/18/1929
                          ------------------------

          J H Shepherd              to  A B Follett(all except 848acs'83
          J H Shepherd              to  A G Follett
          A G Follett               to  Follett, Holt & Hoskins 1/2
                                         of all except 848 acres    1884
          M E Hardeman DCM 7280     &&
           325 acres. (500 acres Dist. Crt.              6/18/1895
          J F Forney  175 acres
                          -------------------------

33/243    L R Bryan & M S Munson 80 acres   (map shows*      10/14/1895
34/396    L R Bryan & M S Munson 58 1/3 acres (158 1/3)       5/12/1896
                          -------------------------

128/13    M E Wiley   245 acres     from Hardeman             8/15/1912
                          -------------------------

82/246    Follett, Holt, Shannon etal  to A McFadden as Follows
82/246    300 acres                                          10/26/1908
79/599    1986.25 acres                                          9/5/08
79/602    693.75 acres                                           9/5/08
          ----------------
          2980  acres                                           9/-/08

     note below:
          J H Shepherd        609
          F H & S            2980
          M E Willey          245
          L R BRyan & Munson 138 1/3
          A B F               20
          Stevens            300
          J J Forney         116.50
          O F Shannon         20
          ----------------------------
                   3819
```

Stephen F. Austin League Abstract No. 29[7]

Alonzo Beckford Follett
"Died trusting in the Lord."
Born December 1, 1819
Died December 8, 1890

Lydia Follett, Infant 1898
"From loves shining circle the gems drop away."

There were no stones at these graves:

Mary Thompson, Fiancé of
Alonzo Beckford Follett
Buried about 1850

Isabel Follett Burr
Buried about 1861

Charlotte Follett Shannon
Buried about 1861

Anne Louisa Follett
Buried April 1875

Lutie Follett
Buried September 1875

John Follett
Buried 1884

Mrs. Alexander Glass Follett
Buried November 23, 1889

Julia Hye,
Ex-slave, who never left Follett Family after being freed, is buried at foot of
burial plot. Oct 18, 1889

Sometimes the information comprised sparse tidbits, which combined to create a fuller picture. A handwritten account states three additional burials, along with notes about the family's history with various vessels:

Boats Uncle Johnnie was Captain of: *Boats Uncle Escher was Captain of:*
Saint George   *Flower of France*
Lucy

Mrs. Sproule's Birthplace:
Armagh
Ireland
Came to Haversville, Kentucky, then to Harrisburg and died in Quintana.

The Census from July 2, 1860 gives another glimpse of the family.

Dwelling 154 at Peninsula

Anne Follett	*age 64*	*Alonzo B*	*age 35 a stock raiser*
Isabella Burr	*age 27*	*Joseph B Follett*	*age 30*
Mary L	*age 17*		

Dwelling 155 in front of The Boilers

A. G. Follett	*age 33 Farmer*	*M. J.*	*age 35*
Ema	*age 7*	*J. E.*	*age 3*
S. W.	*age 1*	*WAB*	*age 1/2*

The Follett family's cemetery was marked by "Tract 4" 20 AC, first located near "The Cedars" on the east end of the Peninsula very near San Luis Pass.[7]   Pharr is in Brazoria County. The Holt family lived in the city of San Luis. Julia Hye was an American Indian servant to the Follett family.

The best way to avoid cemeteries altogether is to remain in good health. When faced with illness or injury, the islanders often medicated themselves, or employed the help of a neighbor such as Alexander Glass Follett who arrived armed with a medical journal and past experience. For those with chronic conditions, new technology offered an

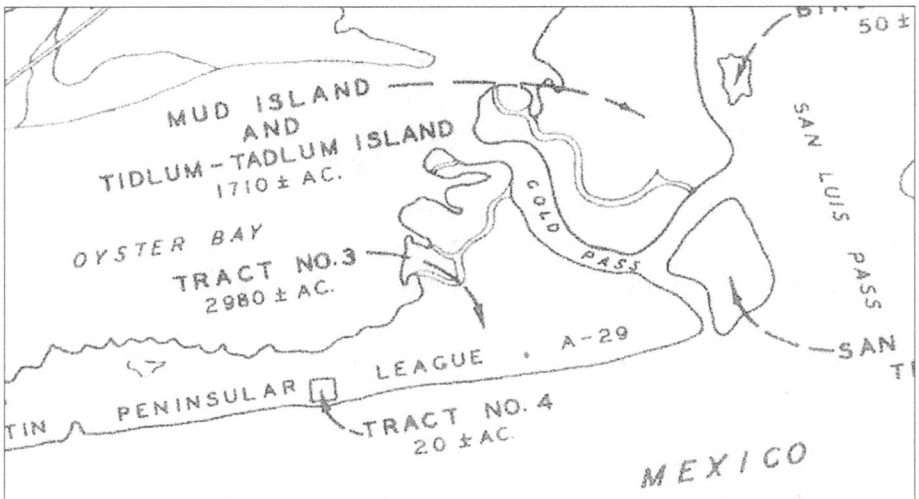

Follett Family Cemetery
Army Air Force Base, Subgroup G-4-Property Acquisition records of the Galveston District Office. Record Group 77. Records of the Corps of Engineers, in the SW Region (Fort Worth) National Archives and Records Administration.[8]

alternative means of cure.

> *The Texas Planter, Brazoria, Texas, January 25, 1855, recommends:*
> *Hydro Electric Voltalic Chains for instant relief from short acute pain and permanently curing the following:*
> *For use of Chronic Rheumatism.*
> *All Neuralgic Diseases*
> *The use of the Electro Chains for Female Diseases. Simply apply one end of the chain to the abdomen and the other upon the spine just above the hips. It is most important to moisten the chain with common vinegar before applying. A 36-page pamphlet can be had from Patrick McGreal, sole agent for Brazoria County.*

A more practical improvement for life on the island, came in the form of a lighthouse. As navigational instructions were passed from ship to ship through journals, newspapers and word of mouth, the storms added an element of uncertainty to even the most thorough descriptions. The channel depth could shift and common landmarks like trees and houses could be blown away. An uninformed captain could easily loose cargo and lives. It was time to create permanent and universal guideposts for every ship that navigated the area.

(Photo courtesy of Brazoria County Historical Museum)
Photograph of the Brazos River Light House, date was around 1909.
Accenssion No 1985.999p..002

Journal of the Texas Legislature
Jan 20, 1858
Page 212

Resolved, That the Committee on Commerce be instructed to inquire about the necessity of establishing lighthouses and placing buoys at the entrances and in the bays of Galveston, Matagorda, Aransas, and Corpus Christi; also at the mouth of the Rio Grande and Brazos rivers and at San Luis Pass, and that the Committee report by bill or otherwise.

Although San Luis did not get a lighthouse, Velasco (Surfside) certainly did. Construction began in 1895, and the tower was first lit on May 30, 1896. Dow Chemical Company was conveyed the property on March 7, 1967, and the light tower was then dismantled. The lens is on display at the Brazoria County Historical Museum in Angleton. The top portion of the structure (the lantern room) sits on the museum grounds.

Though the lighthouse added a new element of safety to the county, other measures were already in place to enhance the safety of its citizens. Forts were built in three separate areas,

Resolved, That the Committee on Military Affairs be instructed to report by bill, or otherwise, providing for the erection of suitable fortifications at the mouth of the Brazos River, San Luis Pass, and Passo Cavillo, in Texas.

The flourishing county had good reason to protect its assets. Between 1849 and 1859, plantation life in Brazoria County had developed impressively in a very successful way. The County became the wealthiest in Texas. Forty-six plantations produced some of the finest sugar and cotton. These agricultural plantations grew up along the rivers and creeks on which crops could be shipped by barges. Between 1850 and 1860 the numbers included nineteen sugar plantations, sixteen cotton plantations, and three plantations that produced both sugar and cotton. Many plantation owners also raised cattle and some cultivated oranges, lemons, pecans, figs, peaches, plums, rice, grains, sweet and Irish potatoes, and wild grapes. Old Velasco and Quintana served as Gulf seaports and resort centers for an antebellum plantation society. One story during this research tells of a petrified Irish potato found at San Luis.

This map shows the City of Galveston, with San Luis near the far left of the map. Though goods could certainly be imported, often the county was often able to meet its own demand for supplies.

Nottingham featured a lace factory, which was built in 1892 and operated briefly. After Hurricane Alicia in 1983, the final remains were washed away. We also note in this map the entire Island of Galveston seems to be connected to Follett's Island, and they both are connected to the mainland at the Brazos River. It seems even the island itself had adapted to offer its inhabitants a time to flourish.

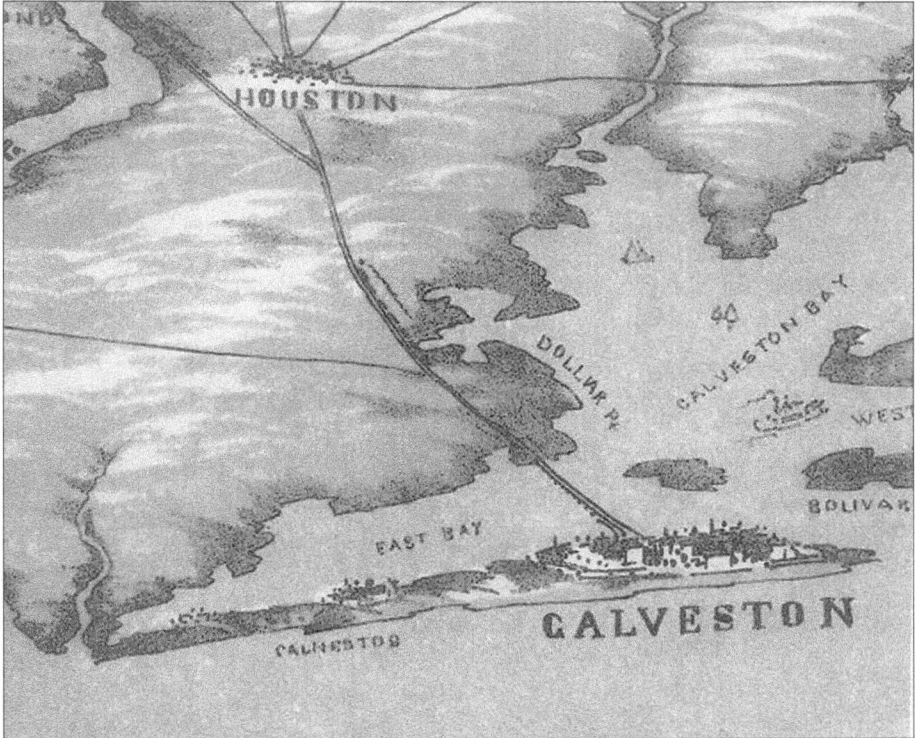

Map Notes Nottingham - 1861 Military Battles and Campaigns Map 9 of 26

Panorama of the seat of war: Birds Eye View of Texas and Mexico/ Drawn from nature and Lith., By John Backmann. New York, Publisher © 1861

Entered according to act of Congress in the year 1861 by John Backmann in the Clerks Office of the District Court of the U.S. for the Southern District of New York.

Chapter 5
Surviving the Storms of War and Nature
The War of the Rebellion: The American Civil War - 1861-1865

In 1861, the United States split into the Civil War, dividing the North and South. The natural portages of Galveston and San Luis City for cotton and tobacco to Europe, as well as the receipt of industrial and war goods, such as powder, guns, cannon, etc., were certain to draw the area into the conflict. In preparation for war, Texas built a fortification on Mud Island, just inside San Luis Pass.

Fort Randall on Mud Island, Texas[1]

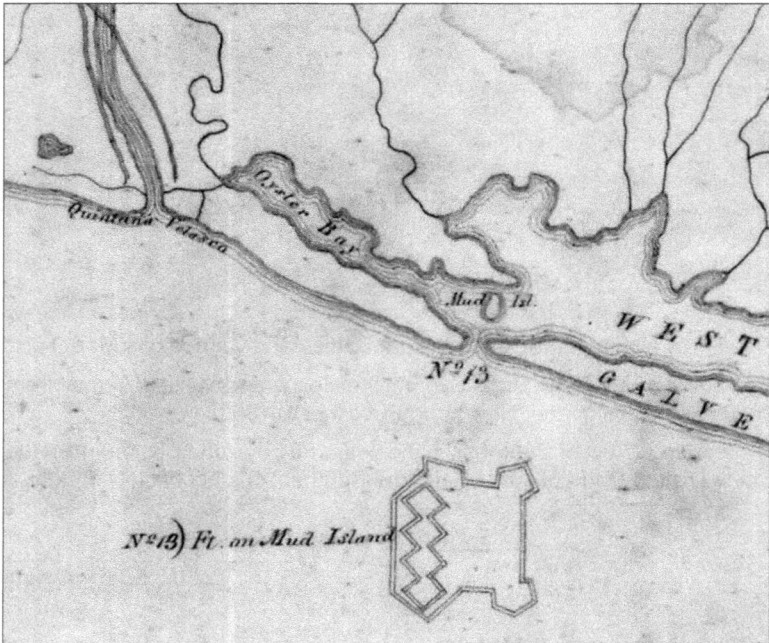

Titlum-Tatlum Bayou 1861-1865

Creator, Jeremy Francis, 1818-1883. A map of the coast of Texas and its defenses, drawn under the direction of Captain Tipton Walker, Chief of Topographical Bureau of Texas, New Mexico and Arizona, by P. Helferich, Assistant Engineer (hand-drawn and colored).

As the focus shifted from trade to defense, a Matthew Hopkins Survey recorded the renaming of Mud Island to "Navy Island," on October 26, 1836. However, by the time of the Civil War, the original name, Mud Island, was used by the Confederacy. The Confederate Army erected a small earthworks camp on Mud Island. An 1864 map, including a detail, indicates the strategic importance of the Fort on Mud Island. Additional Confederate fortifications were drawn and mapped as seen in the Official Military Atlas of the Civil War.

War of the Rebellion[2]

Though entire books have been written covering the conflict of the Civil War, surviving letters offer information concerning specific events on San Luis. The ports continued to import supplies, making the area a potential target for Northern troops. As military forces branched out, the placement of troops on the island required special care to ensure that they could withdraw if necessary.

The following twelve Letters of Command are from the Confederate Army Record

HEADQUARTERS,
Velasco, Tex., November 13, 1861

General Hébert:

I have not ordered another company to San Luis Fort, and the reason of the delay is I have not been able to place at the disposal of the troops that I may station there any safe mode of retreat, should it become necessary to do so. I have it in contemplation to place a small steamer there in a very few days, which will enable me to afford all necessary means to the troops in case a retreat should become necessary. This is a matter of much importance to Galveston, as well as the county of Brazoria, and you may rely upon my constant efforts until I shall have two companies on the island ready for active service.

Very respectfully,

J. Bates
Colonel Fourth Regiment Texas Volunteers.

HEADQUARTERS MILITARY DEPARTMENT OF TEXAS
Galveston, Tex., November 15, 1861

Major MACLIN, Chief Q. M., Com. of Sub.,
and Acting Chief of Ordnance, Department of Texas:

SIR: I have been directed by the commanding general to furnish you with the following memorandum of troops to be called into service, if possible, for the defense of the Department of Texas, with their respective rendezvous: First, Sabine Pass, one battalion, to consist of one company of artillery, one mounted and three infantry companies; second, Galveston Island, Bolivar Point, and Virginia Point, not less than 4,000 men, to consist of eight mounted companies, one regiment of artillery, and the balance infantry; third, at or near

Harrisonburg, 2,000 men, of which one regiment should be mounted; fourth at Spring Creek, near Hempstead, 2,000; fifth at Victoria, 2,000; sixth, on coast from San Luis to head of Matagorda Bay, four mounted companies, six companies of infantry; seventh, on Rio Grande, not less than 3,000, of which one regiment should be mounted; eighth, at Pass Cavallo, three companies; and Aransas, two or more companies. The relative number of rendezvous or stations of these troops may be changed, as circumstances may require, and will be provided for by the proper departments, upon the above basis, until further orders.

I have the honor to be, very respectfully, your obedient servant,

SAML. BOYER DAVIS,

Major, and Acting Assistant Adjutant-General.

HEADQUARTERS MILITARY DEPARTMENT OF TEXAS
Galveston, Tex., December 3, 1861

Col. H. E. MCCULLOCH,

Comdg. First Reg't Texas Mounted Rifles:

Sir: I have been directed by the commanding general to furnish you with the following memorandum of troops to be called into service, if possible, for the defense of the Department of Texas, with their respective rendezvous.

First, Sabine Pass, one battalion, to consist of one company of artillery, one mounted, and three infantry companies; second, Galveston Island, Bolivar Point, and Virginia Point, not less than 4,000 men, to consist of eight companies mounted, one regiment of artillery, the balance infantry; third, at or near Harrisburg, 2,000 men, of which one stead, 2,000; fifth, at Victoria, 2,000; sixth, on coast from San Luis to head of Matagorda Bay, four mounted companies, six infantry; seventh, on Rio Grande, not less than 3,000, of which one regiment should be mounted; eighth, at Pass Cavallo, three companies; Aranzas, two or more companies

The relative number, rendezvous, or stations of these troops may be changed as circumstances may require, and will be provided for by the proper departments upon the above basis until further orders.

I have to honor to be, very respectfully, your obedient servant.

SAML. BOYER DAVIS,

Major, Assistant Adjutant-General

HOUSTON, TEX., October 26, 1863

Colonel SULAKOWSKI,

Chief Engineer :

COLONEL: I am instructed by Major-General Magruder to say that he has received information, deemed authentic, that the enemy is moving on Texas, via Niblett's Bluff. Col. A. J. Hamilton and staff are at New Orleans. This indicates that the whole expedition will move against Texas. The general is extremely apprehensive that an attack will be made by water, and that the enemy will enter at San Luis Pass. The general wishes to know your views in regard to the nature of the defenses which can be made there, and wishes you to attend to that matter if your health will permit.

Please answer by telegraph.
I am, colonel, very respectfully,

EDMIND P. TURNER,
Assistant Adjutant-General

VICTORY, TEX., *December 3, 1863*

Brigadier-General SLAUGHTER :
The general directs that you throw scouts down as far as San Luis Bay, and also well down on the inside of the island to Oyster Creek, so as to communicate to you with rapidity the approach of the enemy.

You will keep artillery in readiness to defend the bridge. Should the enemy cross San Luis Bay, you will have time to throw troops into Virginia Point from the garrison, but should he not cross over, he will move up more rapidly and give you little time.

You will see that all necessary arrangements are made by which a sufficient number of steamers are ready and on hand to assist and remove the garrison should the communication with the mainland be severed.

EDMUND P TURNER
Assistant Adjutant-General

HOUSTON, *February 29, 1864*

Brig. Gen. H. P. BEE:
I am instructed by the major-general commanding to say to you that the want of the necessary depots of supplies will delay the contemplated expedition against Indianola, and to direct you to let the horses of the cavalry remain in their present position a few days and order Pyron's, Woods', Gould's, and Buchel's regiments to concentrate at Camp Dixie (the former camp of Colonel Debray) for the other troops will remain in their present positions.

You will however, countermand the order for Debray's regiment to proceed above the railroad and retaining it where it now is, and order the detachment now at Velasco to rejoin the regiment wherever it may be. You will have Brown's regiment mounted, and direct them to perform all picket and outpost duty on the coast from San Luis Pass west to the peninsula, inclusive. Buchel will take his horses with his regiment to Camp Dixie. You will, after giving the necessary orders, in accordance with these instructions, report in person without delay, in company with Brigadier-General Green, at these headquarters, for consultation with the major-general commanding turning over the command from San Luis to the peninsula to Colonel Bates, the next officer in rank. Colonel Bankhead will give the necessary orders in regard to the artillery intended for the expedition.

Very respectfully,

STEPHEN D. YANCEY
Assistant Adjutant-General

HOUSTON, TEX., April 22, 1864

Brigadier-General Hawes:

I issued an order a few days since in reference to the defense of certain works under your command. I repeat them now and beg that you will have them carried into effect so far as it depends upon you, with the greatest vigor. The order to Captain Kleinpeter will go through Brigadier-General Hebert. You will use the troops to carry them out. Those in relation to the covering troops protecting themselves with rifle-pits at San Luis Pass you will have carried out yourself, calling upon the engineer department for such assistance as may be necessary. A copy of the orders* for General Hebert is herewith furnished you. I am thus urgent because I think Commodore Faragut will make an attack upon this post in a few days. It will be purely a marine attack, as the enemy appear to be evacuating the coast and may go to Louisiana with re-enforcements.

I entertain no apprehensions from a navel attack, if these precautions are taken. Should the enemy's marine and sailors land upon the island (which I do not contemplate), you can easily concentrate your troops in the most favorable positions and defeat him. Direct the officer in charge of the post not to throw away their ammunition, particularly on the enemy when out of reach. Report the commencement and progress of these works every three days. Additional axes, spades, &c., can be had of Captain Garey, quartermaster of this post, upon proper requisitions. Correspond freely with me through Brigadier-General Slaughter, chief of staff.

B. MAGRUDER
MAJOR-GENERAL, COMMANDING

Hdqrs, Dist. of TEXAS, N. MEXICO AND ARIZONA,
OFFICER OF THE CHIEF OF ARTILLERY
Galveston, August 6, 1864

Brigadier-General Hawes,
Commanding, &c.

GENERAL: I am instructed by the major-general commanding to inclose the within order. The major-general commanding desires the 8-inch shell gun from South Battery (Fort S. Sherman) to be sent as early to-morrow morning as possible, on a steamer, to Mud Island

---

HOUSTON, TEX., May 5, 1864

Col. S. S. Anderson,
Assistant Adjutant-General, Shreveport:

Dispatch received. Arrangement already made to drive enemy from the Calcasieu River. Colonel Griffin attacks in the morning. Enemy's force increased on the peninsula; much larger number of tents; force estimated now by officers there at 5,000 to 6,000. Whole available force between Sabine and Colorado does not much exceed 4,000. Sabine Pass, Galveston, San Luis Pass, Brazos, Caney, &c., to defend. Prisoners expected at Hempstead must be guarded by *an efficient force. Order issued for Waul's Legion to move. Hope it will be countermanded. Bradford's and Terry's regiments not yet complete. Terry's five companies had already been ordered east of the Sabine.*

P.O. HEBERT
Brigadier-General, Commanding.

(Inclosure.)
SPECIAL ORDERS,   Hdqrs. Dist. of the Tex., N. Mex., and Ariz.,
    No 218   *Houston, August 5, 1864*
In pursuance of orders from department headquarters all siege guns mounted on siege carriages will be collected at Houston without delay, with their caissons and appropriate ammunition and all equipments. In addition to the above guns, the following guns, ordered from department headquarters, to be mounted on siege carriages, will be sent to Houston, viz:

The 20-pounder and 30-pounder Parrotts from Mud Island; 30-pounder Dahlgren from Fort Sulakowski; 30-pounder Parrott from steamer J.F. Carr; 30-pounder Parrott from Sabine Pass; Sawyer gun now at Houston. The ammunition and implements and all equipments of these last-mentioned six guns will be sent with these guns, but not their carriages. On their arrival at Houston they will be turned over to Capt. H.T. Scott of the ordnance department. Their ammunition and carriages, implements, and equipments, will be examined and put in the best condition. The two 32-pounder field howitzer from Sabine Pass will be sent to Houston, carriages and everything complete. Commanding officers of the posts at which these guns are, and officers having them in charge, will be held responsible that they, with their ammunition, implements, &c., as above specified, are transported with-out delay to Houston.
    By command of Major-General Magruder:

EDMUND P. TURNER,
Assistant Adjutant-General

A day-to-day, step by step account of the Civil War at San Luis Pass's Fort on Mud Island is provided by officers' letters of command to their troops. We see the initial placement of soldiers with a side note to provide a steamer for possible relocation, turn into frantic preparations as the letters' tone turn from caution to baited breath. The officers took every measure to create what fortification they could and hunkered down to wait for the attack.

As we have seen, Titlum-Tatlum Bayou runs from Bastrop Bay to the east end of Cold Pass, just above and set back a bit from San Luis Pass. Titlum-Tatlum Bayou separates Moody's Island to the south-south-west from Mud Island to the north-northeast. "Ships loaded with cotton entered waterways around Titlum-Tatlum Bayou, and hid among willows, out of range of observers with spyglasses on the tall masts of

Federal blockading ships. On dark nights, or in bad weather, blockade runners would slip out of the Bayou to the open seas, hugging shores, sometimes being towed by men on land until water was reached. Cotton taken overseas by such ships would buy for the Confederacy (hampered as it was by lack of manufacturing facilities) guns, gunpowder, medicines, coffee, cloth, hardware, and shoes. Purchases came into Texas by the same route that cotton was freighted out. Aside from such havens as Titlum-Tatlum, blockade runners needed every advantage over the foe, for they supplied life-blood to the "Confederacy."[3]

Local residents joined the imported soldiers to defend their land and lifestyle. During the War of the Rebellion, Alexander Glass Follett enlisted as a Confederate Soldier and served in General Bates's regiment, stationed at the mouth of the Brazos River. He was taken prisoner by a gunboat at San Luis Pass. A copy of the initial Confederate record of Alexander Glass Follett dated September 17, 1861, states that Alexander was a private of Capt. S. L. S. Ballowe's Company and Colonel A. Bates's Regiment in Texas. In April, Colonel Bates, reported from Velasco that a large steamer anchored off San Luis Pass the day before, displayed an English flag, a Confederate ensign, and what appeared from the shore to be a white flag. He further informed that Lieut. O. W. Edwards, with seven men, and Mr. Alexander Follett, a citizen in that vicinity, were decoyed aboard the vessel and held as prisoners. That night, when volunteers and (M) Company B, 13th Regiment, Texas Infantry came on, a party of the enemy in Edwards's boat, passed the battery on San Luis Island, and captured and burned the schooner *Columbia* which was laden with cotton, at the rear of the island. "Finally," said he, "owing to disobedience of Major Perry's orders by Captain Ballowe, the enemy escaped to their ship, without loss." Several shots were then exchanged with the Federal steamer, but without effect. The captured crew and passengers of the were put ashore, after which the steamer stood out to sea.

Addie Hudgins Follett[4]

Alexander Glass would twice be held by Northern soldiers on a ship. The second capture is recorded in *Pleasant Places, A Goodly Heritage*, by Anne Ayers Lide McCurdy, who explains that during the Civil War, Alexander Glass Follett was taken prisoner and spent three or four months on a Yankee gun boat. Follett was treated as an officer, was fed the best food, and slept in officers' quarters. His wife was pregnant and Follett worried much about her. When he was finally released, Follett returned home to a new baby boy.

It has been said that there are two sides to every story. A *New York*

Times article published on October 26, 1863, gives a Northern point of view of the Blockade Runners off San Luis Pass.[5]

Texas Blockade Runners

From the New-Orleans Era, Oct. 16.

The United States gunboat Tennessee. Lieut.. Commanding Wiggins, arrived yesterday from a cruise off Galveston. It appears that our gunboats in the Gulf have been after the rebel blockage-runners in an active manner. On the 12th inst., when about ten miles off San Luis Pass, a schooner was discovered in sight. Chase given immediately; and on coming up, she proved to be the rebel blockade-runner Friendship, bound from Havana to Matamoros. But, as she was evidently steering for Velasco, and was heavily laden with munitions of war, the Captain acknowledged he was a fair prize. The Friendship was taken in tow, and the Tennessee proceeded on her cruise. In half an hour more a sail was made about ten miles off. Chase was given; and on coming up within about three miles she was discovered to be on fire. A boat was sent out to board and try and save her; but when the launch came within about 400 yards, the schooner blew up with a terrific explosion. From the magnitude of the noise and concussion, it was thought the schooner was heavily laden with powder. The missiles from the destroyed vessel were scattered around on the sea for hundreds of yards. There were also a quantity of percussion caps including in the cargo, which was evidenced by the sound of small and continuous explosions heard after the grand flareup. The wreck proved to be the June, of Nassau, N.P.

The Cayuga also chased two schooners, which were fired by the rebels, and blown up.

Also the United States blockading schooner Kittatinny flushed a schooner which the rebels succeeded in beaching and blowing up.

This closes the career of five venturesome vessels, whose owners believed in the "paper blockade" theory. They have come to grief. The Friendship was left at Quarantine by the Tennessee.

The once-peaceful port became a battleground for many chases such as those described in the papers. As the war continued and supplies dwindled, the list of captured and destroyed vessels continued to grow.

BLOCKADE RUNNERS IN THE GULF COAST

Name	Class	Capture Date	Where Captured	Capture Vessel	Known Cargo
Acadia	steamer	Feb. 6, 1865- burned	San Luis Pass	USS Virginia	
Alabama	steamer	Dec. 6, 1864-forced aground & captured	San Luis Pass	USS Princess Royal	iron bars, rope, flour and soda
Catherine Holt	sloop	Feb. 29, 1864-burned	San Luis Pass	USS Virginia	
Emily	schooner	Oct. 19, 1864-captured	San Luis Pass	USS Mobile	150 bales of cotton
Excelsior		Jul. 13, ?	San Luis Pass	USS Katahdin	2 bales of cotton
Exchange	schooner	Dec. 24, 1863-captured	Velasco	USS Antonia	coffee, nails, shoes, acids, wire and Cotton goods
Friendship	schooner	Oct. 16, 1863-captured	Rio Brazos	USS Tennessee	munitions from Havana
Henry Colthirst	schooner	Feb. 22, 1864- captured	San Luis Pass	USS Virginia	gunpowder, hardware, provisions
Jane	schooner	Oct. 16, 1863-burned by own crew	Rio Brazos	USS Tennessee	
John Douglas	schooner	Feb. 29, 1864-captured	Velasco	USS Penobscot	cotton
John	schooner	Sep. 11, 1864-captured	Velasco	USS Augustus Dinsmore	cotton

Blockade Runners[6]

Fannie Mae Follett Gilbert
(2006)
Photo by Eilleen Benitz Wagner

One such vessel, the *Acadia*, embodied the ghosts of these ships, standing in tribute to those who disappeared beneath greater depths. These 2006 watercolors are based upon the girlhood memories of Fannie Mae Follett Gilbert, who was born in 1921. Fannie Mae recalls being seven or eight years old when she was able to observe the two stacks and paddlewheel still visible from the beach. Observed by the residents, the *Acadia* Blockade Runner became known as "The Boilers."

The sunken *Acadia* became a local landmark that lasted several generations. This River Clyde type steamship was built at Sorel, Quebec, Canada, on May 10, 1864, by Jacques Felix and William McNaughton. The following are nautical specifications for the Acadia:

Signal Letter- V.H.P.M. Number of Ship 46.239, Port number 17 of 1864 British Built-Steam Powered with a Paddlewheel.
One poop and promenade and hurricane, two masts, schooner rigging, round stern, carvel-built, no gallery, no head, wood framework. Port of Registry:

Acadia and *Fannie Mae*
2006 Watercolors
Courtesy Fannie Mae Follett Gilbert

Montreal, Canada.
Dated 14th July, 1864. One Transaction Title Derived from Jacques F. Lincinnes
Wm. McNaughton –64 shares
Registry Date 31st October 1864 – At 1'clock PM
Certificate of Sale
Dated 31ˢᵗ October 1864
She was 211 feet long, had a 31-foot beam, and her hold was 12-feet-deep with a 900-horse-power engine. She was built to be a blockade runner and was faster and larger then other ships of her class. The Acadia had two masts that could be lowered when under steam power. Finishing touches were made as they sailed from Halifax to Nassau.

Her first and only Captain, Thomas Leach picked up cargo in Nassau and then headed to Velasco. They sailed along the coast to avoid Federal Blockade Ships. In the night of February 5, 1865, a heavy fog sat in along the coast and she ran aground in 15 feet of water near San Luis Pass. There were no serious injuries or damage, but she was stuck beyond hope. Word was sent to the forts at Quintana and Velasco for help. The coastal patrol came and by daylight most of the cargo was unloaded. Gunfire from the USS Virginia disabled the Acadia as daylight came. Her cargo consisted of marble doorknobs, brass locks, keys, brass lamps, large jars, olives, and spirits.

Wendell E. Pierce examined the wreck during the late 1960s and early 1970s under permit from the Texas Antiquities Committee and under the supervision of Frank Hole, an archaeologist at Rice University. Artifacts are now held at the Brazoria County Historical Museum. An ornate stack was still visible in the late 1970s and early 1980s. Even in these later years, this wreck was a favorite fishing spot for many. After Hurricane Alicia in 1983, the Acadia disappeared from sight over one hundred years after her sinking.

Harve' Brenton of Sherbrooke, Quebec, is a dear friend of the author and father-in-law. After retiring as a naval officer from Canada, he researched for nearly three years to find a photo of the *Acadia*. Such a photo was not to be found. Though the vessel is lost, some of its artifacts have been retrieved.

The *Acadia* carried goods that could be sold at various ports. Building materials were hard to acquire and truly a treasure. Michael Bailey, Curator at the Brazoria County Historical Museum, allowed the author to photograph several of these precious artifacts. He held the porcelain toilet (head) that was recovered from the *Acadia*. After Hurricane *Ike*, our Texas General Land Office sonar flyover rediscovered the *Acadia*. She sank in 1865 and this is the first partial/full image ever taken!

The *Acadia* after Ike 2008 as seen on the ocean floor exactly where she sunk many years ago.

Image of the *Acadia* taken during a sonar flyover conducted by the General Land Office following Hurricane *Ike* in 2008.

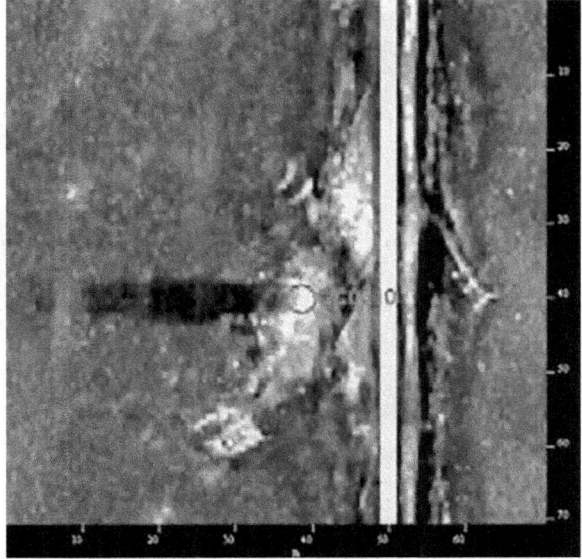

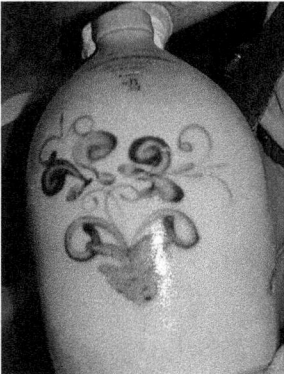

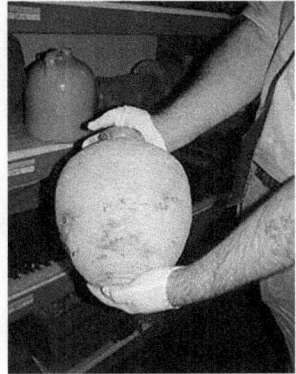

Michael Bailey, Curator Brazoria County Historical Museum shows artifacts from the *Acadia*.

109

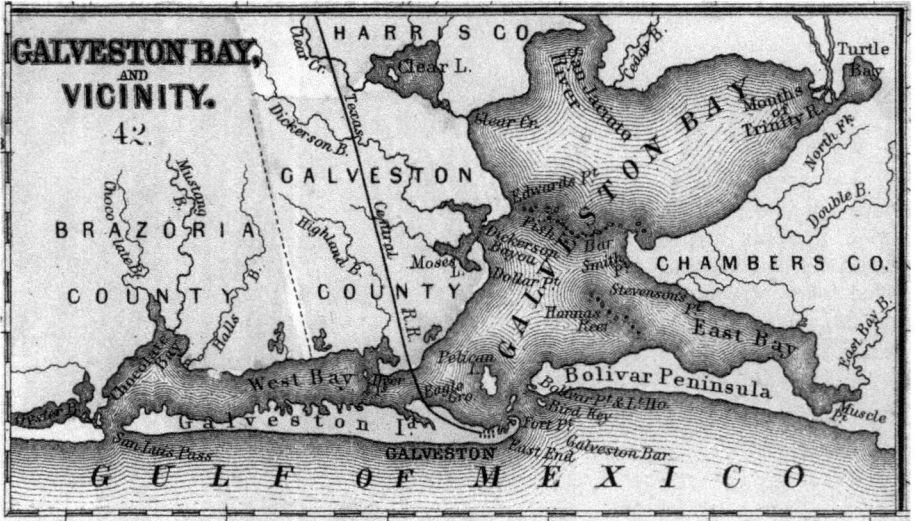

1870 Map of Texas Counties[7]

The war changed life in the South as it depleted the South's supplies and forever altered their economical structure. The North gained victory, and on June 19, 1865, a date which became known as Juneteenth, Union Major General Gordon Granger landed at Galveston. He raised a flag symbolizing the restoration of Union control and proclaimed freedom for the slaves. As noted earlier, it would be five more years before Texas would be fully readmitted to the United States.

As the war ended, the families of Luis Pass began to rebuild their lives. Alexander Glass Follett turned his attention from national wars to more local affairs. In her book, *Alexander Glass Follett*, author Mrs. Shannon states: "In 1878, Alonzo B. Follett was appointed Deputy Customs House Officer at San Luis Pass. He held this position for several years."

The August 10, 1870 Census, Precinct No 5, names the remaining families on the peninsula.

Dwelling House 1716
Follett:

Alonzo 35 a stock raiser	*Joseph 45 a stock raiser*
Wife Mary	*Harriet Sproll 23*
Ann Louisa Fownes 74	

The Census also notes that Alto Getz, was the Collector of Customs in 1870.

Ten years after the end of the war, the island was hit by another devastating storm. The trees, which had been planted to shield crops from the winds, saved several lives as homes were swept away in what was thought to be the worst storm the island had experienced so far.

Sept 21, 1875
Galveston Daily News

From Oyster Creek

The news is indebted to Rev. L. H. John for the following information:
Our party from Galveston, consisting of myself, Dr. E. P Angell and family several ladies and gentlemen, in attendance on a camp meeting, found a refuge at the house of Rev. P. E. Nicholson at Oyster Creek, four miles from Velasco. At that point the water was five feet higher than ever known before. Thirty-three persons found refuge in his house---Mr. John Hudgins and family having reached there on a raft coming two miles across the prairie, crossing Oyster Creek three times. When the storm subsided we could see but three houses in Velasco standing. Major Henderson's residence swept away. Could learn nothing from Quintana but could see by glass that few houses were gone. No lives lost in Velasco. On our return we found Fred Reeve's house on the canal swept away. Also Corrigan's at Christmas Point. We learned after we reached San Luis Island that Reeves was at Corrigan's in the storm and that he and the whole family hung in the salt cedars all night. At Velasco Capt. Lyons hung 11 hours in a tree. At Follett's on the end of Velasco Peninsula the water was 30 inches higher than in the storm of 1867. All government property saved. The old Follett House, which for 30 years has been a land mark on the coast, was swept away. Frank Holt's house on the peninsula also gone. Mr. Follett, who has lived on the coast place since 1880 says that large logs had drifted from above--logs which had been left by storms before the settlement of the country-- which fact indicates the water was high if not higher than in any storm that has swept our coast within the knowledge of this oldest inhabitant.

We learned as we were leaving Oyster Creek that Herndon's and Mrs. Wartoo's sugar house eight miles from the mouth of the Brazos, were swept away. The water was six feet higher at that point than ever known before. A number of houses were carried across the prairie, some within two miles of the Oyster Creek Harbor. We hear of the loss of but one life, an oysterman called Tony, who was at Corrigan's at Christmas Point.

About 3 A.M. Friday, while the storm was at the height, a skiff with nine persons in it, three women and three infants, endeavoring to reach Mr. Nicholson's where our part were, was swamped within about three hundred yards of the home. A rescue party consisting of Mr. Nicholson, Dr. Angell, Rays, Williamson and Phair, went out and found them clinging to some trees with the swell sweeping over their heads. After a desperate effort all were saved.

At every point from the mouth of the Brazos we found the people in great destitution, some living on the potatoes which must soon rot from the effects of salt water. Mr. Nicholson leaves today at 12 N. Provisions of any kind will aid the suffers, and Mr. Nicholson will faithfully attend to their distribution among the families who need aid.

One span of 135 feet of the Galveston, Harrisburg and San Antonio railroad bridge, over the Brazos river at Richmond, was blown down by the storm on Friday. It was the span on this side of the storm therefore it is more accessible, and will be repaired good. A strong force of mechanics have already been put to work. It is impossible to obtain any tiding from points on that road, as the damage to the telegraph line covered a space of forty miles, between Eagle Lake and Pierce's Junction.

Word of the storm reached all the way to the North and was recounted across the country. An article from The *New York Times* describes the Hurricane of September 23, 1875, detailing how it completely washed away the town of Velasco. Here are a few excerpts of this article:

New Orleans, Sept 22---The storm, cyclone appears to have taken in it course, a belt of county some forty miles in width, from the north of Galveston island extending to the north of Houston. The hurricane swept over the entire section of coast to the west of Indianola into the Gulf. Galveston was to the south of the more severe part of the gales. The steam-ship Harlan, before leaving Indianola, gave all her provision which could be spared to the sufferers. Four persons were lost at Indianola in addition to those already reported. Mr. Sondow Barrans, father and son, and teamster, now unknown. The entire list lost at Lynchburg. Morgan's Point, and Bay Souen as follows:

Information received from East Bernard County states that that entire section is under water from Brazoria. The town of Velasco is entirely swept away, and not a house is left to indicate where it stood. Not a life was lost and 173 persons, among them Judge Gus Cool, and the Criminal Court, and family were miraculously saved. When the storm had raged for some time, and the surging sea had entirely surrounded their place and billows, and began to invade the hoses, the entire population were huddled in the upper apartment of the largest building in town. But when it was seen that the sea and storm were about to sweep it away, men who were up to their necks in water with the aid of a small boat, got aboard themselves.

Among them was Col. Cook. He lashed the schooner to the first one tree and then another as they were pulled up by the roots, and thus rode the storm. The house from which they escaped was washed away shortly after they left.

The article goes on to state that warehouses, Sugarhouses, over 200 houses were lost. At Saluria the loss of life was approximate 150 to 200. The wharf had the entire planking torn off. The railroad office was broken down and all railroad books lost.

The destruction of the island was severe, leaving only one surviving settlement on the Peninsula, as reported in 1878. The storm had reduced the flourishing island back to a smaller town of twenty-five houses and one hundred and twenty-five people. The lack of manpower often led to difficulties in covering even the most important jobs.

Sanitary Inspector. Dr. T. J. Turner,
Secretary National Board of Health, Washington, D. C.
Galveston, Tex., August 1878
Sir: I have to report the following result of inspection of San Luis Pass, mouth of Brazos River, and mouth of San Bernard.

San Luis Pass is the entrance from the Gulf of Mexico to Galveston Bay, between west end of Galveston Island and the peninsula. The water is from 8 to 15 feet deep, and there is good anchorage inside. There is only one settlement near here, that of Captain Follett on the peninsula. It is 30 miles from the city of Galveston. The mouth of the Brazos River is 15 miles by land and 21 by the bays and canal southwest of San Luis Pass. The village of Velasco is on the East bank, and the village of Quintana is on the west bank of the Brazos, near the mouth. The two places together contain about twenty-five houses and one hundred and twenty-five inhabitants. There is also during the summer a transient population of twenty to fifty from the towns in the interior, sojourning here for benefit of sea-shore. There is but one small store-house, doing only a retail trade. The post-office for both places is at Velasco.

Yellow fever was brought to Velasco from New Orleans in 1853. There is a steamboat (the Thomas) making weekly trips from Galveston through the bays and canal to Velasco, and landing on the Brazos, as high up as Columbia. Coasting vessels from Galveston and the country (Louisiana) also enter here with general merchandise and lumber. Brazoria, the county seat, is 21 miles up Brazos River from the mouth. Columbia is 9 miles above Brazoria. There is a railroad from Columbia to Houston.

Mouth of San Bernard is 10 miles down the Gulf beach from Quintana. There are only two houses at this point, and one about a mile from it, since the destruction of the village by cyclone in 1875. The river is about 80 feet wide and 4 to 8 feet deep at the bar, the depth depending on the tide and the direction of the wind. This stream is navigable for about 80 miles.

Quarantine at San Luis Pass, mouth of Brazos and mouth of San Bernard, is under control of the county court of Brazoria County. On July 18, that body appointed Dr. R. G. Turner, of Columbia, health officer at the mouth of Brazos; Capt. Alonzo Follett quarantine guard at San Luis Pass, and Mr. Lanrent Decraw quarantine guard at mouth of San Bernard.

When I arrived at Velasco Dr. Turner was absent, having gone, I was informed, to move his family from Columbia to Velasco. Quarantine matters were left in the hands of Dr. Jager, whom Dr. Turner sent or brought down from Columbia, as his assistant.

Observation, confirmed by subsequent inquiry, led me to believe that Dr. Jager's *habits were not temperate, and that quarantine was not safe in his hands. Dr. Jager informed me that he represented Dr. Turner in his absence, and that his guard and boatman was a Mr. Metcalf, the merchant of the village. On the other hand, Mr. Metcalf says he is not an appointee and has no authority to act. I also heard from Dr. Jager that there was a guard under Dr. Turner's orders at San Luis Pass; but on my arrival at this point, Captain Follett told me that he had informed the county court that he, being inspector of customs, could not accept another office of profit. Since that time nothing has been heard from the authorities, and no one here considers it his business to act as quarantine guard. Captain Bissell, mounted inspector of customs, had just returned to Quintana from the mouth of San Bernard, and from him I learned that Lanrent Decraw, the quarantine guard at the mouth of San Bernard, had been several days absent at Galveston, leaving quarantine matters in the hands of his son, sixteen years old. Mr. Decraw's salary as quarantine guard is $15 a month. He is also pilot at this entrance, and receives $10 for every vessel that enters the mouth of the river. There has been no commerce between these three points and Mexican or other foreign ports. Only coasting vessels have entered. They would become very important points for quarantine, if yellow fever should appear on the Louisiana or Texas coast. There is also the contingency, remote, but possible, of small vessels from Mexican or other ports being turned away by the quarantine at Galveston, Indianola, &c., and trying to land at some of these unguarded entrances.*

Today I have called attention of State health officer to the condition of affairs, as above detailed.

In the meantime I requested the collector of customs of this district to instruct his inspectors to cooperate with the local authorities, and to act as quarantine guards in the absence of local quarantine guards, until the matter could be attended to by the State health officer. There is no quarantine establishment at any of these points. When a suspected vessel arrives, she is sent to quarantine at Galveston or Indianola.

The entire expense of quarantine at these three points can be made efficient for $150 per month, being $50 for each place. I am informed the county negotiated with Dr. Turner for $300, to pay all expenses; Dr. Jager told me this.

Since there are no quarantine quarters at any of them, and vessels are not placed quarantine here, but are sent elsewhere, there is no need of a physician. The sanitary condition at the mouth of Brazos is good and no special work is needed on this point. The few houses are scattered over a considerable area.

There have been heavy rains throughout this inspection district. My latest advices are that the general health is good.

My last report was dated August 13, and was mailed on the 14th. I leave for Indianola by ship this evening; thence I go to Corpus Christi. If consistent with the law, I would be pleased to receive about thirty envelopes and wrappers, with the stamp and "frank" of the National Board of Health. Please mail me

*the Bulletin" regularly. Would also like to have it sent to C. W. Short, mayor of
Indianola, Dr. T. E. Burke, H. O., Corpus Christi, and Thomas Carson, and Dr.
C. B. Combe, Brownsville, Tex.*

*I have requested the secretary of state to forward yon the governor's quarantine
proclamations up to date, as well as any that may be issued in future. I have the
honor to be, very respectfully, yours,*
Jno. H. Pope

With the poor economy, the spread of yellow fever and malaria, and the harbor filling in with sand, it became dangerous for ships to enter. The residents began leaving San Luis and homes were dismantled, moved, or left to decay.

Meanwhile, technology was advancing all over the country, much of it beginning in the cities around San Luis. Telephone service in Texas began in Galveston. On March 18, 1878, A. H. Belo, publisher of the *Galveston Daily News,* installed a phone line between his home and his newspaper office. It was the first in Texas and one of the few nationwide. The first telephone exchanges were built by the Western Union Telegraph Company. Southwestern Telegraph and Telephone Company was organized in 1881, to operate exchanges in Arkansas and Texas, and then spread to outlying cities. Later you will view two cables stretched across San Luis Pass on a map, no doubt the telephone cables to connect the Coast Guard Stations from West End to Surfside.

The Follet family who still resided on the island must have watched the developments with interest. They also informed the newspaper of events from what was left of their little village. A January 30, 1878 issue of the *Galveston Daily News* reported the following:

Brazoria County
*Capt. A.B. Follett writes to the News: The body of a man, apparently about
thirty years of age, was found ashore in San Luis Pass, near the residence of Mr.
Follett, by Capt. Ayers, of the sloop Little Arthur. An inquest was held by J. L.
Huggins, J.P., of Brazoria County and a verdict returned of "found drowned:
Deceased was about the medium size, stout built, had red hair and whiskers:
had on a blue coat and gray jeans pants: had in his coat pocket a package of
cards of the New Orleans House, corning of Bath Avenue and Strand.*

News of drowning highlighted yet another aspect of the island officials' attempts to keep their residents as safe as possible, even amidst the dangers of war and natural disaster.

The San Luis Lifeboat Station was one of five stations erected in the 8th Life Saving District during 1880. First designated as Station No. 3 of the 8th District, the Station, located at the West end of Galveston Island was first named "San Luis Lifeboat Station" in the Annual Report of June 30, 1883. The Station was actually opened on October 15, 1880, and the first keeper was John R. Van Siene. He succeeded a watchman Richard O. Hanlan who had been in charge of the premises during construction of the Station. The first crew of the San Luis Lifeboat Station that reported on that date were:

Keeper J. R. Van Sien
1st Surfman – William Evans
2nd Surfman – Otto Muller
3rd Surfman – James Thompson (also Cook)
4th Surfman – William Peterson
5th Surfman – John Ericson
6th Surfman – Henry Heinroth
Near southwest end of Galveston Island, 2¾ miles from entrance of San Luis Pass. A 100 foot strip of land comprising of 14 acres across the west end of the Island from the Gulf Shore to the Bay shore.
Conveyed in perpetuity to the government by Ceiphas P. Adams

Quoted directly from *History of San Luis Lifeboat Station Galveston,*

San Luis Lifeboat Station[8]
United States Coast Guard Courtesy Gallaway Collection- March 13, 1879. (F. A. Leamy, Captain, U. S. Coast Guard Chief of Staff Eight Coast Guard District letter, May 16, 1950)

Steamboat Hiawatha[9]

As the area began to rebuild and return to prosperity, boats offered opportunities for socialization as well as trade. Docked at Velasco, the steamboat *Hiawatha* advertised a Grand Ball. The *Hiawatha* was built in 1890 and sank in 1895.

Men often gathered in hunting parties to take advantage of the abundant game of the area. Judith Willy Bielstein's great uncle, Mr. Wharton Hoskins is seated in the foreground of the photo. William Wharton Hoskins was born in 1864, but he left home never to be heard from again. No one knew what happened to him. The game was killed near the Bernard River in 1894.

It does not often snow along the Texas coast, yet on Valentine's Day in 1895, residents were surprised to witness snowflakes drifting onto their shores. This is a newspaper clipping which tells the story of this huge snowfall.

St. Valentine's Day - -Galveston's Great Snowstorm of 1895
Today the seventeenth anniversary.
Business was suspended
Today St. Valentine's Day, is the seventeenth anniversary of the great snow-storm of Galveston. At 1 o'clock on the morning of Feb. 14, 1895, snow began falling and continued throughout the day. The total fall was 14.4 inches but in many places the drifts were four and five feet high. Business was almost totally suspended. The banks and wholesale houses opened their doors in the morning, but closed again. The streetcars could not run and there was no service until

Morning Hunt[10]

the next day, when the tracks were cleared by an improvised snowplow.

The day was spent in snowballing and no one was spared.

The News of Feb. 15 introductory to its account of the storm summed the situation up as follows:

Wagons up to their hubs in snow' improvised sleighs; skiffs pulled though the streets a/la Laplander; snow drifts four feet high; snowballing parties; Tom and Jerry's: street traffic suspended: trains snowbound; banks and wholesale houses closed up; shoe store sold out of gum boots and overshoes; riots over loaded snowballs; general suspension of all business save at saloons and restaurants -- such, in brief, is the record of St. Valentine's Day. 1895 in Galveston.

The oldest inhabitant could not remember such a climatic phenomenon. In 1886, according to the record of the weather bureau, there was a fall of six inches, and it was remembered by some inhabitants that in 1852 or l855 there was a heavy snowfall but not so heavy as that of 1895.

The storm was general throughout Texas. At Beaumont 28 inches was the record. All lines of business were affected.

Another article gives a more elegant description:

Valentine's Day Snowfall February 14, 1895

San Luis Island Received 15.4 Inches of Snow - Record Snowfall

Snow--real, white, swirling, fluffy, snowy snow, of the kind that delights the heart of the Northerner and startles joyously the heart of the Southerner; that makes the blood tingle as it races through the veins and makes the muscles long for a good handful to aim at some unsuspecting passer-by -- snow of the 'only original' brand, fell in Galveston Tuesday night and covered the streets and roofs with a thin mantle of unaccustomed white that in its novelty far exceeded the beauty of blossoming oleanders and swaying palms.

Following the flurries of snow and sleet that had made winter in the South seem an actuality throughout the day, the real snow started about 11 o'clock, and it was still falling at midnight, making the heaviest snowfall on Treasure Island since 1895 when 15.4 inches came down.

Swirling downward with the gusts of the norther, the flakes fell upon the throngs of Mardi Gras merrymakers on the downtown streets and were greeted with wild salvos of delight. Parties of costumed fun-seekers, uniformed soldiers and the plain, ordinary, everyday citizen, joined in the unusual fun of snowball fights, which added to the general hilarity of Mardi Gras night.

United States Weather Observer Steward reported that two-tenths of an inch had fallen up to midnight and that this amount would be materially increased when the snow finally ceased.[11]

The snowfall added a fond memory to all who experienced the day. Nearly exactly four years later, another unexpected freeze would again blast the island, this time layering everything in ice.

On February 12, 1899, an Arctic air mass swept south from the northern and central plains to the state of Texas. The 8-degree bitterly-cold air mass plunged as far south as the upper Texas coast, where a thin layer of ice coated most of Galveston Bay.

Both of the cold spells fell between a series of tropical storms that battered the coast. Hitting in September 1887, June 1888, July 1888, July 1891, August 1895, September 1897 and in June 1899, the weather offered little respite. These storms were directly responsible for San Luis Pass filling with sand.

Brazoria County Map, 1899[12]

This map shows that by 1899, Little Pass had sanded in and San Luis was no longer an island.

Though the newspapers of the area continued to delight readers with descriptions and details, the telegraph was employed to report current and urgent news. Western Union is little used today, but it was a very important tool to communicate in the late 1800s. Reporting on July 5, 1899, a Western Union telegram from John Phillips, mayor of San Felipe, to Governor J. D. Sayers expresses the grave need for help after this horrific storm:

We have a thousand sufferers from the Brazos flood, five hundred In immediate need of food and clothing, starving. Help us. We have Done and are doing all we can but our resources have all been swept Away.

John Phillips, Mayor

120

Tropical storms and hurricanes were responsible for widespread damage, but even a heavy rain could swell the Brazos River enough to flood the area.

From June 17 to June 28, 1899, between 10 and 20 inches of rainfall poured onto the area from Temple to Palestine and south to Victoria and Houston, with approximate 30 inches falling in Hearne. The Brazos River overflowed its banks and inundated 12,000 square miles. Damage to crops, farm equipment, and homes was estimated at over $9 million. Killed were 284 people, and thousands more were made homeless, with African American tenant farmers especially hard hit. At some points, the water rose above all available flood gauges.

In July, 1899, in an overflow of the Brazos River, inundating the country for hundreds of miles, the service men were instrumental in rescuing with the surf-boats 257 persons, and with other boats in their charge 300 persons (for a total of 557 rescued). Their operations covered 150 miles over a country completely devastated.[13]

Coast Guard Operations
During Natural Disasters & Events of National Significance

The destruction introduced by the tropical storms foreshadowed the utter devastation that would hit the region in September of 1900, when the worse hurricane ever recorded made landfall.

On Monday, September 10, 1900, the New York *Brooklyn Daily Eagle* ran an article regarding the 1900 Storm. Page 8 tells of a cyclone that traveled from the Brazos River Bottom for 100 miles of its length, destroying farmhouses, crops, and everything in its path. Most of this entire issue was dedicated to the 1900 Storm at Galveston, Texas.

Benjamin Hardy Carlton recalls the horrifying details of the day as he journeyed between Quintana and Velasco:

The year was 1900. On September 5th (Editor's note: Actually it was September 7th), the wind was blowing from the north and the water was rising. I consulted the old settlers of Quintana, asking them if it wasn't a storm coming. They said no, it was impossible to have a storm with the wind coming from the north. Well, I wondered what was going to happen. The wind was getting stronger and stronger and the tide was inundating the lower part of town. If it continues like that, what are you going to call it?

At that time, we had two homes, one in Quintana and another in Velasco. On September 6th (actually the 7th), I went to Velasco to attend the Masonic Lodge, taking with me my wife and my two small daughters, Doris and Myrtle. I left the two boys, Marion and Columbus at Quintana. After the close of the meeting I took a sick headache, which I had periodically for a number of years. We decided to stay overnight with my brother-in-law, C. C. Johnson.

The next morning (September 8, 8 AM) the wind was stronger than ever and I attempted to go back to Quintana. Reaching about half the distance I discovered that the water was all over the prairie and floating logs made it impossible to go on. By the time I got back to Velasco the river had become so rough that the ferryboat could not operate. There were two government boats anchored in the river so I asked the officers if they couldn't go down to Quintana and reach my sons and the other folks that were there. They said they would take great pleasure in doing anything for me they could and immediately began to get steam up.

I sent word to Lena that if the storm increased, not to attempt to go to the Velasco hotel as I considered it unsafe, but just to remain in our home. Upon arriving at Quintana they attempted to anchor the steamboat just opposite the lighthouse. They threw ropes over the piling and it snapped like a pipe stem. The boat was drifting rapidly out towards the gulf. The captain turned into the wind and put on all the steam they had. Throwing out the anchors they finally brought the boat to a standstill. The captain ordered his men to get me ashore in a lifeboat.

Arriving on shore I found that everything in the lower part of town was under water. I met my son, Columbus, telling him to stay in a certain house nearby. I had my boatman take the quarantine boat and help to remove his family, including a baby just several days old. When we got there, water was up to the door. After getting them to the boat we proceeded to try and reach higher ground. We hadn't gotten far when the boat swamped. I was holding the little baby and trying to walk with the wind in waist deep water. Every thirty or forty feet the wind would blow me down...the baby being completely immersed each time.

I finally reached Captain Bowers house completely exhausted, but I still had the baby. I expected that the baby had not survived the ordeal but when I unwrapped it, it was sound asleep. The mother and father with several others were fortunate to reach higher ground. In the excitement they lost one little boy but later found him clinging to the branches of a salt cedar unharmed. At this time most of the houses were being blown away and Captain Bowers' house was a two story one. Near his house was a one-story house that was supposed to be storm proof that was built by a syndicate during the construction of the jetties.

Thinking that the Bowers house would soon collapse, we made several attempts to reach the other house. When we were about to make a dash for it we looked out and the house was gone. We went back upstairs and shortly afterwards a two by four was blown through the double walls, through a double partition, and into the piano. Soon after, a lull came and there was not a breath of air. I tried to reach the baby's mother and father to tell them that their baby was safe. On the way the water was up to my chin. They were very happy to learn that their baby was safe.

The lull lasted for about 15 minutes, and then the wind came back from the South at the same velocity that it had been coming from the north. Amazingly, my watch, which had been immersed in the water several times, was still running. It and the clock on the wall both said 8:10 PM. We had all gone through so much, it felt like it should be about twelve o'clock. There I was and I did not know if any of my family was living or not. (Editor's note: His family had all survived.)

Ruby Lide's account of the storm offers details about its effects on those still living in San Luis.

Ruby Lide was living with her Grandfather Alexander Glass Follett at the time of the 1900 storm. His home was about four miles west of San Luis Pass and only a block and a half from the Gulf of Mexico. Ruby recalled the initial exceptional beauty of the day of the hurricane. The water appeared to her to be draining out of the Gulf, leaving an immense beach. It was as though the Gulf were drawing back a fist to strike a heavy blow.

Much like the home of Alexander's father, John Bradbury Follett, the shipbuilder, Alexander's home was built as securely as a ship, with water tight walls and floors. All of which was anchored to heavy pilings. As the strength of the storm grew, the main house and two large barns blew down. 'We were in a storm house also built on pilings and connected to the main house by a platform.' Alexander had built the storm house after experiencing the storms of 1875 and 1886. The storm house withstood the first waves and wind, though it shifted several times, and was left leaning. Ruby was convinced the reason the storm house was saved was that her grandfather had a fencing system. He used a double row of Salt Cedar trees planted very close together. The double row with a driveway between acted as a breakwater that trapped drift material that broke the force of the wave action. When the hurricane came on shore, the surge was so great, it temporarily cut a new channel into West Bay, in addition to San Luis Pass. When the storm passed, Ruby said as far as the eye could see, the prairie was littered with furniture, washtubs, and pianos, even a brickbat from a house with several fireplaces. They counted thirty bodies visible from their door. Only one was identified. Her grandfather had large herds of horses, cattle, sheep and Angora goats. The only animal that survived was a pet lamb that was kept in the storm house with them. As food became in short supply, the pet lamb was eaten. Not one of her best memories.[14]

Another account of the storm at San Luis Pass was given by Joseph Follett, who witnessed "40 to 50 foot waves breaking over San Luis Island."

Uncle Joe (Joseph Boswell Follett) recalled on September 6th, he came out of Galveston harbor with a cargo for Corpus Christi. The barometer was falling and when he entered the Gulf there was a very heavy sea and ground swell, but not much wind. The horizon was hazy as they sailed westward. The barometer kept falling signifying a storm approaching. He decided to cross the San Luis Bar and go into Galveston Bay to wait for smooth weather. He anchored on the seventh bar. The surf was heavy and came over the beach with a loud roar. There was an immense tide and the wind kept increasing. By the morning of the eighth, the wind was from the North, which was off the mainland and should have been driving the tide out; instead it was increasing very fast and rapidly spreading over the mainland. In the afternoon the hurricane struck. There was a fleet of eleven schooners lying at anchor.

There we were and it was no time hardly before the wind had reached a velocity of one hundred miles an hour. The surf was breaking over Galveston Island forty or fifty feet high. Shortly one of the schooners picked up anchors and the wind swept her toward the island to her doom. One by one the others broke loose. All of the sailors stayed with their ships to their demise. Now the Lucille was the last one still holding her moorings. He had her anchored with four anchors, two with chains and two with hawsers. First the chain anchors snapped and then the hawsers began chafing. It was only a matter of time. Captain Joseph made the decision they had to abandon ship. His crew refused at first but he persuaded them they must go. Then he and his crew decided to get into the yawl and go adrift. When the Lucille broke loose, she seemed to drift as fast as a sea gull could fly. Suddenly the yawl swamped and they were left to swim in the darkest of ink black nights he had ever seen. He knew this land well and swam toward a grove of hackberry trees that he knew was on higher ground. Everyone had become separated when the yawl capsized, but when he finally reached the trees he heard his sailors yelling for him. They all gathered in the trees, which were in about twelve feet of water and waited. The clouds began to break up and in a couple of hours they were on dry land. With most of the skin gone from there faces from the salt spray, with no shoes, feet burning from prickly pear thorn, their clothes torn to shreds, they made it to a home that had been under water about four miles away that was still standing and the family alive. All the food was soaked with salt water but they managed to make a cornbread and find a jar of honey to sustain them. This was the pasture where he and his Uncle Alonzo grazed their cattle. That is when he realized that all of his cattle and a thousand head of Uncle Alonzo Follett's cattle had drowned. He was totally broke. He and his crew then walked twenty miles to Angleton where Uncle James Boswell Follett took care of them until they found work. Alexander built a new home at Velasco.[15]

Although Halfway House was repeatedly damaged by storms for more than fifty years, the Follett family continued to live in, repair, or replace the damaged sections. Halfway House remained until the 1900 Storm, when it was washed away. The hurricane dismantled the few families who had clung to their island, shattering their homes and thrusting the once thriving village into the slow decline of a ghost town.

The island lay quiet for the next fifty years. It became a prime fishing spot for those in "the know" and no doubt a bird paradise. During the same period, Brazoria County saw tremendous growth in all directions.

Photo gift from Mary Cannon taken in August 1976

Oil Rigs in Back Bay

As lucrative as trade had become for the Texas Coast, another source of wealth was uncovered as oil production in Texas began as early as 1877. San Luis Island was just on the outskirt of this "Black Gold" oil-rich area. This photo's "pumper rigs" could be seen from San Luis Island, just to the North beyond the Permit Houses located on Titlum Tatlum Bayou. They remained active until the 1980s.

Natural disasters were happening often, dampening, but not dissolving the spirit of the residents. In this photograph, snapped between storms, fishermen take a moment to seine San Luis Pass for fresh fish.

The years just before and after the turn of the century continued to offer a bizarre and harsh series of natural events, as snow fell between the periods of Tropical storms, and a meteor strike occurred a year or so before the Great Storm. As recalled by Mrs. Addie Hudgins Follett:

Other tragic and strange events seemed to cluster during or near this year of 1909. One afternoon I was lying across my bed nursing a headache. Vida was asleep, and Carrie Mae, Joe, and Baddy were playing around in the house. Suddenly, a bright glare shone in my face through the window, and the heat was so intense that I felt like my clothes were afire. I raised up and looked out. A big body of the brightest light I ever tried to look at was passing out into the Gulf, or so it appeared. I had to close my eyes, and when I opened them again the light was not directly in front of our house and the heat through the window was not so fierce. I looked around for the children. They were okay, and not having been near outside doors or windows had not noticed anything wrong. When I looked out again the light was gone. Later when I went to bring in some clothes,

125

Courtesy Gallaway Collection

Seining San Luis Pass - 1908[16]

mostly diapers, from the line in the back yard, they fell to pieces when I touched them. They were burned to an ash, but still held together. The curtains on all of the front windows were the same, even the one by my bed where I had been resting. Lon was not at home. The children and all the rest of our clothing were alright. Mrs. Scogsburg reported a washing on the line at her house that had the same fate as mine. I always thought it was a meteor that fell in the gulf. The foregoing event fits in with my memories of the adversities that beset us in the year 1909. However, in recent years as I read of the great, brilliant body that exploded over Siberia in 1908, I am not sure that my experience could not have occurred in that year.[17]

In 1909, the coast witnessed yet another hurricane that swept across its shores.

A storm was noted entering the Eastern Caribbean on the 13th of July. It moved towards the west-northwest, passing over the Isle of Pines on the 17th.... The westerly storm motion continued, and on the 21st it made landfall near Velasco...." One-half of the town was destroyed. "The calm of the eye passed over the city for 45 minutes.... The storm surge was as high as twenty feet.... At Bay City, the pressure fell to 29.00" at 2:30 PM.... Property damage was estimated at 2 million dollars and 41 lives were lost...." The storm surge at Galveston was 10 feet; five people perished there.[18]

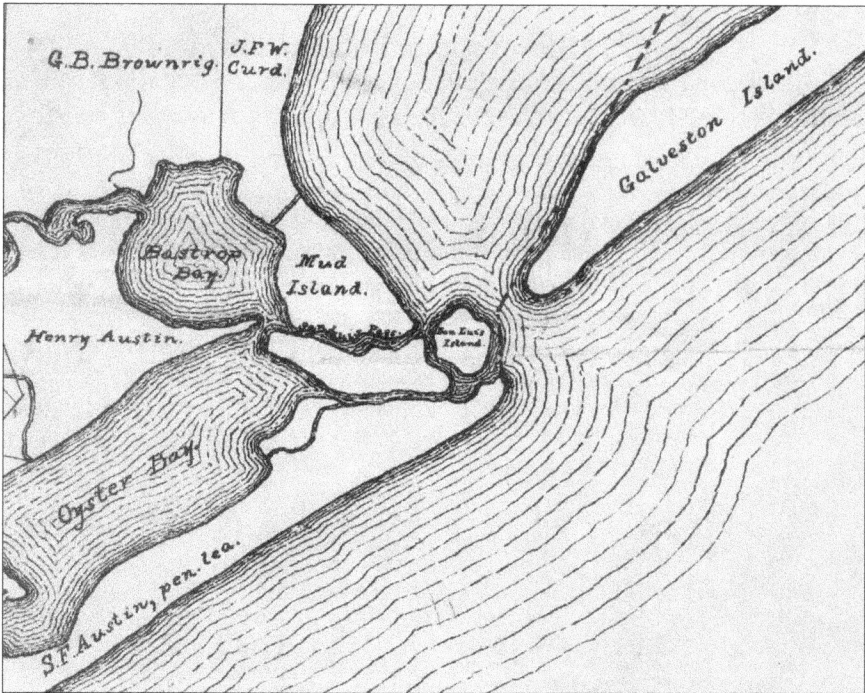

Please note, San Luis is an Island again in this map from 1909.[19]

Courtesy Gallaway Collection

San Luis Pass Coast Guard Station, 1941

San Luis Coast Guard Station[20]

1909 Storm at San Luis Station

Coast Guard Station is now located at the west end of the Peninsula which was the city of old Velasco. Today it is known as Surfside, Texas.

This station suffered the most seriously of those in the track of the storm. Salt cedar trees near the station reservation measuring more than 10 inches in diameter were snapped off like reeds. The sand under and around the station buildings was cut out by the sea to a depth of several feet and the building itself moved out of position and left standing out of plumb at an angle of about 5°. All outhouses, consisting of a stable, boathouse, and workshop combined, an oil and paint locker, a pump house, and a cistern of 3,000 gallons capacity, were demolished and swept away, as was also all fencing inclosing the station quarters. The station horse went with the stable. The Race Point surfboat and

San Luis (1879 to 1940; No. 218)

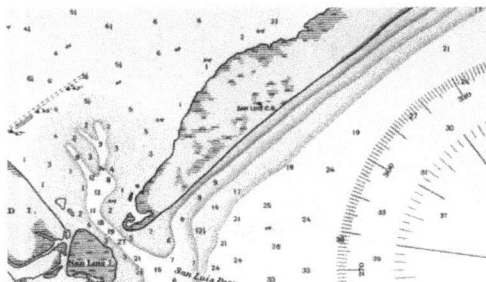

Rescue Boats Assigned [21]

1880:	27ft. Long Branch type pulling surfboat
1888:	26ft. Higgins & Gifford type pulling surfboat
	17ft. skiff
1893:	23ft. "cat" type sailboat
	11ft. skiff
1897:	24ft. Race Point type pulling surfboat
	30ft. sloop "Hornet"
1898:	23ft. Monomoy type pulling surfboat
1913:	Beebe-McLellan type motor surfboat No. 1166
1915:	Beebe-McLellan type pulling/sailing surfboat No. 1302
	Race Point type pulling surfboat No. 1307
1925:	Type H motor surfboat No. 2175
	Race Point type pulling surfboat No. 2841/CG24007
1934:	Type S motor surfboat No. 4487/CG25570

Rescue Boats San Luis Station

its carriage, the supply boat, and an 11-foot dinghy were also carried away. The first-mentioned boat was subsequently found at Hitchcock, Texas, 18 miles from the station, and a portion of the supply boat (a sloop) was picked up 16 miles from the station on the water front of the mainland. The 1,100-foot wharf on the bay side of the station was practically wrecked, except the extreme outer end, which supported a small house containing a 23-foot Monomoy surfboat. This boat was damaged considerably. In addition to the foregoing losses a quantity of property consisting of miscellaneous small articles belonging to the station equipment was also destroyed. The keeper of the station, as well, suffered great personal loss, his cottage—a new building—and everything in it having been carried away by the elements.

On the day of the hurricane Surfman Oscar Stromberg was in charge of the station, the keeper being absent from his post on account of disability. During the morning of the storm and before it was at its height six fishermen sought refuge at the station when the rising water of the Gulf began to sweep across the island. Stromberg ran the surfboat out of its quarters, anchored it clear of possible obstruction in case it should go adrift, and got in it, together with the fishermen, fearing to remain in the station building. While they were aboard the boat, the storm tore it from its moorings and swept it clear over the island and across the bay to the mainland, providentially without mishap to the occupants. When the wind and sea moderated, they pulled back to the station, where they found another man who had got ashore from a capsized sloop. All seven men remained at the station overnight, and on the morning of the 22d Stromberg carried them to Galveston in the surfboat. On their way they found two men in a sloop who had cut away their mast during the prevalence of the hurricane to keep from being turned over. These men were taken into the surfboat and landed at Galveston, where Stromberg reported to the district superintendent the state of affairs at the San Luis station.[22]

Though the majority of lost ships met their fates through such storms or by running aground, they also faced the dangers of fire. The Coast Guard Station #218 was set up to offer rescue to sinking vessels and aid during storms. Ironically, however, their initiation also formed to counteract what was considered a force potentially as destructive as the massive storms: the consumption of alcohol.

On January 20, 1915, the U. S. Revenue Cutter Service and the U. S. Life-Saving Service were merged to form the U. S. Coast Guard. Their first major task began in 1920 with Prohibition, the banning of alcoholic beverages in the United States, which was known as the Rum War. This war ended in 1933 when 11 patrol and picket boats left Galveston signaling the end of prohibition and rum smuggling times. As San Luis Pass shoaled up and was no longer usable for rum running, the station was closed. It was never rebuilt after a fire in 1946.

Most records state that this station was abandoned in 1950.[23]
Adding insult to injury of the memories of the Great Storm survi-

vors, another hurricane hit the coast in 1915. The following account of
the destruction of the Station in the Hurricane of August 16 and 17, is
taken from the Annual Reports of the U. S. Coast Guard for the fiscal
year:

> *Loss of Life and Property During 1915 Hurricane on Gulf Coast.*
>
> *Established primarily for the saving of life and property of the public from the
> perils of the sea, the Coast Guard is not infrequently, itself, the victim of serious
> disaster through the ravages of the storm and flood. Probably the most notable
> instances of the kind in the history of the service have been caused by the tropi-
> cal hurricanes which occasionally visit the Gulf coast of the United States. The
> most disastrous of these storms in recent years so far as concern the service,
> swept the Gulf coast on the 16th of August, 1915, entirely destroying the Velas-
> co, San Luis, and Galveston stations, with practically all their equipment, and
> claiming the lives of two members of the crew of the Velasco station and of four
> members of the crew of the San Luis station. Several members of the families of
> the Coast Guardsmen and a number of persons who had sought refuge at the
> stations also perished.*
>
> *Upon the occurrence of these hurricanes, the crews of stations within the storm
> area have been accustomed, under extreme conditions, to man their larger boats
> at the beginning of the flood, taking with them such refugees as have sought
> protection, in the hope of surviving the storm, riding at such available mooring
> as seemed to offer the best holding ground. The predicament of the crews during
> these trying occasions can well be imagined. Driven from their stations by the
> rise of water, there is nothing else for them to do, on the low, flat beaches of the
> country, but to take to their boats, make them fast the best they can, and trust
> to good fortune to bring them through the storm. The story of the storm of 1915
> is practically a repetition of the incidents of former hurricanes occurring on the
> Gulf coast and adds another thrilling chapter to the annals of this branch of the
> public service.*
>
> *Upon this occasion of total of 21 persons, members of the crew of the Velasco
> station and refugees, sought safety in the Coast guard boats belonging to that
> station. At the height of the storm the station was carried away by the wind and
> flood, and both boats, which were moored to the building, were capsized, result-
> ing in the drowning of 16 persons. Surfmen Christian P. Oddershede and The-
> odore Gust, and the wife and daughter of Keeper Steinhart, were among those
> who lost their lives. Two of the surviving members of the crew and a young
> woman who was with the party, all having life preservers, floated about in the
> waters of the Gulf for 20 hours, finally drifting ashore on Galveston Islands,
> some 25 miles to the eastward of the station.*
>
> *At the San Luis station, on the West end of Galveston Islands, the crew and oth-
> er also took to the lifeboats in the same manner. Four members of the crew, Surf-
> men Edward Boetger, W. J. Cochran, Jerome Cl Maddox, and Maraus Olsen,
> perished, following the overturning of their boat which, as in the former case,*

was caused by the collapse of the station building. The wife of Surfman Krouse, the wife and child of Surfman Boetger, and camper names Richard Hanson were also drowned. The surviving members of the station crew, badly cut and bruised, reached land 18 or 20 miles distant from the station after drifting in the Gulf for periods varying from 24 to 46 hours.

No loss of life occurred at the Galveston station.' On the contrary, it appears that in the early hours of the hurricane the station crew effected the rescue of 18 people, carrying them from the island upon which the station stood to the city of Galveston. If the crew had remained at the station doubtless some or all of the men would have perished, as the station was swept away by the flood. At the Velasco station temporary quarters were immediately secured at the Brazos Lighthouse, through the courtesy of the Bureau of Lighthouses, permitting an early resumption of station duties. A new site has been secured near the moth of the Brazos River which will afford the best obtainable facilities for the work of the Coast Guard. Plans have been prepared for a new station.

At the San Luis station a building was at once erected to provide temporary quarters for the crew. This will serve as a boathouse when the main station building, for which plans have been completed, has been erected. The new buildings will provide better facilities and designed to afford great protection against such contingencies of the future.

Temporary quarters were immediately obtained for the keeper and crew of the Galveston station in the immigration station adjoining, through the courtesy of the Bureau of Immigration, enabling that unit of the Coast Guard to continue its operations without serious interruption. Negotiations are in progress having in view the permanent occupancy of this building, which is found to be well suited to the needs of the service.

A new station was immediately built after this disaster and reoccupied and ready for service by November 18, 1915.

Despite the losses caused by wind, rain and floods, a few surviving photos give us a visual picture of a bygone era. This photo was taken during the 1899 flood. Buildings in the new town of Velasco, Texas are shown, including (lower right) S. T. Coldwater Boot & Shoe Store, (Center) Velasco Bank; (center right) Snyder building; (center) McRae Hardware; Masonic Hall behind McRae Hardware (left) Methodist Church, during the 1899 Brazos River flood.

Always resilient, the town was quick to rebuild after every disaster. This photo shows the interior of Velasco Bank which was built in 1912 with five employees tending to the store. Everything from bolts of fabric, to daily necessities are for sale. William Wharton Hoskins is sitting on the right of photo.

Future generations would continue to recount the details of the storm as hindsight formed a larger picture. A later observation of the

Flood[24]

1915 storms reports:

August 16-19th, 1915: A monstrous hurricane formed near the Cape Verde Islands on the 4th and moved just south of the greater Antilles, to reach the Texas coast near Galveston on the 16th. It was a storm of great diameter. In Galveston, many people, with memories of the 1900 hurricane still fresh in their minds, fled for the hills. . . Storm surges of 12 feet overwashed the island, inundating the business district to a depth of five or six feet. Many houses were demolished and all beach front bathhouses were washed away.

The Bolivar Point lighthouse, near Galveston, became a refuge for sixty peo-

Interior of Velasco Bank[25]

ple during the hurricane. *The oil supply for the light was carried away by the storm surge. This caused a two day outage of the light during the critical period following the storm.... The cistern of the Redfish Bar light was torn away. The superstructure of the Galveston Jetty light was damaged. Within days, the city began recovery. A storm surge of 15.3 feet above mean low gulf was noted at Virginia Point.... The Trinity Shoals buoys, weighing 15 tons including the chain, was dragged ten miles west of its prior location.*

Velasco had the pressure fall to 28.14". Houston reported winds of 62 mph.... Despite ample warnings from the Weather Bureau 24 hours in advance, 275 people died in the storm (only twelve died in Galveston, with no one behind the seawall taken victim). Damage was estimated as high as 50 million dollars.

The Coastal Bend had felt protected from the worst hurricanes in its early history. Corpus Christi, with its high bluff and the protective barrier island, felt particularly secure. Quickly forgetting the Hurricane of 1874, local newspapers in 1886 referred to Corpus Christi as 'the only really safe place on the Texas coast.' An article in 1909 continued to sing praises as 'the oldest inhabitants cannot recall a storm of sufficient severity to alarm even a timid woman' and 'nine-tenths of the area of Corpus Christi is on a bluff 30 feet high, probably the safest point in saltwater America,' or so they thought.[26]

Prohibition Years[27]

Despite the efforts of the Coast Guard to prevent the importation of alcohol, the Prohibition only increased the income from the forbidden trade. From 1919 to 1933, Galveston profited from rum runners from Cuba, Jamaica, and the Bahamas. The ships would drop anchor thirty-five miles out. They would then load their cargo into small powerboats or flat-bottom boats for delivery along the miles of deserted beach. The crews would wrap their booze in burlap sacks; two sacks were tied together for easy handling. Crews would wade out and carry the goods to shore. Sometimes they would use the coves near San Luis Pass to come on shore. Here in this map, San Luis is shown to still be an Island.

Opening another tale of the beginning chapters of San Luis, we come to the story of the Stevens family and Treasure Island. As recorded at the Brazoria County Abstract Company Inc., Hennell Stevens purchased 2,685 acres of land on San Luis and the Peninsula on November 2, 1876, for twenty cents per acre. General Analysis of the Title of San Luis Island shows that it is the eastern portion of S. F. Austin Peninsular League, Abstract 29, Brazoria County.

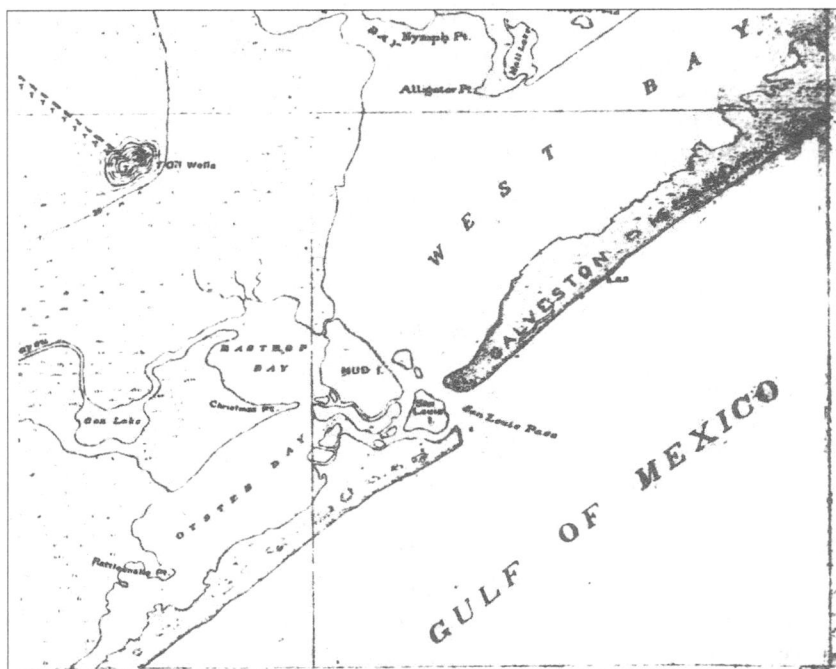

1916 Map San Luis Pass[28]
Note that San Luis is spelled "San Louis" on this map.

At the request of the author, Eleanor Stevens Vaughan wrote the following passage in August, 2006 for this book:

Dr. Hennell Stevens, a Medical Storekeeper in the Union Army during the Civil War, had visited Texas during the war and had fallen in love with it. At the close of the war he moved with his family to Texas, settling in Brazoria County. He was an avid reader and educated in many fields. He first tried farming but had little success. He was a Postmaster in Columbia in 1867; appointed County Judge in 1869 and was County Surveyor of Brazoria County 1872 to 1876, locating many original surveys in the county. He was appointed Postmaster in Brazoria in 1882. In 1883, he and J. H. Shepard founded The Brazoria County Abstract Company, which is still in existence. He also opened a drug store in Brazoria which he managed until his death in 1897.

Very likely with his close involvement with land in the County he saw San Luis Island, or Treasure Island, as a good investment and purchased it November 2, 1876.

Dr. Hennell's son, Frank Wilson Stevens, also did some surveying but after his marriage engaged in real estate and the abstract business which his father had

134

Mr. M.H. Rouse, baby is Flo Terry, Mrs. Gertrude Terry & Bill Rouse. The Brazos River between Velasco and Freeport Texas was in flood stage in November 1918 when this picture was taken. The bridge was completed in 1916.

Freeport Swing Bridge

Photo of the Brazos River Railroad and Auto Swinging Bridge. Photo from Mrs. Ivah Terry Powell. It was sent to the author via e-mail from Dan Kessner, Clute, Texas. According to neighbor Jack Wagner, this is the bridge he used to cross to get to the Peninsula, and then drive to San Luis Island.

THE PROSPECTORY
MAP
BRAZORIA COUNTY
TEXAS

1919 Map[29]

begun. With the big boom in Real Estate around the mouth of the Brazos River it was decided to open a branch of the Brazoria County Abstract Company in Velasco. He moved to Quintana to be close to the new office, but it soon became apparent that the mouth of the Brazos was too prone to becoming quickly clogged and unnavigable to be a good port and the Real Estate Boom soon burst. About this same time, there was much dissension in the County about the location of the county seat, and finally it was moved to Angleton, the geographical center of the county. The Brazoria County Abstract Company also moved there, as did Frank W. Steven with his family, to manage it there.

Frank W's son, Frank Kirkland Stevens, who was working for an architect in Houston was recruited by his father to come home and help in the Abstract business. He agreed to do so, but was able also to enjoy building many houses and overseeing the rebuilding of the First Presbyterian Church in Angleton, of which he was a member all of his life.

He had an avid interest in many civic things pertaining to the county, but the completion of the Intracoastal Canal was high on his list of priorities. Starting when he was 20 years old, he was interested and involved in the buying and selling of land. He was successful enough to provide a comfortable living for his family with this business. Apparently in the early 1960s he decided it was time to sell the island of San Luis (or Treasure Island), and did so in June 26, 1962, which ended 90 years of ownership of the Stevens family.

Eleanor Stevens Vaughn

Hennell Stevens was founder of Brazoria County Abstract Company in 1873, along with Mr. J. H. Shapard. Here is a photo of the abstract company building after they moved from Brazoria to Angleton in 1896.

The vast amount of horrors seen on the island have naturally created local legends and ghost tales. One of these enshrouds the Salt Marshes and is recounted to this day.

The Legend of Salt Marshes (San Luis Pass, Brazoria County)
By Bertha McKee Dobie

This legend was told to me by Mrs. A. F. Shannon of Velasco. San Luis Pass is the narrow entrance from the Gulf into a small sheltered bay on the Texas coast. It is a wild and mournful spot, where sea gulls scream and breakers roar. It is especially wild and mournful when the wind is east, as the few settlers say. Then three great billows roll in successively from the Gulf, overtake each other on the bar, and break together with the sound of thunder. This breaking together of the billows is called the boor on the bar.

A great many years ago a fisherman lived with his wife and young child at the Pass. One day when the wind was east and the boor was on the bar, he went out in his boat to fish. The wind blew stronger, the billows rose higher, and a great tide came in, flooding the salt marshes that border the Pass. The fisherman did not return. A few days later other fishermen found the young wife, quite demented, wandering in the salt marshes and calling, "Come back! Come back!" Since that time, when the wind is east and the boor is on the bar, the white form of the woman flits over the marshes and cries, "Come back! Come back!" in warning to fishermen whose boats are on the water. It is probable that the white wings and the hoarse cries of the giant gulls that come in to the marshes only when there is a high east wind and the lives of fishermen are threatened have given rise to the legend of the salt marshes. Such an explanation, at least to Mrs. Shannon, by Mr. Lon Follett.[30]

Though logical explanations are often offered with the story, it does not take a long stretch of the imagination to admit that the island's history is fertile soil for tales of the supernatural.

Hennell Stevens[31]
Oct. 28, 1832-July 9, 1897
Brazoria County
Historical Museum

Frank W. Stevens[32]
Feb. 27, 1859-Dec. 30, 1928
Gifted from
Eleanor Stevens Vaughn

Frank K. Stevens[33]
Sept. 24, 1885-Jan. 1, 1975
Gifted from
Eleanor Stevens Vaughn

This photo collection of the Stevens men is available only because of the collaboration between Eleanor Stevens Vaughan and determination to make all three photos together for the very first time.

Brazoria County Abstract[34]

Chapter 6
Two World Wars, Thirteen Hurricanes, A Military Reservation and New Dreams

During the twentieth century, two world wars impacted the residents of San Luis. Indeed, San Luis found itself in the middle of these wars, as a strategic point of defense for the military, just as had been the case in the Civil War. Thirteen hurricanes ravaged the area during this period. The 1915 Storm was the last hurricane with a direct hit until 1932.This hurricane, named "Number Two" on the Texas coast, was a Category 4 storm with 140 mph winds with a loss of life at forty.

During the lulls in bad weather, fishing piers and airstrips were constructed. The dreams of transforming San Luis Island into a resort community were envisioned by two different developers and initial steps were taken to see these come to fruition. The progress would become slowed as the world erupted into its first global war, known then as "the Great War."

In World War I,

Unfortified coastal artillery stations were established at key points on the Texas coast to prevent U-boats or commerce raiders from approaching Texas ports. This included Freeport, Sabine Pass and San Luis Pass. Then in World War II, unfortified coastal artillery stations were established at key points on the Texas coast to prevent U-boats or aircraft from approaching Texas ports. This included Sabine Pass, Port Arthur, Baytown, Freeport, Port Aransas, Port Isabel, and San Luis Pass.[1]

San Luis Pass Military Reservation
Mouth of the Brazos River

According to some references, a World War I battery of two five-inch guns was originally at Surfside Beach. In World War II, a two gun battery was placed at Quintana with one 180 degree and one 360 degree Panama mount (a gun mount developed by the U.S. Army in Panama during the 1920s for fixed coastal artillery positions) was located there, the first set of guns were World War I French 155 mm GPFs (Grande Puissance Filloux). These were later replace by two 6-inch naval guns and still later by two towed 155 mm American howitzers . These were manned with personnel for the 20th Coastal Artillery.[2]

There were three towers built to support the World War II Quintana gun emplacements. The twenty-foot command tower was located behind the guns. The "A" station was forty-five foot tall and located 10,000 feet northeast of the Quintana guns. While "B" station was a twenty-three foot tower located 7,800 feet southwest of the battery.[3]

The quiet period between the two wars was punctuated for the coast by another hurricane on August 13-14th. With winds roaring at 145 mph, it ranked it as a Category 4. It was the second in a series of seven storms that would enter the Gulf of Mexico during the summer of 1932.

The following is a record of the storm:

1932 Storm Texas Hurricane History by David Roth, National Weather Service Meterologist - Forecast, NWS/HPC Forecast Operations Branch, 5830 University Research Count, College Park, Maryland 27040. August 13-14, 1932 a disturnbed area of weather was noted near Belize and Honduras on the 10th it moved northward across the gulf before intensifying rapidly about a day prior to landfall. A ship 200 miles southeast of Galveston radioed in a pressure of 28.88 on the morning of the 13th. The center passed slightly east of Freeport and directly over East Columbia where winds were estimated at 100 m. p. h. with a lowest pressure of 27.82 in Galveston. Telephone and electrical service were out for days. The storm was very compact. Eight hundred birds died in Wharton during the rain. As the system continued north into Oklahoma, an additional twelve inches of rain fell. Forty dies in Brazoria County and total damage was $7.5 million.

Precautions were wise, for the New Year brought no respite from the storms.

> After the "July 6,1933 Hurricane which made land fall between Brownsville and Tampico, the July 22-26 1933 Hurricane, (the fourth of the season) crossed the Yucatan peninsula and began to recurse northward through the western Gulf of Mexico. This tropical storm moved up the Texas coast for several days and brought heavy rains and flooding to extreme eastern Texas. At 6 AM on the 22nd the pressure at Freeport reached a minimum of 29.63.
>
> An area of 25,000 square miles saw rainfall amounts of 12.5. As much as twenty inches were reported in east Texas and western Louisiana. Corn, cotton and watermelon crops were in ruin.[4]

Once again, the storms had reshaped the island. Little Pass had sanded in, but this 1936 map[5] shows the location of a second Little Pass cut to the Gulf of Mexico.

Hitting a year before America entered the Second World War, then August 7-8th, 1940 hurricane formed over North and South Carolina.

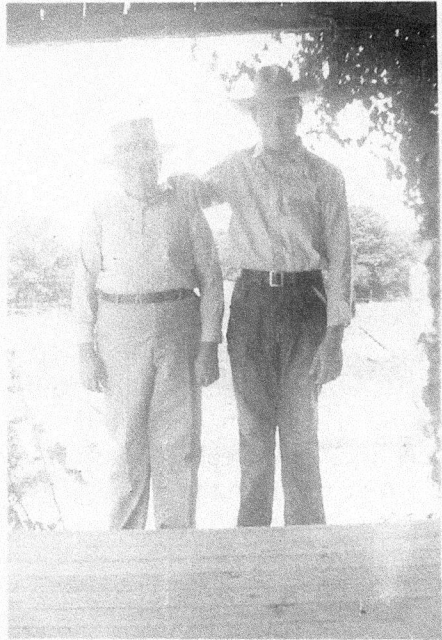

Brazoria County Deputy Sheriff Steve Roberts, shared photos of the storm house his family erected near East Bernard.[6]

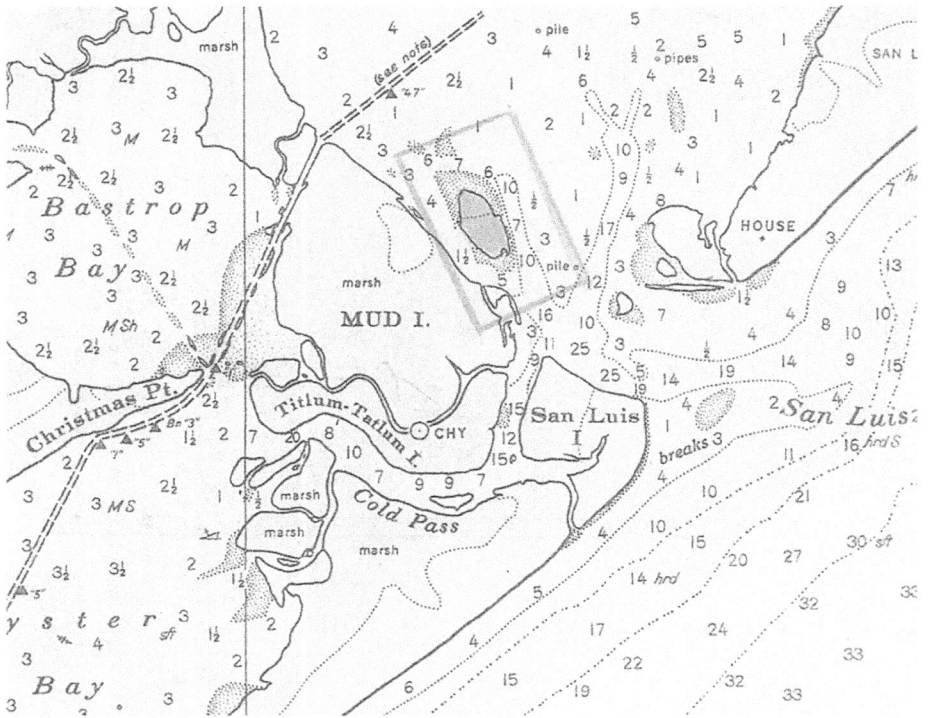

1936 Map
Texas General Land Office, Galveston Bay and approaches no. 1282, August 22,
1936, Audubon Society K-6-1292C.

Making landfall as a Category 2 hurricane east of Sabine Pass, the storm was recorded as the "wettest hurricane on record."[7]

This fishing guide illustrates the coastal terrain just before the hurricane. Though having no date, the "FISHGIDE" is believed to have been made between 1937 and 1940.

A detail from the previous Gulf Oil Company map drawn by Ronnie Luster names "Cold Pass," but does not name Little Pass. The Intracoastal Waterway is in place. The road is noted as "Beach Drive to San Luis Pass On Low Tide Only" and the San Luis Pass Bridge has not yet been built. The best information available indicates that this is a Ronnie Luster map.[8]

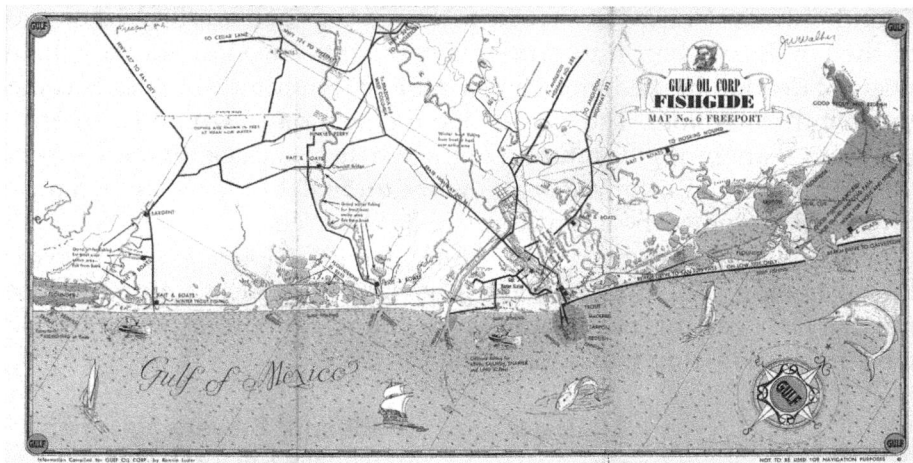

Who would believe this fish story? A 65 Foot, 70 Ton Whale Beached[9]

Though residents were familiar with the destruction brought when wind and rain hit their shores, they were surprised in 1940 by a very different sort of visitor. The tale is recounted with permission from Mr. Robert L. Wright who took this photo.

Yes, it was true. The Friday, August 23, 1940 issue of the *West Columbia Light* newspaper reported this whale beached a few miles from Velasco. The beached whale was about sixty feet out in the water, spouting water twenty-five feet into the air. One person climbed on top of the whale and began to carve his name into the skin. As the whale was not dead, it immediately threw him off. Hundreds of people came to view the mammal. The whale died the next day. Two powerful motor boats were brought in to move the whale to a dock where viewers would be charged fifty cents to view the animal, but the two-inch rope broke after moving the animal only about two feet.

Mr. Robert L. Wright of West Columbia took photos of the whale for his newspaper. The now retired Mr. Wright from West Columbia told me that he began this newspaper at the young age of fourteen years. He gave me his blessing to use his work.

The Houston Press

HOUSTON, TEXAS, MONDAY, AUGUST 19, 1940

25-Ton Problem Gives Velasco the Blubbers As Beached Whale Draws Crowd, No Buyers

The Houston Press article, 1940 also ran the story.[10]

Eleanor Stevens Vaughan Recalls the 1940 Beached Whale Incident

Eleanor recalls her son was about two years old when her father took them in his boat to see the whale. They were living in Port Arthur at the time and made the boat ride from there. Eleanor told Sam how someone climbed onto the tail and began to carve his initials into its hide when the whale "that was not dead," flung him off!

Eleanor Stevens Vaughan, at ninety-one years of wonderful life in 2005, shows Sam Boyd (my grandson) her prized 1940 newspaper story of a whale, beached a few miles to the east of Surfside.[11]

Third Whale Washed Ashore[12]

Buddy Schuster is a surfside native who live his entire life outdoors. *The Facts*, Brazoria County newspaper, featured Buddy Schuster standing with a whale bone over his shoulder at the beach. Buddy lived out of doors in a "lean-to" on Follett's Island near Surfside for most of his life and was a voracious story teller. He once said when rattlesnakes came into his "lean-to," he just let them be. They didn't harm him. He

Buddy Schuster[13]

fished every day and could read the water like the back of his hand. While at the Bright Lite Store at San Luis Pass he would chat with local male fishermen, but he was very shy and would not talk with women.

The excitement of the beached whale lingered until another storm landed in 1941, and the weather demanded the spotlight once again.

A storm formed over the central Gulf on the 17ᵗʰ. It made a counter clockwise loop, moved west, then northward to near Matagorda on the 23ʳᵈ. On the 22ⁿᵈ, a ship near 27.1 N 93.7W recorded a force 12 northeast wind, and a pressure of 29.11. Winds were estimated near 100 mph at several locations along the coast. A ship at Texas City reported a pressure of 28.66" and winds at 83 mph. The pressure fell to 29.05" at Matagorda, 29.1 at Port O'Connor and 29.31 at Freeport. Port Arthur saw winds of 73 mph, 6.68 of rain, and tides of 5.4. Freeport had a tide of 9.9 feet while very high tides were experience from Matagorda to Galveston. Galveston measured a seven foot tide. The rice crop was ruined.[14]

Another storm hit on August 21, 1942. Due to WW II, this storm was small and went unreported until it struck Bolivar peninsula with 72 mph winds and tides to seven feet at High Island. Damage to the rice crops totaled $790,000. Eight days later, the Hurricane of August 29-30, 1942 crossed Matagorda Bay with hurricane force winds covering 150 square miles. About 50,000 people were evacuated from Galveston alone. Freeport had an 11.8 foot storm surge.

Deep Holes in Christmas Bay!

We heard about fishing the deep holes in Christmas Bay, but never

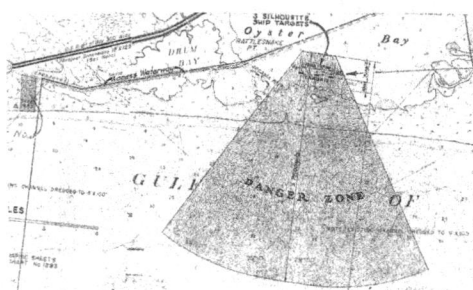

Bombing Range

War Department Map
Drawing No. BRZ-CM-1
Temporary Harbor Fortification-
Freeport, TX (07-06-1945)

War Department Map[15]

knew how they got there. Ronnie Reed explained that it was the location of an Air Force practice site for bombing. According to resident Frances Lawson, three large battleships were shaped from pilings in the water for this purpose. Everyone was notified not go into Oyster Bay (Christmas Bay) on Thursdays.

The First World War brought a new method of locomotion to the island. Ellington Field is located fifteen miles south of Houston, near current I-45. The airport was established during World War I, and it totally burned in 1927. In 1941, military combat training for pilots, gunnery, and bombardiers began again at the newly constructed Ellington Field.

Mr. Mitchell T. Hail, historian, Texas Military Forces Museum, of Angleton, Texas, shared the following maps, which have been saved at the National Archives Building in Fort Worth, Texas. As told to me by Mr. Hail, these historical papers were about to be burned when someone said, "Stop! This is history!" I continue to be amazed how the evidence of history is spared.

The Army Air Corps., separated the trainees from the trained bombardiers. The trained pilots were moved to Lake Charles, Louisiana. The Galveston Air Force would leave Lake Charles, fly in from the North, drop their bombs, pull up immediately and then land at the airfield at Hoskins Mound. Hoskins Mound is a natural suphur mound and a perfect landing field. The War Department map is a very special one to share.

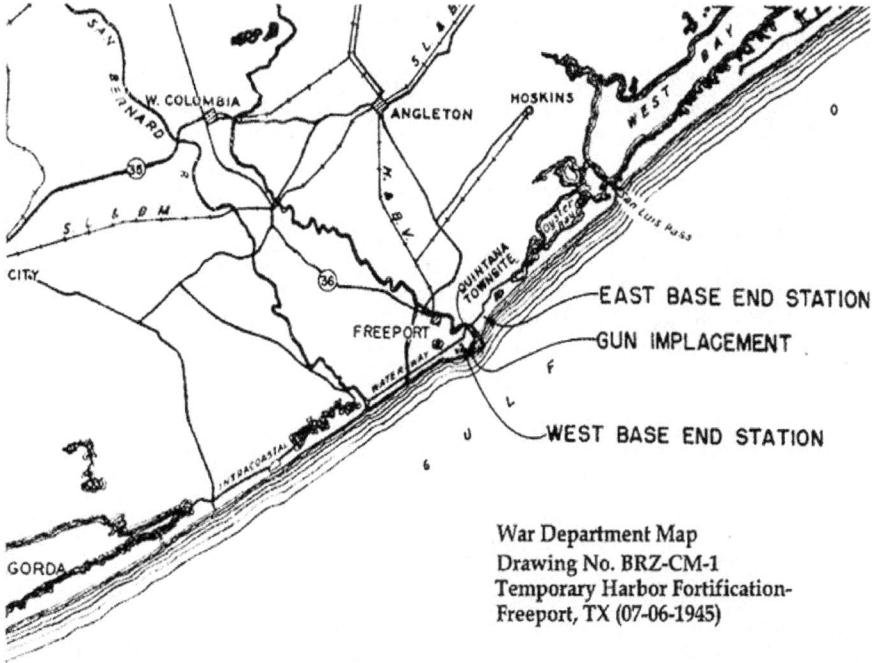

EAST BASE END STATION

GUN IMPLACEMENT

WEST BASE END STATION

War Department Map
Drawing No. BRZ-CM-1
Temporary Harbor Fortification-
Freeport, TX (07-06-1945)

War Department Map[16]

The Bombing Range Map shows Bird Island to be fifty acres.[17]

Additionally, the map shows the location for the Follett Family Cemetery, which is in the twenty acre Tract No. 4. As noted earlier, the Cemetery was located at the site called "The Cedars."

Notes read:

"April 10, 1943

"Tract number 4, comprising 20 acres, A. F. Shannon Estate, c/o A. F. Shannon, Velasco, Texas, has an old cemetery located thereon. It is situated in the salt cedar breaks, and the number of burials could not be determined. Some old markers remain.

USE0 A HOUSTON LETTER[18]
COMMANDING GENERAL

USEO HOUSTON TEX   HO 126 APRIL 9 1943   14007

COMMANDING GENERAL
FORT GEORGE WXXXX WRIGHT, WASHINGTON

REURTT (Ruertt is an abreviationADDRESSED TO GALVESTON, TEXAS, DISTRICT ENGINEER RELATIVE T: REsponse yoUR Telegraph) O BOMBING RANGE FOR GALVESTON AIR BASE, OYSTER BAY, SOUTH

OF ABANDONED INTRACOASTAL WATERWAY AND SOUTHWEST TEN MILES FROM SAN LUIS, FIVE THOUSAND SIX HUNDRED THIRTY FIVE ACRES, MORE OR LESS, IN BRAZORIA COUNTY AND BIRD ISLAND CONSISTING OF ABOUT FIFTY ACRES IN GALVESTON COUNTY, ALL COMPRISING FIVE TRACTS WITH EIGHT OWNERS, AND ONE TRACT OWNED BY STATE OF TEXAS. LAND VALUED AT APPROXIMATELY 22,000, ONE SET OF CAMP IMPROVEMENT OWNED BY UXX HUNTING AND FISHING LESSEE VALUED AT $1200 ON STATE CLAIMED LAND. PRIVATE LAND LEASED FOR WINTER GRAZING. NO XXXXX MINERAL VALUE. APPROXIMATELY TEN MILES OF TWO-WIRE TELEPHONE LINE IS LOCATED ON AREA, REQUIRING ABOUT 25 MILES OF RELOCATION AT COST OF ABOUT 42500.

> MESSAGE NO. HS0 177
>
> RANTZOW
> HEAD, DIVISION REAL ESTATE SUBOFFICE
>
> END CCW
> ,443/8 wa rcd msg ok at 0914072
>
> 3/8 0

There were no improvements located on the above, except the 2-wire telephone line parallel to the Gulf shore, which connected the

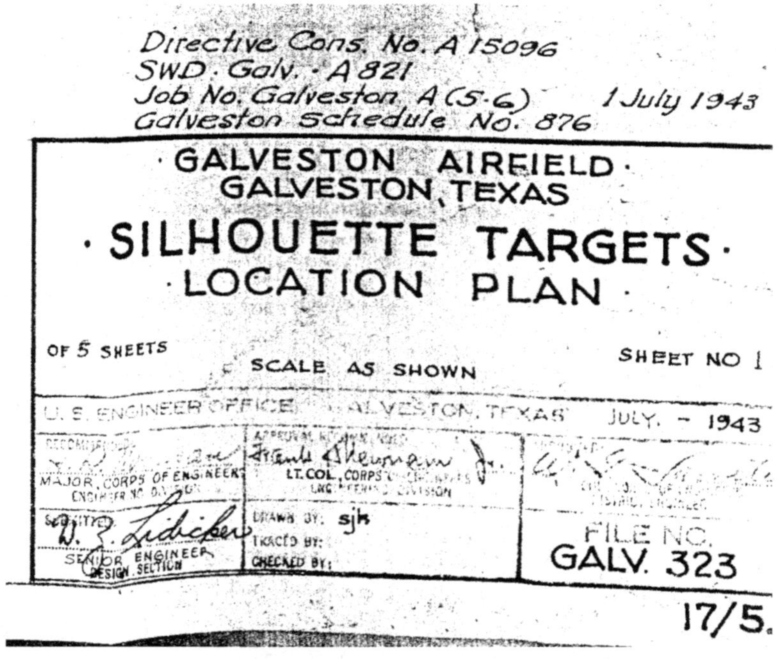

West End Air to Ground Gunnery Range[19]

San Luis Coast Guard Station on Galveston Island with Freeport Coast Guard Station at Velasco (or Brazosport), Texas.

The west end of Galveston Island, from the old Coast Guard Station to the tip, was leased as an air to ground gunnery range. It started in the summer of 1941 in an informal fashion, with unit commanders negotiating for the use of the land while they were deployed to the Galveston Municipal Airport for air to air gunnery over the Gulf. Later a formal lease was signed and the range was used by different units assigned to the Galveston Army Airfield during World War II.

When the observation squadron performing anti-submarine patrols, that used the gunnery range, was moved and replaced by a light bomber squadron, a bombing range rather than a gunnery range was needed. The Oyster Bay Bombing range was set up. In 1943 the anti-submarine patrols went back to the Navy and the bombing and gunnery ranges were used by different training units in the United States. The B-26 training unit at Lake Charles used the bombing ranges around Galveston extensively.

The silhouette targets originally had plywood tops, but the Hurricane of 1943 took the plywood off and left it floating everywhere in the bays. It was never replaced. Local residents wrote letters asking to keep the plywood for their own use, and permission was granted.[16]

In 1943, another hurricane formed. Its details have been reported by NOAA.[20]

July 27-28th, 1943: War censorship came into question during this hurricane. This storm was detected just off the Mississippi Delta on the 25th of July. It formed into a hurricane rapidly and moved inland in Chambers County. Its eye was 13 miles in diameter as it passed inland, yet the storm itself was no more than 70 miles in diameter. It was considered the worst storm in the area since 1915, and at La Porte, worse than the Galveston Hurricane of 1900.

The brunt of the storm passed over the Houston Metropolitan Area between noon and 4 P.M. (population was 600,000 at the time). Gusts above 100 m.p.h. Occurred in the Galveston-Houston area. Two utility towers over the Houston Ship Channel were blown down (these were rated to withstand 120 mph winds). Four cooling towers at the Humble Oil and Refinery Co. (now Exxon) were demolished as they reported wind gusts to 132 mph. The anemometer at the Metropolitan airport also saw a gust to 132 mph. Oil derricks across Chambers and Jefferson Counties met their fate during the hurricane (Fincher et.al).

Beaumont received 19.48" of rain on the 27th and 28th - establishing daily rainfall records that still stand today. Winds there gusted to 54 mph. La Porte saw over 17" of rain. Ellington Field had the pressure fall to 28.78", where 5 planes were destroyed. A number of brick business buildings and churches collapsed

Titlum
Tatlum

Be sure to notice the direction of the shoals! [21]
1944 Texas General Land Office Photo

on Galveston Island. Winds caused much of the damage, which totaled $17 million (U.S. Army Corp of Engineers).

Due to the northerly winds across Galveston Bay, tides were extremely low. On Galveston Island, a storm surge of 6 feel was experienced. The U.S. Army Corp of Engineers' hopper dredge, "Galveston" broke up on the north jetty, taking 11 lives. The tug Titan foundered between Corpus Christi and Port Neches, causing 3 more lives to be lost. Nineteen victims in all. This was the first storm in which aircraft reconnaissance was used, flight level was between 4000 and 9000 feet.[22]

Once more, the hurricane rearranged the topography of San Luis. The 1944 Texas General Land Office photo shows San Luis to be an island, but Little Pass is again sanding in. This area, known as Little Pass, was considered to be fifty acres. Titlum-Tatlum Bayou is shown separating Moore's Island from Mud Island and emptying into Cold Pass. A landmass in the San Luis Pass channel is clearly visible. The western tip of Galveston Island is quite a distance from this landmass in the photo.

The Hurricane of August 26-28, 1945 was the worst storm along

Fishing camp at San Luis.[23]

the lower Texas coast since September of 1933. Two-thirds of the coast experienced hurricane force winds, with highest gusts noted at 135 mph. Tides as high as fifteen feet inundated Port Lavaca and rainfall amounts of thirty inches were common along the coast. The coastline retreated as much as fifty feet due to the storm.[24]

Though the island was no longer inhabited, neighbors Jack and Hans Wagner started coming to San Luis Pass as children. Mr. Owen Barton owned the Velasco Tackle Shop near the bridge in Velasco where the Wagners would get into the back of Mr. Barton's pickup truck and drive to San Luis Pass. With no beach road, many times they would have to wait for low tide to drive the long way along the beach. Barton would catch tarpon and jewfish in the Pass. They recall one such fish weighed nearly 600 pounds. Barton would rig his line with wire cable and a large spring to set the hook. There were no limits on how many fish you could catch, so fifty to a hundred trout was a normal fishing day or night, as it may have been. Years later, they would pick up Ronnie Reed (child friend and other children and bring them to San Luis Pass to learn to fish. Now we know why Ronnie is such a great fisherman!

After such brutal storms, the August 24, 1947 hurricane landed in Galveston, bringing minimal winds of seventy-two miles per hour. Wind-driven rain caused most of the damage to the interior of home as windows were blown out.[25]

Another hurricane hit in 1949, which was marked by its unusual

151

Bait Camp Enlargement photo.

path.

October 3-4, 1979 This system formed in the eastern Pacific Ocean before cross-
ing into the Gulf west of Vera Cruz. Only three other storms are known to make
such a crossing from the east Pacific to the Gulf of Mexico. Freeport was struck
by the storm hurricane. Winds were estimated at 135 mph five miles west of
Freeport.[26]

Despite being a haven for fishermen, San Luis would not remain a ghost town. The island was leased, and began to slowly revive as hunting and fishing rights were granted. Though inhabitants hesitated to relocate to the island, accommodations for tourism began to dot the landscape. Bait and a boat rental business, along with a café, and tourist cabins sprang up.

According to page 502 of the Deeds and Records of Brazoria County Courthouse, Gladys S. Terrell and husband Nelson J. Terrell of Houston and Frank K. Stevens and H. R. Stevens of Angleton, Texas, leased San Luis Island to K. A. Moody and Paul F. Schroeder of Harris County, Texas for the following purposes:

1. To conduct a bait & boat rental business.
2. To build and operate a café.
3. To construct and operate a number of tourist cabins.
4. Hunting rights for the Island with right to sub-lease for hunting purposes only.

Rentals for the property shall be payable annually in advance and shall be $300 for the 1st year; $400 for the 2nd year and so on up to & including the 10th year, increasing $100 each year. This lease for ten years also had an additional five-year option attached.

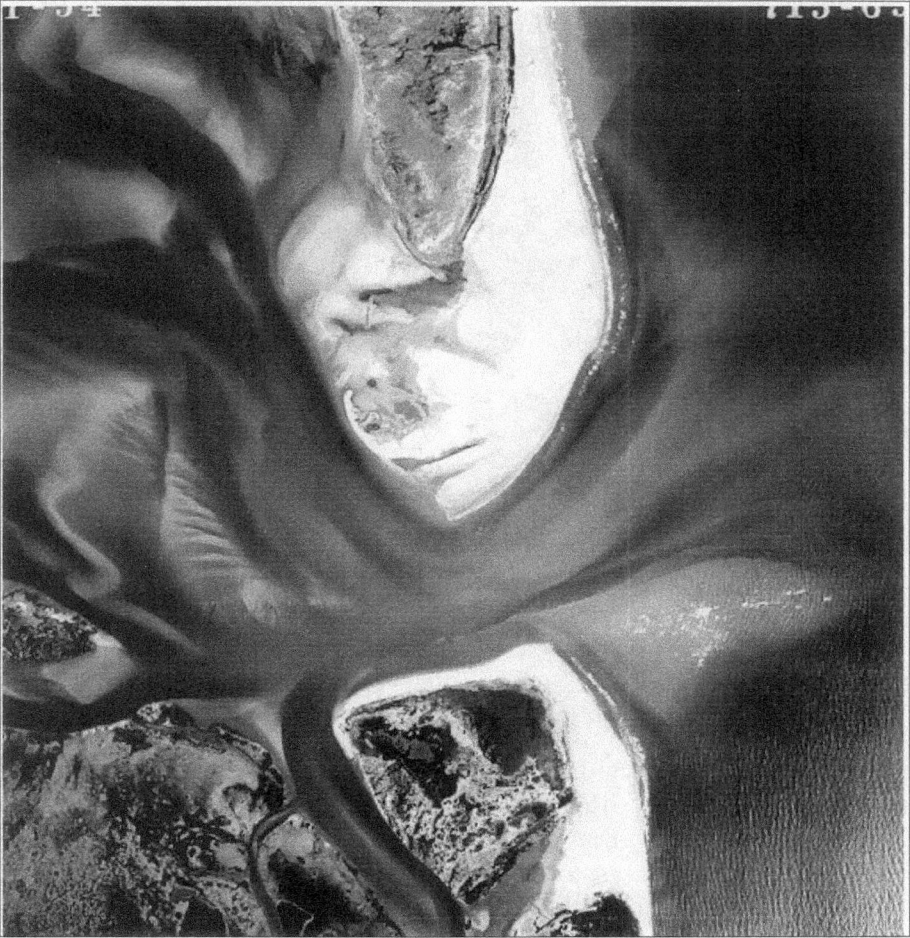

Smiling Lady Aerial[27]
1954 Texas General Land Office

A surviving photo offers a peek at the new accommodations.

Bait camp, café, and tourist cabins are visible at the end of the white shell road.

This area is in the Proposed Section IV Treasure Island and the County Park would be in the white sand area in the upper right of the photo. The entire point of land is now eroded away.

Judge Robert Lowry said when he first came to San Luis Island that there was nothing on the bay side but an old bait camp on the northwest corner, and it was owned by Ezra Ballard and his son Ben, who was the shrimper.

The "Smiling Lady" in the middle of the picture, at the end of Gal-

THIS CHOICE WATERFRONT PROPERTY
TO BE SOLD AT PUBLIC AUCTION
BY ALBERT E. KUEHNERT
AUCTIONEERS, INC. HOUSTON, TEXAS

Cassidy Development[28]

veston Island, is sculpted in the sand. Little Pass is almost completely closed in. San Luis's "Big Pass" is almost closed. It was said that in the 1840s and 1850s that "Big Pass" was so shallow, sometimes you could walk across to the Galveston side.

The idea of creating the island into a tourist destination rapidly grew and by 1954, the land was purchased for $540,000.

J. B. Cassidy Development Corporation, newspaper article read as follows:

J. B. Cassidy Buys Peninsula from F. W. Wheeler and G. D. Prince, Jr., for $540,000 April 7, 1954.

The 1954 Brochure San Luis Beach stretching to San Luis Pass reflected the dream of developer J. B. Cassidy. In this brochure, the property owners plat map marks a "café" and "cabins" marked on the tip of San Luis Island's Bay side point. This is no doubt of Ezra Ballard's location in 1953. Plat dated 1954. This Plat map also shows the names of very successful Texas businessmen. A subdivision that was never completed is the 158.28 acre "Proposed K. S. 'Bud' Adams Development.

Far behind the times, modernization crept forward on the island.

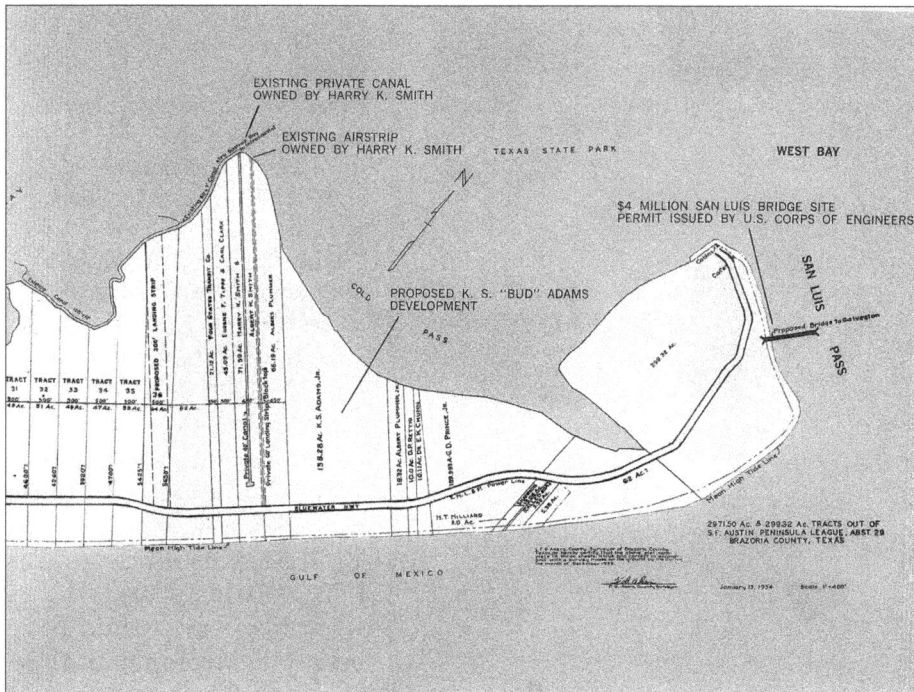

Cassidy Brochure Property Owner's Map, 1954[29]

Our neighbor, Harry K. Smith owned an industrial gas company. A large steel tank readily filled the first gas lights on the Island. Gas lights in the 1950s!

Approximately 3000 acres of land, (the surface estate only) out of the Stephen F. Austin Peninsular League 29, Brazoria County, Texas, was secured with a promissory note in the amount of:

FIVE HUNDRED AND FORTY-THOUSAND AND NO/100 ($540,000) BEARING INTEREST AT THE RATE OF SIX (6%) percent per annum and payable to:

F. W. Wheeler and G. D. Prince, Jr.

The surface only of a tract of 2980 acres of land, more or less, in the S. F. Austin Peninsular League, Abstract #29, situated in Brazoria County, Texas and being the same land conveyed in the following deeds:

(a)   a tract of land of 693-3/4 acres, described in a Deed from Mrs. Mary E. Follett, Guardian, to A. M. McFaddin, dated September 5, 1908, and recorded in Volume 79, page 602, Deed Records of Brazoria County Texas.

(b)   a tract of 1986-1/4 acres, described in a Deed from A. B. Follett, et al to A. M.

Surfside Bridge[30]

McFaddin, dated September 5,1908 and recorded in Volume 79, page 599, Deed Records of Brazoria County, Texas, and

(c) a tract of 300 acres, described in a Deed from Emma B. Follett,

Guardian to A. W. McFaddin, dated October 26, 1908, of record in

Volume 82, page 246, Deed Records of Brazoria County, Texas.

A Plat was filed at Brazoria County Court House by J. B. Cassidy on August 12, 1954. This brochure was J. B. Cassidy's and shows what his plans would have been for development from San Luis Beach to San Luis Pass.

The Island News brought further attention to the island, when it ran a special release depicting the excitement of the new bridge at Surfside. Beautiful women were photographed having the best time ever on the sandy beaches of San Luis Beach.

Adding to the festive feel of the reawaking island, the 1954 Frank Horlock home on the beach near San Luis Pass was quite the party house. Frank's home was one of the first to be built on the Peninsula in nearly 100 years. Stan Begam who was a photographer and Frank Horlock, the Beer Distributor for Grand Prize Brewery, were both from Houston and great friends. Stan said he would drive over in his station wagon to the brewery and fill it to the top with free beer. Then the two of them would load it in Frank's airplane and fly to his beach home, taxi up the airplane right to the door and unload huge amounts of beer. Then it was party time!

Braving the risks of island living, Dr. E. K. Chunn built his beach house and pier in 1954. His pier still stands today and is a favorite flounder fishing spot for many fishermen. His son, Keith Chunn, explained an aerial photo of the Cold Pass channel looking toward San

Frank Horlock home completed at San Luis Beach.

Houston Businessman Frank Horlock Home[31]

Luis Island, which he presented to the author. The first long pier is the Chunn Channel and Chunn Pier. The other pier toward San Luis Pass was the Prince Pier. His pier did not last very long. The Doug Prince Pier went out into Cold Pass near the Prince's caretaker's house. The white line from the Prince Pier is a road from the highway paralleling the beach to the Prince's caretaker's house. This road is still there today.

The island continued to offer ideal circumstances for aircraft. During the 1950s and early 1960s, there were three air landing strips on the East end of Follett's Peninsula. The airstrip runway was immediately beside the Chunn land on the Prince side of the property line and went from Cold Pass toward the Gulf immediately behind and in line with the Chunn Pier. When the airplanes landed, flying toward the Gulf or into the wind coming off the Gulf, they would fly over and along the Chunn Pier and land on the Prince side of the Chunn Pier. The electric lines along the road that paralleled the beach were underground for about 200 feet to allow the planes to take off and land without hitting the electric wires. This runway was designed for small planes such as "The Piper Cub." He told me that the dogs always chased the planes

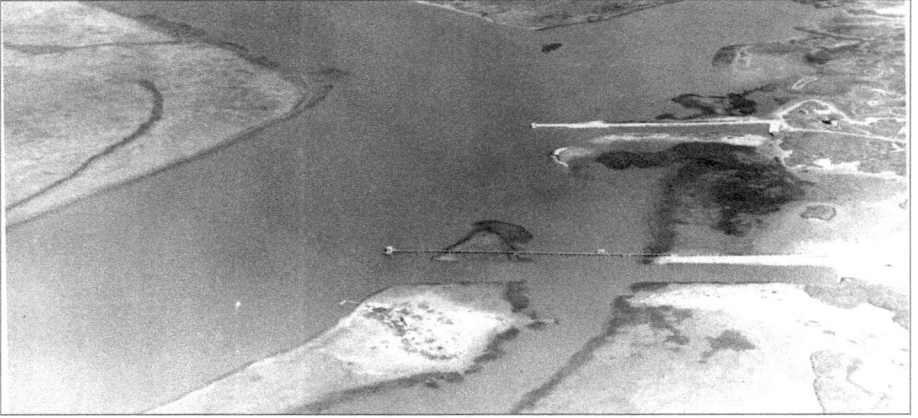

Chunn's Pier and the Airstrip, 1955.[32]

Doug Prince's San Luis Beach house nearing completion.[33]

on takeoff. But on the other hand, Garvin Germany of Angleton, Texas, tells that when he would land there, the Prince caretaker would run out to the runway shouting to "Get off!"

Mrs. Chunn had a yellow Cadillac, and one day a high tide left a deep water pond over the normally traveled beach road. Frances Lawson, long time Treasure Island resident, saw her coming and said to her friend, "She is not going to stop!" Sure enough, Mrs. Chunn became stuck in the temporary pond. The only nearby help was the electric power company truck. They gladly pulled her out.

The road ended at the San Luis Beach Subdivision and residents drove the beach to get to their property. Dr. Chunn said you really had to know where you were driving, as there was quick sand, and he saw many a car simply get stuck and disappear from sight!

One by one, houses were rebuilt along the shorelines. No longer a temptation for farmers, the island still attracted the attention of an individual heading quite a different another aspect of the food industry: Doug Prince, the King of Hamburgers.

G. D. (Doug) Prince founded Prince's Hamburgers in Dallas, Texas, in 1929. He expanded to Houston in 1934, with carhops and window trays for his drive-in on Main Street. It was a "big deal" for his business to be featured in a 1941 issue of *Life* magazine.

Our famous neighbor, Doug, began building his beach home on the Gulf Side of the would-be highway near San Luis Island in 1954. He built a seawall in front of his home. He also placed short pilings close together from his house to the surf blocking all traffic. The state of Texas made him remove his pilings and open the beach to auto traffic.

He loved diamonds and wore a twenty-two-carat yellow diamond stickpin on his shirt and wore one in the zipper of his pants, so the story is told. They had a Ford Ferguson tractor, and he loved to mow grass.

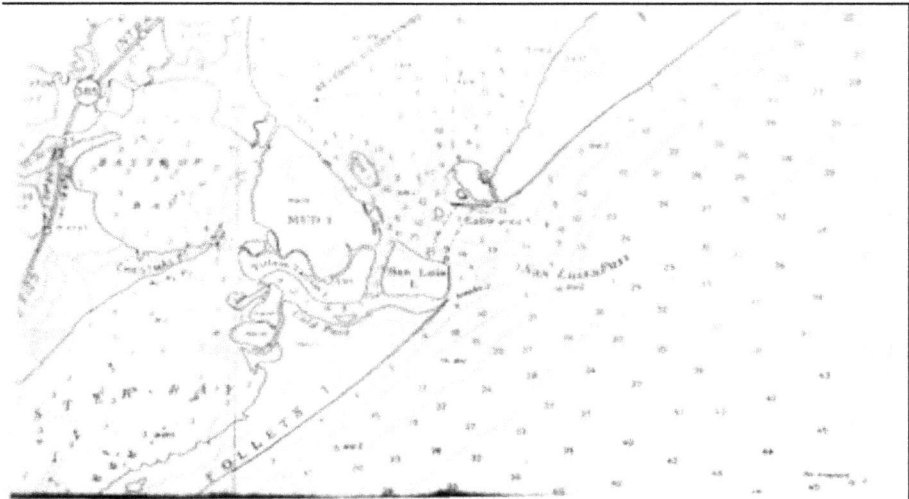

January 1955 folio of Maps Gulf Coast Waterway issued by the U.S. Coast and Geodetic Survey.
Notice that San Luis is an Island in 1955

K. S. Bud Adams Development
Courtesy K. S. Bud Adams

If you saw Doug at the beach, he was almost always mowing his grass.

He built an awning similar to the one for his famous hamburger restaurant Prince's Hamburgers in Houston with enough room to park ten cars under his awning. It didn't last long as storms deemed its "removal."

A January 1955 folio of Maps Gulf Coast Waterway shows San Luis to be an island. The map also shows two cables that cross San Luis Pass. These two telephone cables ran from Galveston Coast Guard Station along the Gulf of Mexico to San Luis Island Coast Guard Station in 1943, as noted from the War Department. This also may explain the "Cable area" markings on this map dated January 1955, U. S. Corps of Engineers, U. S. Army; Port Arthur to Brownsville, Texas. No records prior to S. W. Bell Telephone are available at the Galveston Corps of Engineers.

On June 27, 1957 Hurricane Audrey battered the coast. This storm surge brought high tides from Galveston to Louisiana, proving itself to be unparalleled in the history of Louisiana. [34]

Despite its ferocity, it would take a second storm to thwart the plans of reinvention, or the visions of men like K. S. (Bud) Adams.

Houston's billionaire oilman, and later owner of the Tennessee Titans, Mr. K. S. (Bud) Adams proposed a subdivision near San Luis,

The author, Eileen Wagner with K. S. Bud Adams.

Aerial photo of proposed subdivision layout.
Courtesy of K. S. Bud Adams

which would stretched across 158.28 acres. His vision included three hundred houses. When I met with Mr. Adams, on May 16, 2007, he said he had planned this Subdivision with canals on the Bay side and high-rises and a club on the Gulf side. Adams would fly back and forth in his Bell helicopter, reviewing the property from his beach house at Jamaica Beach, but then along came Hurricane Carla. Adams flew his friend Herb Townsend down to take a look at his home the day after Carla. There was absolutely nothing except bare sand. This was the end of Mr. Adams' planned subdivision. Adams said it scared him to death that he would build it and then lose everything. Adams gave the author photos and an artist's rendition of the subdivision.

His fears were well-founded. The storms continued with unrelenting tyranny. On July 24, 1959 Debra struck the region between Freeport and Galveston. Winds gusted to 105 miles-per-hour near Freeport. Hurricane force winds extended 100 miles inland. The highest reported tide was 7.9 above mean sea level.[33]

Between September 9-12, 1961, Hurricane Carla forged its name into the history of the coast and burned itself into the memories of every life that it touched. With winds of 175 miles-per-hour, this storm came ashore as a Category 5 hurricane. This was the most powerful storm to hit Texas in over forty years. Hurricane Carla made landfall between Port O'Connor and Port Lavaca. The entire coast of Texas was affected. Water levels at Sabine Pass recorded tides were ten-feet above normal, the highest levels since the Storm of 1919. It was the wind, not rain that did the most damage. Forty-three people lost their lives,[34] Vice President Lyndon Johnson was to head a thirty-person inspection.

Many photographic negatives were saved by photographer Nat Hickey of Freeport, and he shared his collection for use in this book. The shoreline and land mass was significantly changed after this horrific storm. You can clearly see where Little Pass reopened. Another photo negative shows San Luis Island to be an island again after Hurricane Carla.

Frances Lawson, homeowner at San Luis Beach, tells a great story about Hurricane Carla: She picked up her insurance adjuster and drove him (as best she could) through damaged roads to view the home of her neighbor at San Luis Beach Subdivision, who had lost almost everything. The roof and walls were gone. A pair of slippers was neatly placed beside Frances's bed on the second-story level and other items still exactly as she left them. Frances placed an extension ladder against the house and told the adjuster to climb up and take a look for himself. He had said all the way on their drive, that he was sure all the dam-

This September 18, 1961 Nat Hickey Ariel after Hurricane Carla shows the west end of Galveston Island is breached and Little Pass has reopened.

age was a tidal surge. She disagreed all the way with him. When he climbed to the second floor, she took the ladder away. When he looked down and asked "What are you doing?" she replied, "Now, do you understand? This was wind and tornadoes!" He gladly agreed.

September 18, 1962. Little Pass has re-opened during Hurricane Carla.

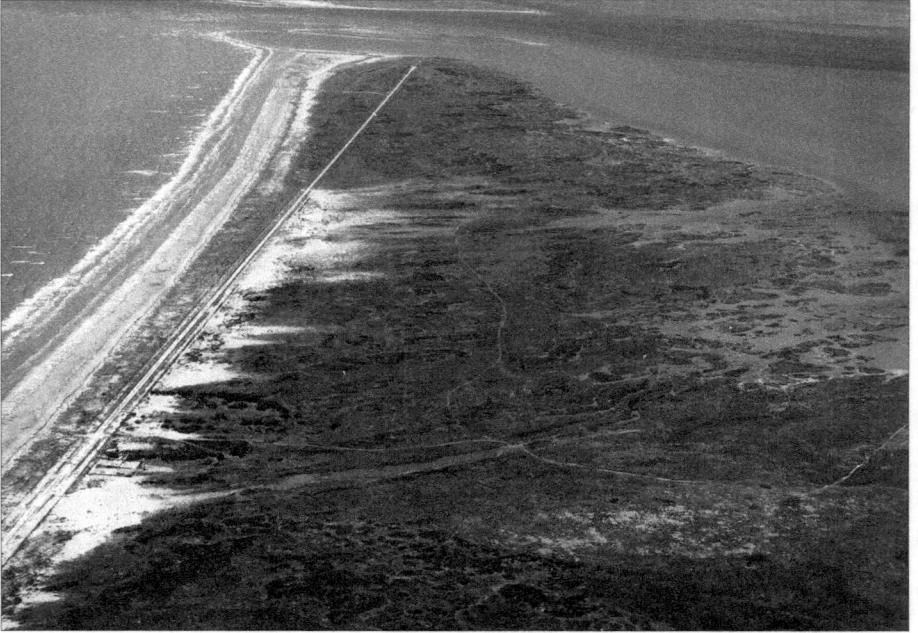

Galveston Highway 1304 built to San Luis Pass[35]

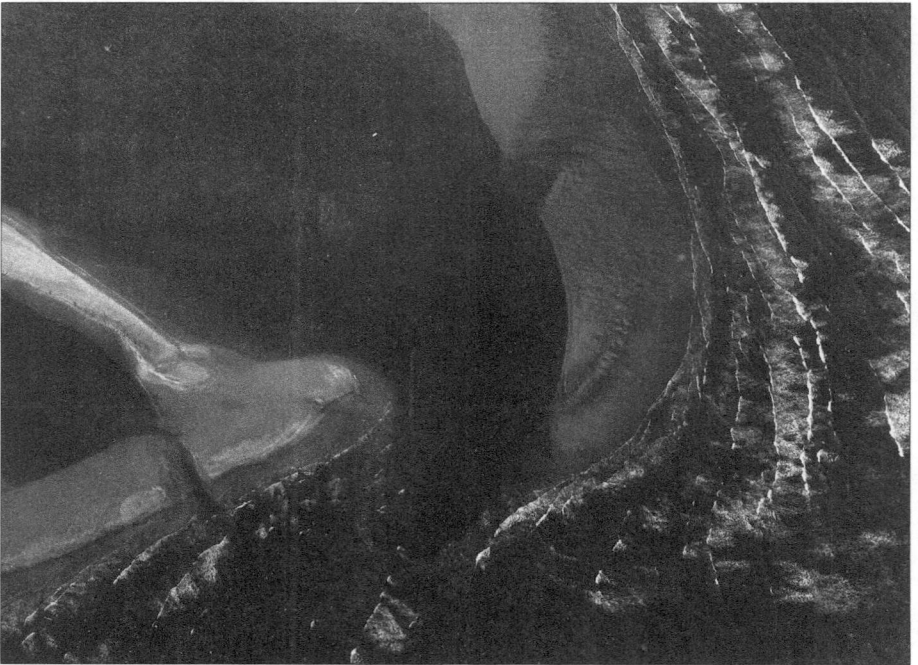

San Luis Pass hugs Brazoria County side and is shown to be very deep.[36]

An aerial photo from 1965 gives a bird's eye view of the island. Nat Hickey provided another link showing San Luis to be part of the mainland with streets laid out and several homes built. "Bluewater Highway" seems to be in the process of being built. San Luis Pass-Vacek Bridge had not yet been built. The San Luis Pass Fishing Pier is visible with the Pier House on the Pier. Several homes on Cold Pass near where Little Pass once flowed to the Gulf of Mexico are barely visible.[37]

Chapter 7
New Beginnings

San Luis Island found itself in a transitional period as it shifted from family-owned establishments to ownership by a development corporation. Many components contributed to converting San Luis Island to Treasure Island. A bridge, pier, highway, and canals were built in order to construct and connect this community's infrastructure. The development of Treasure Island brought a new identity to San Luis Island, along with new people.

This transformation could not have taken place without obtaining the land deed. For eighty-six years, the Stevens family owned the Island of San Luis and the Peninsula until family members consented to sell it to San Luis Island Corporation on October 31, 1962, for $60,000. The family had, no doubt, viewed San Luis Island as a great buy in 1876 at twenty cents per acre.

Little Pass

Beach Road had to wait for low tide.[1]

Treasure Island Plat[2]

Somehow the fifty acre tract of land that was once Little Pass was left out of the sale until March 24, 1963, when the family sold the fifty acre dry land track to San Luis Island Corporation for $500 per acre.

As the new city began, the only way—other than by boat, of course—to get to the finest fishing on the Gulf Coast was to drive the "beach road." The tide schedule was very important in using the "beach road," because drivers would have to wait for low tide to cross the Little Pass area.

Treasure Island Section I Plat was signed by Frederic Wagner on November 26, 1962. There are no pipelines or pipeline-easements in this plat. Also, notice that Gulf Beach Drive was a boulevard.

Lamar Golding had a booth at the Flea Market on Highway 59 and Hillcroft in Houston, where he was promoting the new Treasure Island Resort. Lt. Col. Bill and Mary Cannon found the perfect set of house plans that day. The Cannons immediately bought their lot and began to build their home. Bill took the first aerial photo of Section I, which shows the first roads and large palm trees dividing the Boulevards.

Heavy equipment is seen on the Galveston Island side of San Luis Pass. The San Luis Pass Bridge is in the first stages of construction. The thousand-foot San Luis Pass Fishing Pier is complete.

On April 2, 1963, the State of Texas leased a tract of land to Treasure Island Pier, Inc. to create "an easement for a right of way for a fishing

Equipment

Fishing Pier with Pier House[3]

pier with the right to use, construct, erect, maintain, repair, replace and rebuild same on and across that part of the following described land owned by the State of Texas, in Brazoria County, Texas for $100.00 per annum."

The San Luis Pass Fishing Pier was built in 1963, remaining for forty-five years, though hurricanes and tropical storms destroyed portions or all of it many times.[4]

Any land in front of the vegetation line along the Gulf of Mexico legally considered to belong to the State of Texas. Therefore, the State had to dedicate and approve the "pier" project. The following record indicates that permission was granted to commence construction.

"A tract or parcel of land located adjacent to San Luis Island in the Gulf of Mexico, 1,000 feet in length and 30 feet in width, being 15 feet on either side of the following described centerline. Commencing at the Northwest corner of Lot 1, Block 9, Treasure Island Subdivision. The easement for a right of way is for a total period of 5 years and is renewed with the Commissioner of the General Land Office."

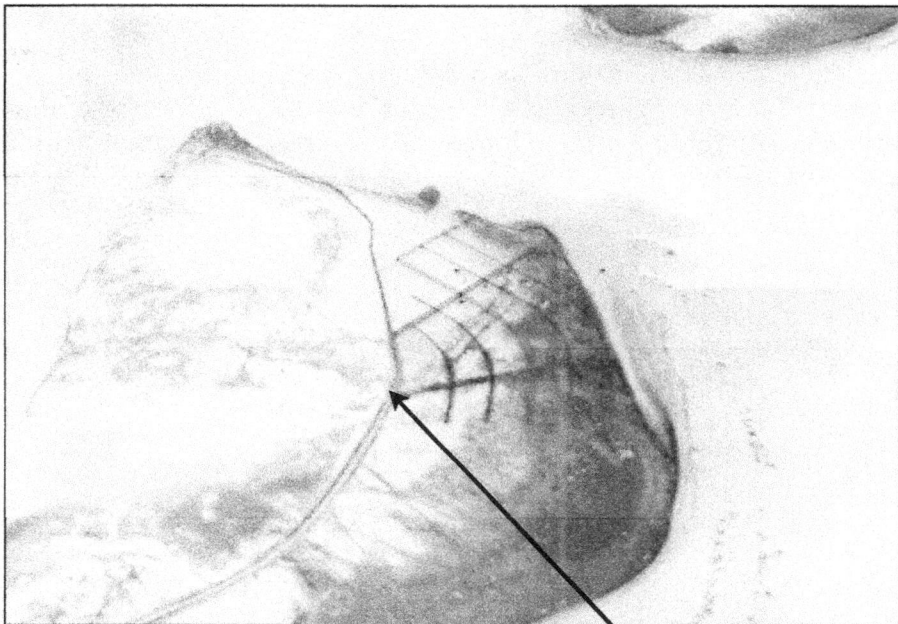

Little Pass has sanded in.[5]

A printed copy[5] of the January 9, 1963 telephone conversation, gives us a unique chance to explore one of the conversations that took place during the development stages. A written request on January 21, 1963, specifies desires for a 1,000-foot pier, 100 bays, ten feet each.[6] San Luis Island Corp. was to build the San Luis Fishing Pier. The permit was granted, and construction began on what would become one of the most popular fishing spots that could be found on the island.

Telephone Conversation   9 Jan 63 3:05 pm
From: Lamar Golding, Houston
To: Col Torbett

Mr. G: We have a development we are doing on San Luis Island. We want to build a fishing pier and we have employed an engineering firm in Houston, Francis Niven. He has done a lot of pier work. This proposed pier is to be along-side the channel of San Luis Pass, which is a tricky situation. We want to send him to Galveston to discuss with your people the steps toward securing permits and we wonder who he should contact.

Col T: When do you expect him to come down?

Mr. G: Sometime this week.

Col T: He should go to our Operations Div and talk to first Mr. Neeley. I am sure Mr. Neely will be able to help him on all particulars. If there are any over-all, policy requirements to be discussed, our Chief Opns would be available or he could come in and see me if he wishes.

Mr. G: I will tell him.

The pier was an instant success, becoming an attraction for residents and tourists. The ghost city began to breathe again, expanding with life. Though the pier no longer exists, a plethora of photographs have survived.

Corp of Engineers - Pier Permit specifications[7]

Fishing from the New Pier in San Luis Pass, photo taken from T-Head.[8]

Fishing on the famous "T" head Pier, Photo taken from T-Head.[9]

TREASURE ISLAND PIER

One of the feature attractions of the planned leisure activities at Treasure Island is its fishing pier. This 1000 foot long structure was designed with the fisherman in mind. This lighted installation parallels San Luis Pass, lying some 100 feet south of the deep channel. The engineer noted in his design that he had provided the pier be only 5 feet above the mean high tide. This fishing pier will be open to the public 24 hours per day for a nominal admission charge. However, this facility will be free to the Treasure Island lot owners and their immediate families. The concession facility will sell bait, tackle, sundries and all the little goodies that are needed for an outing or fishing trip. Management also noted that complete rental equipment would be available so that anyone coming directly from the office to the pier could with convenience partake of the fabulous fishing.

San Luis Island Corp. produced a promotional brochure to begin raising interest in the island.[10]

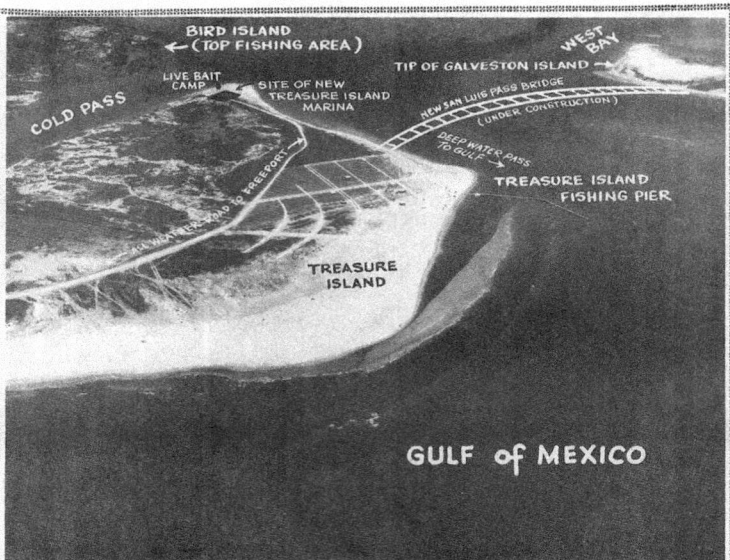

Brochure[11]

Masthead for Treasure Island Times[12]

The advertisement above appeared in what was to become the third newspaper for San Luis Island and was named the *Treasure Island Times*. The newspapers printed brochures for the San Luis Island Corporation and a gift from Welcome Wilson, Sr. A color brochure highlighted the most common pastime offered by the island.[13]

Color brochure produced to highlight the area.

173

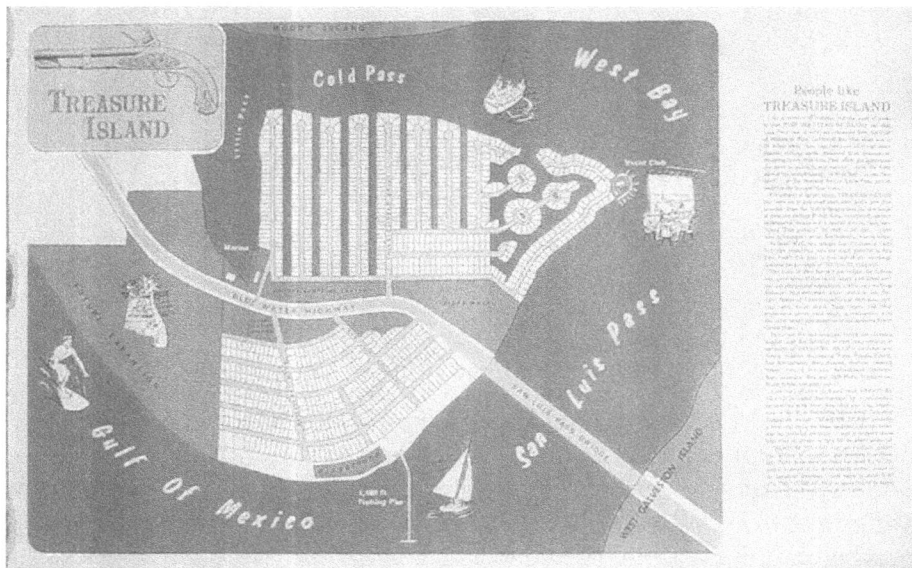

Late 1950s, Early 1960s, Color Brochure for Treasure Island with Seven Canals, Yacht Basin and more.[14]

With the fickle weather and growing traffic, it was a huge job maintaining the streets in the early days of the resort. Red Miller was hired to make the streets passable in 1963. He recalls that they were terrible with holes large enough to contain a small car. He repaired the roads and maintained the grounds for a mere $600 a month. Oyster shell paving was used in Galveston during the 19th century. Hans Hecht said that the roads would wash away during even the slightest storms. A few water supply lines were now being placed underground.

Hans Hecht related that in the beginning people would build a new house, but after finishing them, they sometimes did not visit to their new vacation home for a long time. Rattlesnakes filled the upper decks and even slithered inside the walls of their beach house if they could find any opening, especially in the fall and winter. When people reopened their houses up in the spring, the walls came alive with the rattle of rattlesnakes.

Hans was the first official garbage collector. He would pick up the garbage and place it in a big hole which had been dug in the middle of the bay side of Treasure Island located on what is now Schooner Drive in Section II. There was no development on this side except for the bait camp owned by Ezra Ballard. Hans recalls finding broken shards of pottery and bones while digging the hole for garbage. He believes the bones were Karankawa Indian bones, recalling that someone came and

Treasure Island Color Brochure[15]

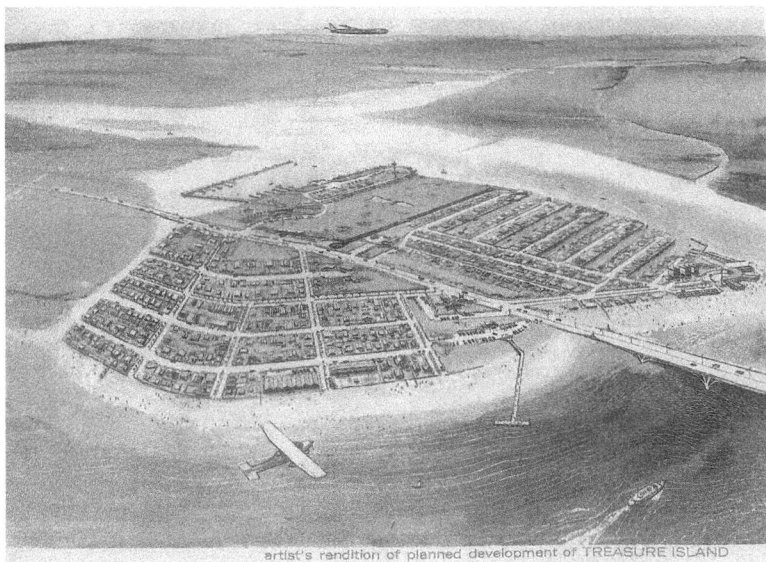

Treasure Island Brochure[16]

took the shards to the Jamaica Beach area.

Treasure Island property owner Curly Dufner and his wife, Robi, owned a hamburger shop and gas station on the Gulf side of "Bluewater Highway" at Lazy Palms three miles west of San Luis Island. Hans said residents would go there in the evenings to play dominos or cards and drink beer.

Hans also worked a second job for Curly Dufner on his shrimp boat each day. He claimed to be the first shark fisherman in this area, talking about a ten-foot shark caught in San Luis Pass. He also said many ranging from fourteen to sixteen feet got away!

Lawrence Cieslewicz, Jr. mentioned that he and his father built a fishing shack on Bird Island, but God burned it! A bad storm, no doubt filled with lightning, struck the shack and burned it to the ground. Lawrence felt it was too easy to fish and hunt with no limits and was standard to spear 120 flounder in one night. Seining was still legal when

Aerial Photo By Lt. Col. Bill Cannon, U.S. Air Force[17]

he was young, and they seined many times. Regarding duck hunting, it was amazing how many ducks would fly in during hunting season. Lawrence and his father, Lawrence, Sr., were considered the "Kings of Hunters."

No doubt, the generous hunting and fishing permits attracted more homeowners, and the advertisements for settling onto Treasure Island continued to entice the public.

Judge Robert Lowry recalled that his friend Bill Cannon served in the Air Force Reserves and was a member of the practice team who used the bombing range three to four miles to the West at Rattlesnake Point (not visible in this artist rendition.) The planes would fly in from the North, drop their bombs, and then fly out into the Gulf of Mexico where they performed a turnaround over San Luis Pass.

During this period, Bill called Judge Lowry and told him work was beginning at San Luis and to go down and have a look. Lt. Col. Bill Cannon took many aerial photos during his missions over San Luis Island.

Please note where the road ends in the upper right-hand corner of this photo. "Bluewater Highway" was not yet built, and the only way to get to San Luis Pass was to drive across the beach. You can also see where the water of Little Pass would still cover the existing make-shift road.

San Luis Pass

Aerial Photo showing nine miles of "Blue Water Highway" completed at San Luis Beach by The Island Development Co. To connect with proposed causeway to Galveston Island.

J.B. Cassidy Brochure[18]

The Highway, County Road 257, was known in the 1930s as the "Hug-the-Coast Highway," the *Freeport Facts*.[19] When Mr. Welcome Wilson, Sr., lived in Brownsville, Texas, all the talk was to have a highway built along the Texas Coast. The plan was to have each county build its own section for its community to connect Brownsville to Louisiana.

The road is mentioned in the amenities brochure for Treasure Island by Jamaica Corp. stating: "County Road 257 from Freeport and points south, joins San Luis Pass Road at the new bridge, providing a hard-surface access to the area." Another description was an "All Weather Road." The master plan called for its conversion to a four-lane State Highway.

With a toll bridge being built at San Luis Pass, along with the new subdivision of Treasure Island Resort Community, there came the need for a highway from San Luis to Surfside was needed. Circumstances, however, were a real mess. Many local area obstacles slowed the transition to the "Bluewater Highway." The distance from the tip of the Peninsula in miles at San Luis Pass to the new Surfside Bridge was fourteen miles. Ten of these belonged to J. B. Cassidy's Island Development Company, and were therefore private property. The other four miles belonged to various owners. Nine of these miles were in the middle section of Follett's Island. In addition, the State of Texas had no interest in helping with the project. As a result, everyone had to use the beach for a road until much later.

Galveston successfully passed legislation to build a toll bridge to a neighboring county, which had a population of 50,000 or more. The city's twelve and a half mile asphalt road was included in the $3.3 million bond issue voted on and approved in 1948. The investment firms of Nongard of Chicago and Louis Pauls of Galveston received a two-year contract with Galveston County covering the San Luis Bridge project. "Galveston County Road District No. 1 was created in 1957 as authorized under the 55th Legislature, to operate the San Luis Pass-Vacek Bridge, a toll facility."

Galveston County's old "S" Road to the end of the Island, a $290,000 road project, became San Luis Pass Road, FM 3005. But, without a public highway on the Brazoria County side, the county could not build the San Luis Pass-Vacek Toll Bridge. Galveston estimated the Brazoria County Highway would cost $300,000 to build. Attorneys were hired. These were the major entities involved in finding a solution:

Brazoria County sought to have Surfside and San Luis Beaches declared a state park.

The State of Texas set aside that the portion of the beaches between the mean high tide and mean low tide were marked as public property.

"The State Parks and Wildlife Commission stated that, if the county could obtain that portion of the beach which was designated for a park, they would accept it as a park.

"Brazoria County Engineers Department objected to the entire project because, even during small storms, the road would be covered with water and too expensive to maintain.

Cassidy claimed all the land at San Luis Beach, stating that he did not want to give up his right-of-way grant because, if a prospective hotel were to purchase land, they would want exclusive rights all the way to the water. But Cassidy did finally counter with an offer of 100 acres for a state park which would become the new highway. He also offered to dedicate access roads from the existing road running down the middle of the Peninsula to the beach on both the gulf and Oyster Bay sides. The access roads would be placed every two miles.

As the new subdivision was being laid out, right-of-ways through the Cassidy property had to be gained. The 120-foot right-of-way easement for the road from G. D. Prince and F. W. Wheeler is dated April 7, 1954. Doug Prince insisted the county fill the big potholes before he would grant his right-of-way. These 120-foot easements were gifted to Brazoria County.

The following quotation is an answer to an inquiry regarding the proposed roads connecting Galveston Island:

> State Highway Dept. vs. County 11-2-55: Motion by Comr. Isaacs seconded by Comr. Danford that information be relayed back in answer to the question submitted by the Texas State Highway Commission that Brazoria County is not interested in either route at the present time, and that in the future the same may be considered; and that the County Judge be instructed to answer same;

> Whereas, Brazoria County has not sufficient funds for procuring right-of-way for either of the Beach Roads on the mainland route from Freeport to Galveston Island; Now, therefore, be it ordered that the Commissioners Court of Brazoria County in regard to these routes go on record as being unable to favor any proposed road at the time, and until such time as sufficient funds may be available; and it is further ordered that the County Judge of Brazoria County transmit this information to Mr. D. C. Greer, State Highway Engineer with the State Highway Department in reply to questionnaire to the Commissioners Court of Brazoria County regarding said roads date October 28, 1955.

The previous owners of San Luis Island for nearly eighty-six years, Frank K. Stevens and Herbert R. Stevens, Sr., issued a grant for a section of land across San Luis Pass on November 17, 1964 to San Luis

Island Corp.

The original San Luis Island Corp. brochure carried many newspaper articles. One 1965 newspaper article stated "Isle-to-Brazoria Bridge Bringing New Beach Boom," and "$13 Million Estimated," which referred to the amount that would be spent on the Treasure Island development over the following twelve to eighteen months.

Despite the delays, the Right-of-Way was granted in 1964:

Motion by Comr. Brown, seconded by Comr. Brigance, that upon the recommendation of the County engineer, the Right-of-Way Deed executed by Frederic E. Wagner, President, attested by Lamar Golding, secretary, for and on behalf of the San Luis Island Corporation on November 17, 1964, and Gladys Stevens Terrell on November 10, 1964, be filed for record at the expense of the County and returned to the office of the County Engineer, said right-of-way deed conveying to Brazoria County a strip of land of variable width across a portion of San Luis Island in the Stephen F. Austin Peninsular League Abstract 29, Precinct 1, Brazoria County, Texas, and it is further ordered that the consideration for said right-of-way shall be as expressed in said right-of-way deed. Motion carried, all present voting aye.

Further complicating construction, by the time the work needed to

Photo of the Original Fishing Pier with Pier House[20]

begin on the road, J. B. Cassidy had filed bankruptcy, and his 120-foot easement had to be reconfirmed by new owners. Each of the individual properties that J. B. Cassidy sold, i.e. Dr. D. K. Chunn, etc. needed a 120-foot easement 'Right-of-Way' recorded at Brazoria County Courthouse. Precinct 1, Brazoria County supplied the funds to build CR 257. The County Commissioners Court continues to ask the state of Texas to accept and maintain "Bluewater Highway." To this date, there is little interest from the state. I can certainly understand why. Portions are only tarmac on sand, making the "Bluewater Highway" a temporary highway at best.

It is my understanding from Keith Chunn, Jr. that the name, "Bluewater Highway" was a request in trade from G. D. Prince for his 120-foot Right-of-Way Grant to Brazoria County. There are no official records I can locate as to who built "Bluewater Highway," or the date it was completed. It is believed that the funds came from that Commissioner's District. We do know it was near the time of the grand opening of Vacek Bridge. We also know that San Luis Island has never been an island again since the elevated road closed Little Pass. Mary Cannon of Treasure Island remembers well her first drive down the new paved highway. By the time she reached Treasure Island, her car was covered

Father, Lt. Col. Bill Cannon and son Bill Jr., caught a twenty-eight pound red drum near the center of the original pier.[21]

with black tar that had splashed up on her car—not a little bit, but a lot! She was furious.

Correspondences for the highway were not the only papers being shuffled back and forth. On April 8, 1963, Treasure Island Pier, Inc. sold the Pier to San Luis Island Corporation (Volume 847 Page 930-931, Brazoria County Records). Then, on June 1, 1964, San Luis Island Corporation sold the Pier back to Treasure Island Pier, Inc. It is recorded as 2.57 acres (13939 Volume 891 Page 32-33, Brazoria County Records).

Red Miller recalls that Benny Brown built the first pier in 1963 for Lamar Golding. Lamar Golding lost heavily when the pier was destroyed by a hurricane. The pier had been built very low to the water. Debbie Barrett, daughter of Judge Lowry, recalls that in the early years of the pier, a baby fell off into the water of San Luis Pass. Judge Lowry jumped in and saved the baby. The grateful father delivered tomatoes as a thank-you for many years thereafter.

Fishing on the pier was great. Bill Cannon Jr. and David Little caught thirty-four stingrays on a nice January 1966 day.

We can hear about an incident, but when we find a photo of the results of that incident, it is a wonderful treasure to share. A photo showing the San Luis Fishing Pier House after it was destroyed by a storm

Pier House is gone.[22]

Reinforced Concrete Seawall along the beach at Treasure Island.

An aerial photo[23] shows the remains of a concrete seawall in Section I, dated June 22, 1967.

was gifted to me by Gaylen Purett on May 12, 2005.

Finally, we have proof there was a concrete seawall on the shoreline of Section I. As published in the *Treasure Island Times*, Volume III,[24] this seawall did not last very long. It simply disappeared into the sand.

With Section I completed and thriving, San Luis Island Corporation Section II Plat was platted on Feb. 1, 1964, and was signed by San Luis

Section II Treasure Island Resort Community - A Gated Community[25]

Island Corp. President, Frederic Wagner, on June 15, 1964. A wonderful artist's rendition of the proposed Treasure Island Marina was gifted to me by Welcome Wilson, Sr. The project was intended to be a $1 million facility, which was to include a yacht and racquet club, exclusively for owners.

A handwritten note on an old plat found at the Brazoria County Engineers Office notes that the names of streets were dedicated to property owners by San Luis Island Corporation on

April 8, 1964. The note also indicated that "Archie Bennett bought the commercial land—legal 621-4406 Section 2 R." This was originally planned to have the shopping center and fine retail stores.

Bill and Mary Cannon's home, located at 13115 Buccaneer Parkway was one of the first to be built in the new Treasure Island Resort Community. Mary said when they first began to build their home in 1965, that there were no pipelines installed for water. All water had to be brought with you. To use the restroom, you had to go find big bushes in the sand dunes.

When construction of the bridge began, the Cannon children would line up old cans on the bridge sand dunes to shoot their BB guns at the cans. What fun! Judge Robert (Bob) Lowry had a go-cart that would go thirty miles an hour and was so much fun on the beach. Their children

MARINA-MOTEL FACILITY PLANNED IN BOOMING BEACH AREA
$1 Million Project Planned for Treasure Island at San Luis Pass

Artist rendition of future Treasure Island[26]

Cannon Home[27]

Footings for Bridge

Boulevard

Water Tower

Footing for new Bridge[28]

Cut for Bridge

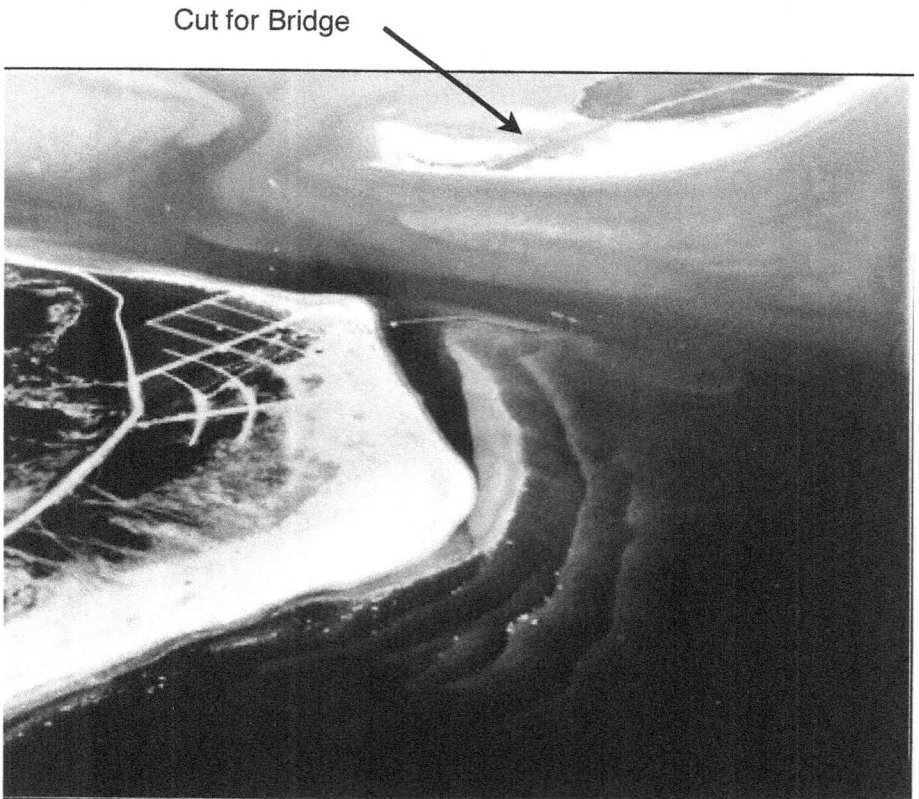

Aerial with western tip of Galveston Island - In this aerial view of San Luis Pass Bridge, the western tip of Galveston Island is clearly visible.[29]

learned to drive here.

The quest to improve the island introduced plans for building a toll bridge. Tax revenue from a bond issue raised the funds in Galveston County for this bridge. It was to be constructed entirely of concrete, 9,045 feet-long, with pre-cast, twenty-four- and thirty-inch square concrete pilings, 125 feet long. The pilings were driven down ninety feet below sea level. This provided approximately a clearance of thirty feet under the bridge. This project provided only a two-foot-wide walkway on each side. Notice the huge amount of sand brought in for the base.

Here is a treasure: a photo of the first concrete pilings being set for the San Luis Pass-Vacek Bridge brings on San Luis Island and the cutaway to set the footings securely into the earth to last a lifetime. The cut away is seen in the distance on the Galveston side for the bridge footings.

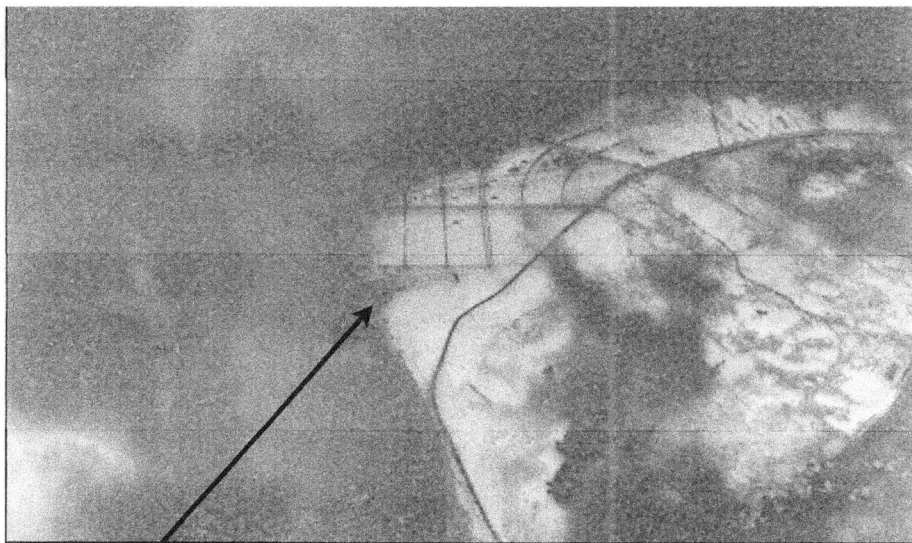

1965 storm destroys bridge work.   1965 storm aerial[30]
Almost covers island with water.

San Luis is no longer an island.

Galveston Island

Another aerial photograph shows the bridge that connected San Luis to Galveston.[31]

Though dwarfed by the new bridge, the pier continued to be a popular attraction for both fishing and photographing. This photo shows the pier in place, forming a "T" head, with a pier house attached, on April 27, 1965 at noon.[32]

T Head at noon - A second photograph offers a close up aerial view of San Luis Pass Pier on January 8, 1966.[33]

On Jan 8, 1966, this stunning aerial photograph was taken, showing Section I with Pier and Pier House visible on pier.[34]

Occasionally, attempts at progress only introduced a new set of problems. Jamaica Corporation bought the assets of Treasure Island from San Luis Island Corporation during 1967 and 1968. As told by Welcome Wilson, Sr., "Louis Pauls put in the small jetties on Galveston Island, and his plan was to charge $2.00 to fish to help pay for the jetties." When those jetties were finished, they caused the west end of Galveston and San Luis Pass to scour, causing much loss of land. Welcome Wilson's brother, Jack Wilson got the idea to use car bodies to stop the erosion. When the sale was made, Jamaica Corporation refused to buy the front lots of Section I which was now under water. According to Welcome Wilson, Sr., "We traded the owners of the underwater lots for lots in the second row not under water. Their solution included a row of car bodies along the East side of Treasure Island facing San Luis Pass. In today's environment, this certainly would not have been allowed.

An aerial shows pilings for the Harold Hudson home and a fence around the perimeter for security. Photographs of this fascinating structure also provides glimpses of the car bodies, waiting to be placed to counteract the erosion.[35]

Hudson finished with concrete bulkhead.[36]

This long line of car bodies is, to my knowledge, the only photo showing their place-ment.[37]

Harold Hudson, a stockbroker from San Antonio, built his home in 1966. Present owner, Sam Guiberson, stated that construction crews camped at the site until it was complete. Because the house was so iso-lated, it had a short wave radio for the Hudsons to communicate with San Antonio and elsewhere.[38]

The *Houston Post* article states that the previous developer had used car bodies for the past four to five years. The developer used them to protect the pier. The car bodies were placed from the edge of the water to 200 feet out. The developer said they spent $40,000 in the previous year alone on this erosion project. He also stated that during the previ-ous few years, they had lost 250 to 300 feet of beach to erosion. [36] New Jersey and Long Beach Island placed automobiles in much the same manner following the 1962 storm, according to a *National Geographic Magazine* article in late 1962.

As erosion began, Lamar Golding hired an auto salvage dealer, Doug Blunck, to bring in car bodies to try to protect the pier and Har-old Hudson's home. Doug owned a Caterpillar bulldozer that had a gasoline engine, which was unusual, as most Caterpillars are diesel. While pushing an auto body out into the water, a large wave swamped his Caterpillar, and Doug went to find Red Miller to help get it out. By the time the two got back, all that could be seen was the exhaust stack. As a result, Harold Hudson hired a helicopter with a cable and hook to

Nearly a quarter mile of sand in front of Harold Hudson home. Col. Cannon standing on sand.[39]

place the car bodies to form a very large square in the water about 200 feet out.[40]

These aerials are priceless because they confirm the stories that we heard for years of what happened. A photo is absolute proof that it did take place. Hans Hecht said 1400 car bodies were placed from just north of the Vacek Bridge, beginning in front of the KOA, to the pier on both sides, up to the Hudson house and beyond. To be wade-fishing here and have your feet get stuck in a steering wheel when the tide was coming in! Now, that is scary! The car bodies present an ongoing hazard because, though they can be buried up to ten feet beneath the sand, even the slightest storm can expose them again.

Despite the barricade of car bodies, erosion continued to reshape the island. Erosion is evident in a photograph of Col. Cannon standing. One would have to wear sandles to cross the hot sand.

Moving forward to 1982, we can still see a tremendous volume of sand in front of this home.[41]

Counteracting erosions effect on travel, the toll bridge was completed to provide better roads to transport traffic. Its Grand Opening was on December 6, 1966, requiring a toll of $0.75. The San Luis Pass "Vacek" Bridge was named after Commissioner Jimmy Vacek. The *Houston Post* feature story showed car bodies placed along the shoreline at Treasure Island to help stop erosion. Jack Wilson, vice president of Timewealth Corp., explained that cars had been used in several developments along Galveston Island by prior corporations. Louis Pauls had also planned to build a bridge from Galveston to Bolivar, but the venture never came to completion.

Tommy Harrison, Seven Seas Grocery, recalled that when the San Luis Pass Bridge was being built in 1966, the concrete trucks would stop by his grocery store on their way back to Galveston. Tommy would trade the drivers a six-pack of beer in exchange for them to empty any remaining concrete in his driveway. He says his driveway concrete is six or seven feet deep. When asked about the weather, he explains, "Oh, that end of the island can get real wild at times!"

The original tollbooth stood for many years until a car hit it head on some thirty-nine years later. To make a "U" turn on the Galveston side before the tollbooth, we had to drive under the bridge and back up the side to the highway, on the sand no less!

The hard roads provided convenience and safety, but the arrival of the water tower contributed a basic element of survival. Before the water tower, the few families with homes brought their potable water

Aerial Photo from General Land Office[42]

with them. There would be no pipelines to their new homes for quite some time. The first source of water was from a well and water tower. The first floor was the subdivision office. The second floor was the home of Roy Otto who acted as security guard, the third floor was a 300 to 400 gallon charcoal filter and the top served as the water tank. Records of Wells and Springs in Brazoria County and Adjacent area show that:

Well No. 64-401 Treasure Isle Depth 275 feet. March 22, 1967 Screen from 258 to 268 ft. Supplies water for 20 homes. (WT Nutt Treasure Island Birdwell Water Well Service (64-402).

Robi Duffner recalled that the nearest place to buy lunch or dinner was where Pergini Condominiums stands today. When I spoke to him on June 27, 2005, Red Miller stated to me that the water tower building was two blocks back from the public Pier House. Red has vivid memories of the building and noted that it had many water leaks and smelled really bad inside. When they demolished the building, Red took the charcoal filter and used it for many years. Just a slab remained with the water pump equipment exposed to the elements.

Hans Hecht remembered the water tower well. There was a small hatch to open to get into the water area. Hans confessed to swimming

Toll Booth Vacek Bridge[43]

in that wonderful, cool water. "Don't tell anyone," he said to me.

Mary Cannon told me a wonderful story, speaking of how, when Judge Robert Lowry with his wife Kitty and the Cannon's were to have a party for fifty to a hundred people, Roy Otto would turn off the water. Mary would say, "Well, it is party day, therefore, I am sure Roy will need to turn off the water sometime today." Red Miller's memory of Roy Otto was that he always had a cigar in his mouth.

Often, the first impression a visitor receives of a town comes from the welcoming sign. The first entrance sign photo that I located came from *The Facts* newspaper. It shows the water tower, as well as Section I, being flooded by high waters. Occasional high water is something we have to contend with.

Office — Information — Water Tower

TREASURE ISLAND

Treasure Island developed by
San Luis Island Corp.
2929 Cedar Springs, Dallas 19, LA 1-9994
P. O. Box 2877 Freeport, Mobile YP 7-5068
Houston Phone   CA 7-5725

The *Sandscript* carried a great story and picture of Roy Otto. Photos of Roy are rare, so I was very happy to find this article.[44]

Only good photo of Roy Otto.[45]

MEETING THE TIMEWEALTH TEAM

Roy Otto in front of Treasure Island Office.

First entrance sign.[46]

Aerial photo taken by Lt. Col. Bill Cannon, showing Section II under construction. Notice the white rectangular area in the upper middle section of the photo. As the lagoon was being dug and the canals were being constructed, the soil was placed between Fathom Drive, Doubloon Street and Pieces of Eight.[47]

Fishing Pier

The pier changed hands when it was purchased by Lester Kamin on September 13, 1967.[45] Again, it was destroyed in 1970 by Hurricane Celia. Red Miller rebuilt the pier in 1970 for Lester Kamin. Red told me on August 24, 2005, that the sandbars moved continuously, causing the pilings to be tight one day and loose the next. Finally, he used a pressurized water hose to create a hole to sink the pilings down deep enough to hold firm. The original Pier House and pilings were very low to the water, just five feet above the high tide line. As Mary Cannon recalled on August 12, 2005, "You would really get wet even with a small wave!" Red put in new, taller pilings. The pier length was 1,600 feet. A full color brochure notes, that the pier was owned by San Luis Island Corporation and was intended to be free for residents. Hurricane Alicia demolished the pier once more in 1983 and Tropical Storm Francis in 1998.

Hurricane Claudette took the pier down again in 2002. With cautious foresight, the new owner, William Mercer, constructed the pier deck with removable sections which could be dismantled quickly and taken to safety in case of another bad storm. Special surveillance was mandatory while installing the new taller pilings, because of numerous sunken ships in the area. However, no sunken ships were encountered where the new pilings were being placed. Some of the best fishing on the Texas Gulf Coast was to be found at the San Luis Pass Fishing Pier. It was always fun to go to the Pier Grill for a hamburger!

Many owners bought and rebuilt the pier. They felt it was important to maintain this bit of history and to enable the public to continue creating memories. These owners, from first to last were:

San Luis Island Corp.

Treasure Island Pier, Inc.

Lester & Hortense Kamin bought the pier on September 13, 1967

Bob Leighton

William Mercer

When development for Section II began, lots, blocks, and roads were laid out. Developer Lamar Golding completed the first of the seven intended canals, known as Canal A, in 1967. Twelve foot concrete panels were brought in for a bulkhead and placed five feet into the ground and in approximately seven feet of water. The center depth of the canal was twelve feet. Underwater lights were placed in the concrete bulkhead of the first canal. Five homes and three boat slips were soon completed on Cold Pass frontage. Each home was built one lot inland from Cold Pass. The housing bulkheads were made of wood and were not placed deep enough to withstand the strong current and rapid flow of water as the tides entered the bays and emptied back into the gulf. Bulkhead guarantee: A news clipping clarified any question regarding bulkheads and their maintenance policies. The bulkheads were guaranteed for one year, and that was about as long as they lasted!

This May 30, 1968 aerial photo shows Canal A built with three boat slips on Cold Pass. Judge Robert Lowry recalls the grand opening was quite a big hoopla. The promoters threw a big party and brought in beautiful girls from Houston to swim in the canals. The girls were doing water ballet shows, but were afraid of sharks. Hans Hecht was hired to place a large net across the front of the canal to keep the sharks out.

The initial roads for Canal A were of crushed oyster shell. Development moved very slowly. Various homebuilders were involved with Canal A, and a few homes were completed. However, several years passed before the second and third canals were built. Harry Bowles, mentioned the second and third canals were built with concrete bulkheads that were only eight feet in length. The bulkheads were placed in approximately five feet of water with three feet in the ground, while

One Canal Aerial[48]

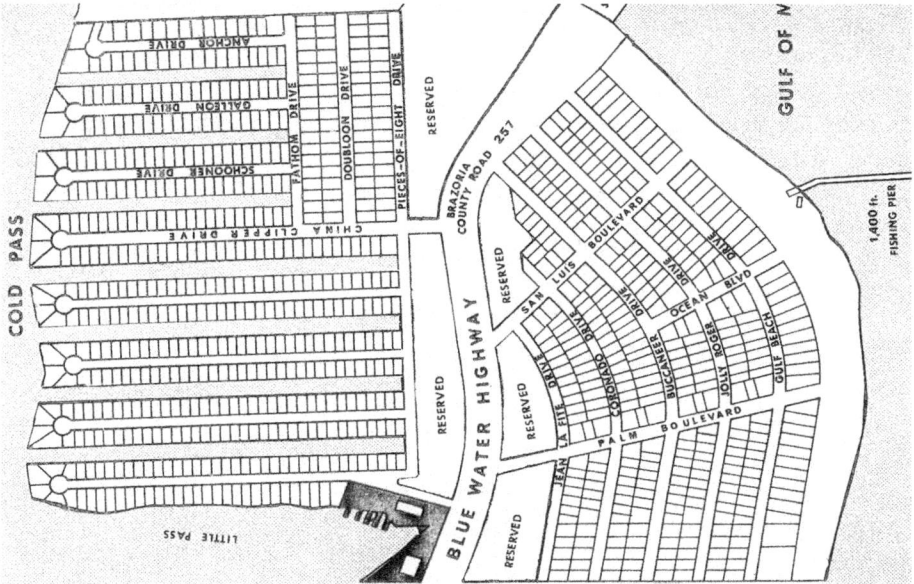

Timewealth Brochure[49]

Undaunted by the slow progress, publications for advertising the future of Treasure Island continued to roll off the press. One of the first brochures for the subdivision by Timewealth Corporation, as seen in this photo, proposed the following: Seven Canals, Yacht Club, Marina, Service Station, Shopping Center, and a Motel.

201

In this brochure, the home on the right looks similar to the one at 223 Schooner Drive, but is not. The house at this address according to Judge Lowry, things are not always the way they look, "Some of these photos are not from Treasure Island." Also in the brochure is the Pier photo looking from the T-head back towards the subdivision. In 1967, and there were grand ideas for the seven canals, a marina, shopping area, and yacht club, etc.

TOP LOCAL MEN HEAD JAMAICA CORP.

W. W. WILSON

The unparalleled success of the Jamaica Corporation is largely due to the effectiveness of the management team. While each man is an expert in his own field, it is the exceptional blending of talents which has brought the Jamaica Corporation to the top in its many endeavors.

At the top of the organizational chart is Welcome W. Wilson, Chairman of the Board for the Jamaica Corporation and for the Homestead Bank, Houston's fastest growing suburban bank. For six years Mr. Wilson was assistant to Mr. R. E. "Bob" Smith, Houston's best known oilman and philanthropist. As a Member of the Executive Office of the President of the United States, Mr. Wilson served as Director of Defense Mobilization for the five-state area including Texas, Oklahoma, New Mexico, Louisiana and Arkansas. In this position Mr. Wilson won the Arthur Fleming Award, the top recognition for outstanding Federal Services.

Executive Vice President is General

EUGENE MAIER

Eugene Maier, U. S. Army, Retired. An urban planning expert, Gen. Maier served for 16 years as a Director of Public Works and Traffic Engineering for the City of Houston. In 1961 he was named among the top-ten public works officials in the nation.

Jack E. Wilson, Vice President, was formerly Director for the Southwestern area, Technical Operations, Department of Defense. He is currently a member of the Civilian National Defense

JACK WILSON

JOHNNY GOYEN

Executive Reserve, and is recognized as one of the most knowledgeable men in the resort development industry.

Johnny Goyen, Vice President, also serves as the City of Houston as an elected Councilman at Large. Mr. Goyen is Chairman of the Board for the Jamaica Apartment Company.

Sherwood Crane, Vice President, supervises all financial activities of the Corporation and serves as Chairman of the Board for the Colonial Savings Association. Mr. Crane is holder of the University of Houston's Outstanding Alumnus Award, issued once annually.

Director of the commercial development division, Henry P. Moore is a graduate of Rice, and the Harvard University's Advanced Management School. Mr. Moore has served for 20 years with Tennessee Gas Transmission Company, with responsibility for sales and property management prior to joining Jamaica.

Comptroller and Director of Administration is Joseph C. Cobb, Jr., a Certified

HENRY P. MOORE

Public Accountant, and a member of the National Financial Executives Institute, Mr. Cobb was formerly executive vice president for Sparkler Manufacturing, the Light House Inc., and an officer with Southwestern Industrial Electronics. Co.

These men head up the 30-man headquarters staff operating from the central office in the Sheraton Lincoln Center. A great number of other friendly and qualified employ es are busily occupied at the various sites and projects described elsewhere in this paper.

SHERWOOD CRANE

Top Local Men[50]

DON'T BE CONFUSED

Early in 1967, the Jamaica Corporation purchased the assets of the San Luis Island Corporation. Chief among these assets was a fine resort sub-division called Treasure Island. Now operated as a wholly-owned subsidiary of the Jamaica Corporation, Treasure Island will become one section of the San Luis Pass Resort Community.

James C. Joy, Registered Professional Engineer, is Vice-President for Engineering and Development. A former Air Force Captain, he is a 1952 graduate of Mississippi State University. He served for 5 years with Engineering Consultants, Dunbar and Dickson, and as City Engineer for 6 years at Freeport, and 5 years at Galveston. Joining the Jamaica group as Director of Engineering in 1967, he was named to a Vice-Presidency in 1968.

As Vice-President for Marketing, Stan McIlvaine is responsible for resort property sales, sales promotion and market research. Formerly General Manager of Astroworld, in Houston, his broad experience in promotional work includes service with the Six Flags over Texas amusement park in Dallas, and as General Manager with the Houston Buffs baseball team.

WALTER GROVER

Walter Grover, Vice-President for Operations, is General Manager for all activities within the resort communities. Another University of Houston man, he is President of Tower Tire Supply, in Houston, and a Director with Galveston's Tourist Bureau.
A former Naval Intelligence Officer, his corporate duties also include supervision of the Utility and Marine Corporations, the Nursery operation, and all concessionaire improvements.

J. C. JOY

DAVE HAMPTON

Dave H. Hampton, C.P.A., is Vice-President and Controller for Jamaica Resort Corporation. A native Houstonian, he is a graduate of Reagan H.S., and Southern Methodist University. Holding membership in the city, state, and national professional accountants associations, he served for 13 years with Drilling Tools, Incorporated, of Houston, including 9 years as Treasurer for that group.

STAN McILVAINE

The Team[51]

The Ghost City of San Luis Island

EUGENE MAIER

Vice-Chairman of the Board of Directors. Eugene Maier is a professional engineer with degrees from Yale and Kansas Universities. A retired Brigadier General, A.U.S., he served the City of Houston as Director of Public Works and Engineering, and as Director of Traffic and Transportation, for a period of sixteen years. In this capacity he was named one of the Top Ten Public Works Officials in the nation for 1961.

President of Jamaica Resort Corporation is Jack E. Wilson. He formerly served as Vice-President for Marketing, and Director for Sales Promotion.

Prior to joining Jamaica, in 1964, he was Director, Technical Operations, Southwestern Area, for the Department of Defense. His background is one of broad-scale operations, programming and planning.

A native Texan, he graduated as one of "Ten Outstanding Students" in the University of Houston class of 1950.

JACK E. WILSON

JOHNNY GOYEN

As Vice-President for Public Affairs, Johnny Goyen supervises all public, governmental, and media relations for the corporation. He also has served for 12 years as Councilman-at-large for the City of Houston, with prior service to the City as Director, Corporation Courts, and Public Properties Department.

A University of Houston graduate, he was the first Director of Alumni Affairs, later served as President of that organization, and was named Outstanding Alumnus in 1954.

Sherwood Crane, Senior Vice-President for Finance, supervises all financial operations of the corporation. He is Chairman of the Executive Committee of the Homestead Bank; Chairman of the Board, and President, of the Colonial Savings Association.

With many years of banking experience, he is a University of Houston graduate, and the 1953 winner of the Outstanding Alumnus Award from that institution.

SHERWOOD CRANE

The Team[52]

The aerial photo of San Luis Island, Cold Pass, and San Luis Pass shows the completion of the second Canal in Section II of Treasure Island. The Ezra Ballard Bait Camp is still operating.[53]

A change in ownership proved to be troublesome for the home-owners along Canal B and C. Keeping the process in order, the canals were built before Trotters Lagoon was dug.

Timewealth bought the assets of Treasure Island from San Luis Island Corporation in 1967, which included Canal A. The first dredging permit for canals that I have located is dated April 3, 1970 and was issued to Timewealth Corporation, who then constructed Canals B & C with no boat launch. The master plan called for a marina with boat launch for use by Treasure Island residents. One letter titled "Background" by Harry Bowles stated the following:

> "Because the boat ramp was never platted in Section II, there were many issues of concern.... A lawsuit could be brought and would discuss the following: 'The suit concerns the legality of closing an existing boat ramp,'" in Canal A.

Prospective purchasers were led to believe that the subdivision would have a full service marina and boat launch privileges at the launch located in Canal A. Most of these people were told that this was a temporary launch until the marina was complete. To solve their concerns about too many boats using Canal A, a cable and lock were placed at the entrance for homeowners use. Another letter from Harry Bowles states that the original brochure by Timewealth placed the boat ramp on the property known as Flounder Flats. Timewealth had an option on this property which expired and was reverted to the F.D.I.C. A third map was distributed locating the ramp with the proposed marina. The Corp of Engineers approved a move to Trotter's Lagoon area between Lot 6 and 7 of Anchor Drive.

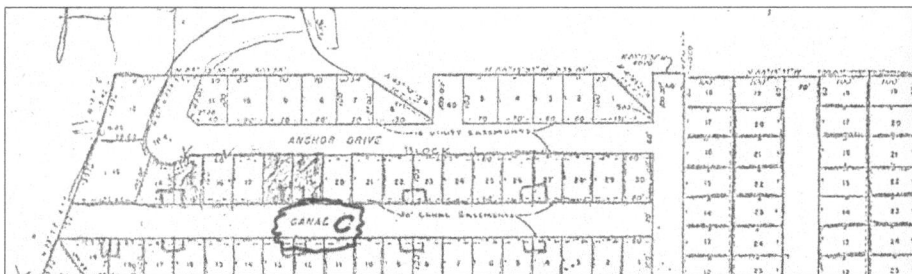

Boat Slip[54]

Welcome Wilson, Sr., as president of Jamaica Corporation, developed Tiki Island, Spanish Grant, Jamaica Beach, Sea Isle, Terramar Beach and Treasure Island.

Many visionaries have failed to see their projects come to completion because of circumstances outside of their control. The downturn in the economy and new federal laws regarding write-offs sent J.B. Cassidy's project into bankruptcy. J. B. Cassidy lost to Plaintiff King Fisher Marine Service Inc., in the amount of $47,008.99. Cassidy's bankruptcy included various lots and blocks of San Luis Beach and was dated October 3, 1967.

The *Angleton Times* served public notice of the auction.

Despite the rise and fall of leadership, the island made slow and steady progress toward becoming a hub of activity once again.

Welcome Wilson, Sr.[55]

Chapter 8
Continued Spectacular Treasure Island Development in spite of nature's onslaughts

Fires and storms that could easily discourage a community from expanding proved to be no hindrance to San Luis and its determined residents. In fact, further establishment of the San Luis community was evidenced through new plats and water wells, which laid the foundation for further growth. Assisting the development of Treasure Island, homes built along Titlum-Tatlum Bayou provided additional landmass protection from the treacherous Gulf Coast. San Luis had been tested by adverse weather and even wars, but the persistent residents remained.

Jack E. Wilson, brother of Welcome Wilson, served as president of San Luis Island Corporation for a short time in 1967, signing approval for Section II Re-Plat. Welcome Wilson, Sr., who became president of

Section II Re-Plat[1]

San Luis Island Corporation and developer for Treasure Island, captured the progression of this development through aerial photos. There is an additional row of lots to the south of China Clipper that is not shown on this plat.

Many changes were about to happen. The KOA (Kampgrounds of America) was de-annexed. Little Pass had been shut off by the "Bluewater Highway," for which there had been approval "to build an elevated road" and which became a dam to Little Pass. A July 1968 black and white aerial photo shows the highway cutting across the former Little Pass with its dam effect. The dramatic length of the San Luis Pass-Vacek Toll Bridge across San Luis Pass is breathtaking. Adding to the excitement of this photo is the view of Titlum-Tatlum Bayou extending from the upper left around to the upper center, thereby separating the lower end of Mud Island from Moore's Island and emptying into Cold Pass. Bird Island is also visible in the upper right. Early developments of both Sections I and II of Treasure Island are clearly visible, including the major streets in I and Canal A opening into Cold Pass in II. The extensive shoal off the beaches of Section I is clearly visible, continuing around the beaches of Follett's Island and extending straight out into the Gulf of Mexico. Today, the remaining shoal runs parallel to the

One canal built 5/30/1968
Please note that the shoals go straight out from the beach toward the Gulf of Mexico.
Mr. Nat Hickey of Freeport owned a blueprint shop and took many aerial photos.[2]

shore.

Please note that the shoals go straight out from the beach toward the Gulf of Mexico.

Mr. Nat Hickey of Freeport owned a blueprint shop and took many aerial photos. Once again, we see treasures of the development of Follett's Island. Here, the shoreline from Treasure Island toward Surfside shows the beginning of a makeshift road that hugs the coastline. The fishing pier and the beginning of the San Luis Pass-Vacek Toll Bridge stand out in the bottom of the photo. Above them are additional views of Treasure Island development, Sections I and II. The picture also shows the deep curve of Cold Pass which flows from San Luis Pass to Christmas Bay. Christmas Bay dominates the top of the photo from far right to just left of center.

Nestled between Section I and Louis Pauls 86.79 Ac. is Section III. Section III lies directly in the path of Little Pass, and if it were ever to open again, all development would be in direct jeopardy. Consequently, this section has never been fully developed. Only three homes were

Christmas Bay

Bluewater Highway[3]

Treasure Island Section III Plat[4]

built, with one blown away during hurricane Ike in 2008.

The deep channel current of San Luis Pass hugs the coastline of Treasure Island. Another aerial photo gifted by Nat Hickey captures the ever-shifting sandy bottom of San Luis Pass. The sands are most

Aerial Canal[5]

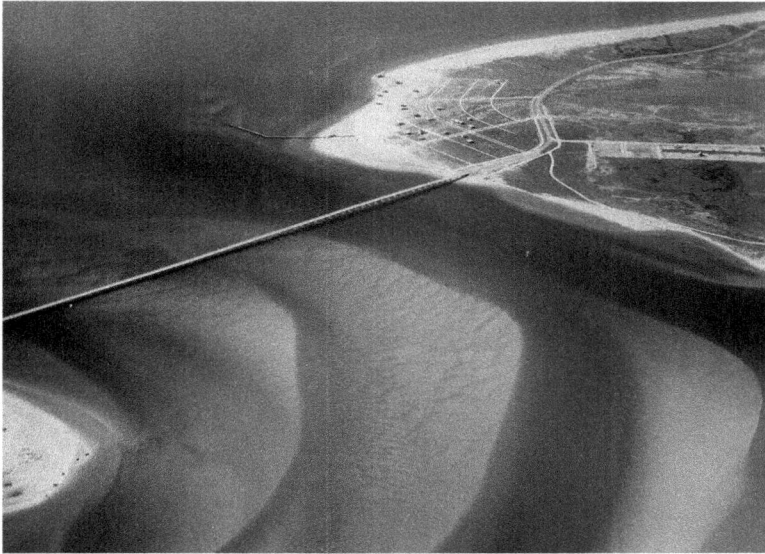

Deep Channels[6]

visible around the western tip of Galveston Island. This aerial photo-graph of Section I shows San Luis Pass-Vacek Bridge complete. Canal "A" is complete with several homes. Sands are also visible in Cold Pass below Canal "A." Canal "A" runs due east and west.

In Aerial No. 4002, 5/30/1968 is a view from the north, northeast of sand channels in San Luis Pass. Three dominating deep channel cur-rents are well defined in the patterns of the sands in this shot looking toward San Luis Pass from above West Bay. These patterns are contin-uously changing. The incredible length of the San Luis Pass-Vacek Toll Bridge is once again dramatically portrayed!

Though the island is surrounded by the Gulf, access to fresh wa-ter remained problematic. The first water well of record was drilled in 1967 and did not have a house covering the pump or equipment. Everything sat exposed in the open, salty air. After Hurricane Alicia, a toilet washed up near the water supply pump housing. Finally, the res-idents working for the Municipal Utility District grew concerned that the water system could be easily contaminated. A pitiful little build-ing was placed over the equipment to minimally meet the community needs. Water Well Building Number II also served as the Office for the Subdivision.

Water-well building[7]

Well Number One With a Replacement Pump House After the Water Tower was Torn Down

Though the pump house was a small improvement, it was not long before storms would put it to the test. NOAA named the May 30, 1968, tropical storm Candy. It moved inland over southeast Texas, causing heavy flooding and crop damage, along with many tornadoes. As Candy roared through San Luis Pass, it destroyed the outer end of the San Luis Pass Fishing Pier. Nat Hickey's aerial photo captures the skeletal remains.

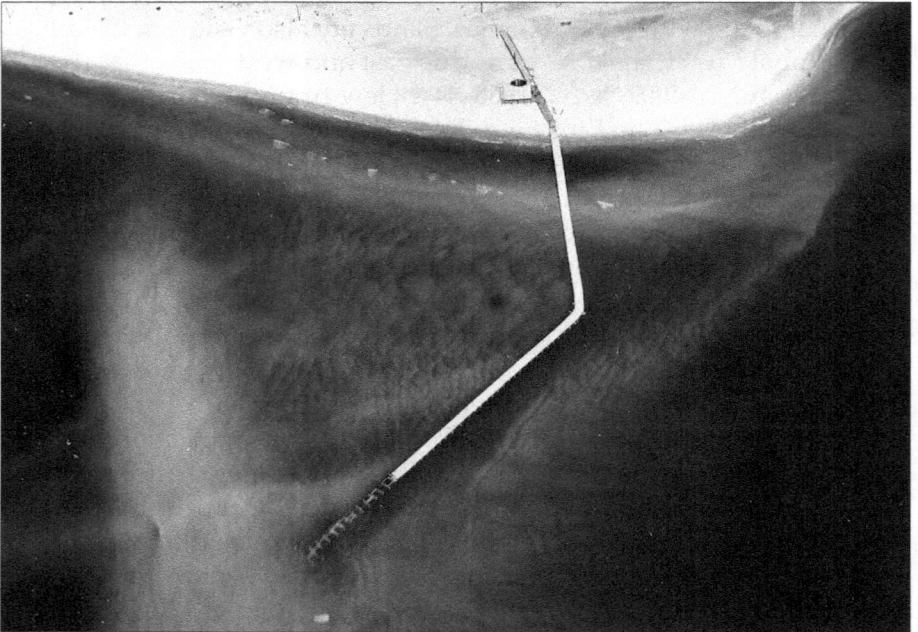

Pier damage from Hurricane Candy.[8]

Car Bodies Aerial[9]

The car bodies are visible in this aerial photo as testimony of the fight against erosion. At that time, little was known about the detrimental effects that the cars would have on the environment. The residents cared deeply about the wildlife found on their island, sometimes sacrificing personal comfort to protect nature.

As the subdivision was being built in Section II on the canal side, there was a large natural white shell parking area. The lot was taken over as a breeding ground by birds known as "Black Skimmers" or *Rynchops Niger*. These birds are best known for their red scissor-like bill. The lower mandible extends farther than the top, allowing them to skim the top of the water for small fish. Residents put out signs asking

Skimmers (Rynchops Niger)[10]

visitors not to drive to their homes for fear of breaking the eggs. They would park their own vehicles some distance away and walk to their homes until the eggs hatched and the baby birds had grown enough to fly away. As development increased, the Skimmers moved to a parking lot at the Dow Chemical Plant near Surfside. Now, when fishing at night, one can see them just a few feet away as they fly up and down our lighted canals. They truly are a marvel.

Skywalk

Cannon Skywalk[11]

A great deal had changed since Lt. Col. Bill Cannon first saw development beginning at San Luis Island during bombing practice at Rattlesnake point. He and his best friend, State District Judge Robert Lowry built beach homes on adjacent lots. The Cannons and the Lowrys had huge fish fries with fresh fish. Judge Lowry told me that he had served 150 people many times. The men built a skywalk bridge walkway between the homes, thus saving their wives Mary and Kitty thousands of steps as they jointly cooked all the meals.

Judge Lowry made national headlines in 1973 by authorizing African American foster parents to adopt a Latino child. The case was the first adoption granted in Harris County under those circumstances. Mr. And Mrs. James E. Adams, fifty-four and fifty-five years old, had cared for little Victor since he was thirteen months old. Brought to them as a battered toddler, they were the only parents he had known. The six-year-old boy was the center of a terrible court struggle between his foster parents and Harris County Child Welfare Unit. The county considered the Adams too old. They also claimed that Victor would be deprived of his Hispanic heritage. Race had nothing to do with his decision. He wanted what was best for the little boy. Lowry ruled in favor of the Adams family in January of 1973.

Judge Robert Lowry was also a director of the Texas State Historical Survey Committee of the Texas Historical Foundation. With an armload of papers, he came to my beach house one summer day and said, "Eileen, here are the early documents of Treasure Island. Write this history. I know you can do it." That is how this book got started.

As developers and promoters were busy executing the new plans for Galveston Island and Treasure Island at San Luis Pass, a huge concert was scheduled for the July 4, 1970. Jerry Jeff Walker, a nationally recognized county and western singer/writer, who was best known for his *Mr. Bojangles*, was to be the lead singer. Twenty-thousand people were expected to attend the concert.

During this period, Rooster Collins had a bait camp near the West End of Galveston Island at the base of Vacek Bridge. Anticipating this huge crowd, he bought a thousand cases of beer in preparation for the big day. With only one cash register, he put up a chain link fence around his property to control the thirsty crowd.

As always along the Texas coast, the weather is never predictable. This 4th of July was no exception. On the day of the concert, a strong easterly wind brought tides from the back bay three to four feet above normal. The high water separated the people from the stage and the band. It was a disaster, and Rooster lost his shirt.

Plenty of tales abound about Rooster. In 2007 I chatted with owner Tommy Harrison of the Seven Seas Grocery, Galveston Island. He noted that Rooster was a true "Old Salt," Admitting, "For certain, Rooster was not very tidy and was very gruff." After December of 1966 when the Vacek Bridge was completed, Rooster's bait camp was conveniently located at the base with a narrow channel running to the bay. Naturally, the cut would need a dredge boat

A Texas Historical Survey Committee Marker

ROBERT L. LOWRY
MEMBER
TEXAS STATE HISTORICAL SURVEY COMMITTEE
DIRECTOR
TEXAS HISTORICAL FOUNDATION
1965

occasionally to keep it open. Hire a dredge boat, not Rooster! He used his shrimp boat propeller to keep the sand from filling it in.

Rooster's shrimp boat was both his savior and albatross. He had an uncanny knack for finding sandbars in the pass, running aground until high tide. He was a resolute shrimper with fresh Gulf shrimp for all of his customers.

His place was always open to fishermen and wayward children. At one time he had ten to twelve young people, most of who only stayed for a few months. However, Rooster had five or six who stayed for years and helped him run his store. One of the older girls helped Rooster look after the younger children, also assisting Rooster when his health went bad. Reggie Corley, a local wade fisherman, recalled that Rooster had a bad temper. If things didn't go his way, you were not welcome to come back. "We used to camp out under the bridge, and in the early morning Rooster prepared a breakfast of steak and eggs. We would trade Rooster our fresh fish for food and bait." He also recalled that, "His store was one of the best for any type of fishing gear, especially lures."

Sports writers and fishermen respected Rooster for his knowledge of fishing, The *Houston Post* and *Chronicle* newspapers called him weekly to get the latest fishing report for West Bay and San Luis Pass.

Rooster used the children to catch mud minnows, one of the many jobs with which they helped. How Rooster identified with children is a matter of conjecture, but his heart was always open for them. He helped many when they were down and out—his way!

Rooster kept a first aid kit and was known as the *local* for cuts and fishhook removal. Reggie noted that while he was camping under the bridge one night, "a Mexican man with three children was wade fishing and got into a school of stingrays. The man pulled the children to the beach where they passed out on the sand in shock. He ran to our fire, took coals with his bare hands and put them on his own sting areas and was still able to run and get the only medical help available at Rooster's."

Tony Perez, a property owner of Treasure Island, tells a story about the time he was in Rooster's store when a young man walked in and bought one item while attempting to steal a couple other items. Rooster saw him, reached under the cash register counter, picked up his pistol and laid it on the counter. He then asked the young man as he was about to walk out the door, "Is that all you're gonna pay for?"

A new subdivision on the west end of Galveston Island began in the late 1980s, causing the property owner to sell the property out from under Rooster. This subdivision project ultimately failed due to a poor economy. He then bought property on Follett's Island, just at the mouth of what had been Little Pass, where he set up shop with his shrimp boat and bait camp. Once again, he used his shrimp boat propeller to cut a channel to his bait camp. Some mornings when we crossed Surfside Bridge, we would see miles of a mud trail from San Luis Pass out in the Gulf of Mexico. We knew Rooster was cleaning his channel again.

Tom Bright, owner of the Bright Lite Store at Treasure Island, had a wonderful dog named Otto who went everywhere with him. Not far away, Rooster now had chickens at his bait camp. Janice Ramey, manager of the Bright Lite, noted that one day the Treasure Island Security guard had to take Otto, for an emergency visit to the veterinarian. It seems as though Rooster had filled Otto's backside with buckshot!

With rumors of his relationships with wayward children and his messy nature, the residents of Treasure Island protested until they forced Rooster to move. He then opened and managed a hunting and fishing camp west of Jamaica Beach in the Bay of Jubilee Cove for several years. His last move was to 61st Street in Galveston where he worked until he died.

This map marks Rooster Collins' former bait camp and boat launch

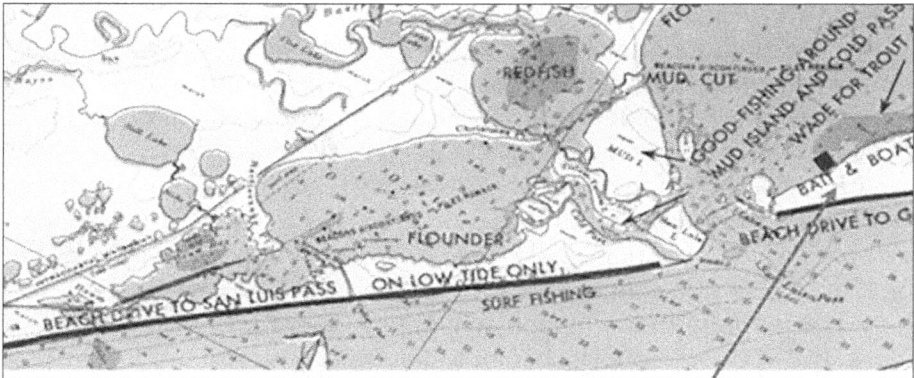

Rooster Collins Bait Camp and Boat Launch[12]

on the west end of Galveston Island. It is believed this Gulf Oil Company is believed was drawn by Ronnie Luster. He names "Cold Pass" but does not name Little Pass. The Intracoastal Waterway is in place. The road is noted as "Beach Drive to San Luis Pass on Low Tide Only," and the San Luis Pass Bridge has not yet been built.

Ronnie Luster who founded the Coastal Conservation Association stated:

> *Cold Pass is the umbilicus to the Gulf for the Christmas Bay complex. Christmas Bay is the central body of a three-bay complex. It connects to Bastrop Bay in the North, and Drum Bay to the South. Bastrop and Drum Bays are tertiary bays but exhibit distinctly different environmental conditions. The lifeline for this system is Bastrop Bayou, which delivers freshwater, nutrients and sediments to the estuary. The freshwater maintains the salinity gradient critical to certain larval and juvenile organisms. The sediments maintain the estuarine marshes of emergent vegetation which provided shelter for these same creatures. The nutrients are the basis of the food web which nurtures these organisms. The bay was studied intensively for a brief period in the 1970s but research has languished since then, only with sporadic, unconnected studies being conducted from time to time. Christmas Bay is analogous to a bi-level bathtub. Bastrop Bayou and Bay is the freshwater spigot delivering various amount of water, at seasonally different temperatures, to Christmas Bay. The water spreads out in the bay but does not always reach the southern tip. Cold Pass forms a two-way drain, removing low salinity water and replacing it with higher salinity water with each tide. Christmas Bay, a small secondary bay at the southwestern extreme of the Galveston Bay ecosystem, has been incorporated into the joint Texas General Land Office/Texas Parks & Wildlife Department.*

Former resident Harry Bowles suggested that because Cold Pass varies from eight to fifteen feet deep and is very narrow, it causes water to move very fast at tide change. The water temperature may vary as much as ten to fifteen degrees colder on the bottom than on the top thus the best reason we can guess for the name *Cold Pass.*

From the dredging of the water, the canal dug into the land, and the cars placed to slow the natural erosion process, the island was reshaped by both natural and man-made forces. Trotter's Lagoon[13] would be the next feature to make an appearance on San Luis. Timewealth Corporation dug the man-made lagoon which was in the shape of a question mark. In 1971, the economy began to falter. Timewealth felt the real estate sales slow so tremendously that they sold the intended Yacht Club land area to Gulf Holding Corporation owners, Fred and Ruth Placke. The Plackes worked with Timewealth's engineer, J. C. Joy, to design a facility to be used as a KOA campground. Trotter's Lagoon was named after Jack Trotter who was originally a partner of Welcome Wilson Sr. Trotter later partnered with Fred Placke to build this man-made lagoon at the mouth of Cold Pass.

This photo is one of the best finds, showing the KOA campground design as it is being created. Here, dredging equipment is shown forming what would become fill from the dredge provided upload for the

Lagoon
Welcome Wilson, Sr., photo

area between Fathom and Pieces of Eight by raising the area by five or more feet. The aerial photo shows Ezra Ballard Bait Camp in the upper left corner.

Fred Placke named the lagoon after his partner and designed the accompanying facilities with many amenities. Accommodations were offered, such as a full stainless steel kitchen, grocery store, a laundry mat, and a propane gas fill station which included a boat gasoline pump. Dockside, another small building known as the Teen Room was connected by an arch to a "Y"-shaped swimming pool, which was deep on one side and shallow on the other. The pool was the delight of Treasure Island children as well as their guests. One of our thrills was being able to wash and dry our clothes at the laundry facility. Boats could buy gasoline at the dock. The KOA acreage was then de-annexed from Treasure Island, and Fred Placke drilled his own water well for the KOA. There was a main water valve at the end of Doubloon Street, intended to be a backup for Treasure Island if its water system failed. The main entrance to the Placke property was through Treasure Island on Doubloon Street. When this road was closed to his customers, Placke had to buy additional land for ingress and egress.

Kampground of America[14]

Vacek Bridge is Completed[15]

This aerial photo from March 8, 1971, featuring San Luis Pass, Cold Pass, Treasure Island, and the west end of Galveston Island, shows the lagoon to be in place and all three canals are dug and full of water.

In 1971, David Feinman of the West Bay Utility Company bought a modular home from a company operating in the K-Mart parking lot on Galveston's 61st Street and "S" Road. They cut the home in half, drove it to the West End of Galveston Island and over the new bridge to 318 Schooner Drive. Later Larry Ham, first president of the Treasure Island Public Utility District, bought the home and a number of years later sold it to Tommy Cashiola.

When Richard Nixon became President, he made a number of changes in the first few months to the nation's budget, causing the Dow Jones to drop by forty percent. People could no longer afford to own a second home. The following depression threatened not only homeowners, but businesses as well. On San Luis, this proved to be devastating for Timewealth. Welcome Wilson Senior, Sr., stated, "We hung around for several years but finally had to liquidate." By October 4, 1971, sales had come to a standstill. Timewealth's dreams were shattered, and they were forced to close. At the time of liquidation, the following companies were named in the bankruptcy:

Galtex Land Co.   Lamar Golding   Main Bank
Main Capitol Corp. Western National Bank, 8 lots
Timewealth Corp.   San Luis Pass Corp.   Stewart Trust Co.
Houston Citizens Bank held papers for 5 lots

Summary for Treasure Island:
Sec I 308 lots   Sec II 250 lots   Sec III 40 lots
Sec IV 6 lots   Commercial 16 lots   HL&P 1 lot
SW Bell Telephone 1 lot
Total assessments 622

Despite the economy's impact on San Luis, progress continued slowly. According to *Sandscript* issue No. 5, dated November, 1969, construction began for telephone service to Treasure Island.

> *There were no phone lines in 1970 when Harry Bowles moved there. I remember when they put the lines in. It was a big topic watching them string the lines from Surfside to us. We were finally getting phone service! As I recall, George Mort, Shirley and Wally Gafner, and Bill De-Mouche got their lines first in about 1972. Lester Kamin was a driving force because he owned the Fishing Pier and needed phone service so his customers could call the pier. We also pressured them from the security standpoint, concerned that we could not call for help to the Sheriff's Office, Fire, etc. As I recall, there were a number of exciting times with a few of our big mouth chatty neighbors, as we were all on party lines.*
> *- Quote from Harry Bowles, December 19, 2005*

After the subdivision came out from the cloud of bankruptcy, a civic club was formed.

Original forms of legal descriptions of districts and boundaries were filed on September 1, 1973, by Dan Smith. The San Luis Island Resort Community Civic Association was now formed with Lester Kamin as president, Dan Smith as treasurer, and Willard Nutt as security guard.

A Municipal Utility District (MUD), was formed. The officers discovered later that the paperwork had not been prepared correctly, and that they were in fact not a MUD. They were forced restart the process to become a legal functioning Municipal Utility District.

In November 10, 1972, a letter from West Bay Utility Company states: "We are pleased to be able to inform you that West Bay Utility Company is the new owner-operator of the water systems at Jamaica Beach, Bermuda Beach and Treasure Island." This letter was signed by David R. Feinman.

On May 25, 1973, West Bay Island Corporation's Stanton Freidman of West Bay Construction Company sold the water well equipment and records to David Feinman, the owner of West Bay Utility Company. Stanton Freidman moved out of the area and left no means to contact him if any problems arose. On May 5, 1973, a resolution was created for Treasure Island Municipal Utility District to acquire the existing water system by Lester Kamin and signed by Larry Ham, secretary. On September 28, 1973, San Luis Pass Resort Community Civic Association sold the water well system to Treasure Island Municipal Utility District (TIMUD).

TIMUD bought lots 7 & 8 in Section I along with all the equipment and records. A loan was made from Greater Houston Bank for the amount of $89,792.17. The history of well drilling at Treasure Island is as follows:

Erosion at Cold Pass[16]

1974 Number 2 Water Well was drilled.

1976 Number 3 Water Well was drilled.

1976 Number 4 Water Well was drilled. It was a dry hole.

1979 Number 5 Water Well was drilled, also a dry hole.

For every step forward, it seemed like San Luis encountered another problem. The original wooden bulkhead frontage on Cold Pass Section II was not deep enough to withstand the strong currents. All three canal frontages fell into Cold Pass. About thirty feet of Canal A, about twenty-five feet of Canal B, and about twenty feet of Canal C disappeared. Finally, the concrete sides collapsed into Cold Pass. Remnants can still be seen on Canal B.

Harry Bowles told me that a crew was hired to rebuild the bulkheads at the frontage of the canal to Cold Pass. This time they were jetted down forty feet with air drivers. During Mickie McCunn's presidency, she gave permission to rebuild the side bulkhead at the front of the canal to a depth of twelve feet.

A very special resident, Paula Carroll, built her house in Treasure Island in 1969 and served the community, both MUD and civic, until approximately 1195, twenty-six years of service. She was the office manager and bookkeeper for those many years. For the first years there was no road to the house and they had to walk across the lot behind the house for access.

This photo shows that nearly one full lot fell into Cold Pass.[17] It did make for great fishing.

Another photo shows the wooden bulkhead and cables at the end on the north side of Canal "B."[18]

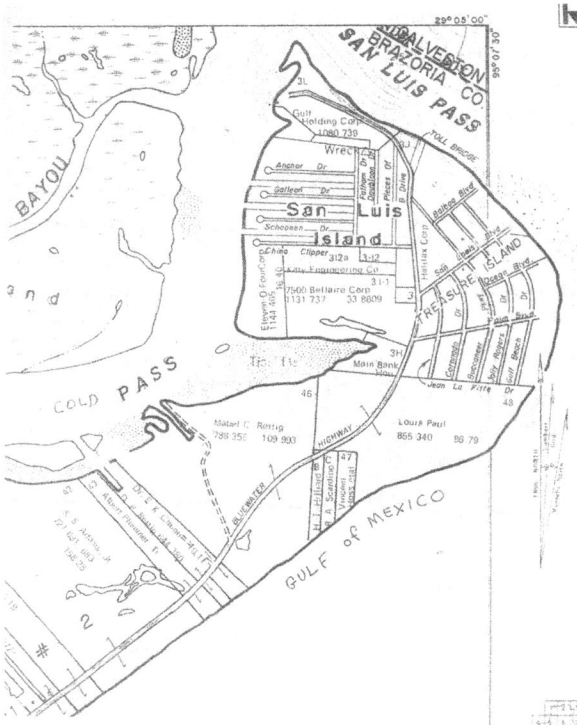

Property Owners 1974

The map above specifies the borders of various property owners in 1974.[19] Number 247

A curious feature shows a label at the north end of Doubloon which is marked "Wreck." I am not sure what this means.

As of September 1, 1973, Treasure Island Municipal Utility Water Control and Improvement District recorded legal description of boundaries for 294.18 acres of San Luis Island, out of S. F. Austin Peninsular League, Abstract 29, Brazoria County, Texas. The KOA was de-annexed on March 2, 1974. It was owned by the Gulf Holding Company and Fred and Ruth Placke. It consisted of approximately two acres, according to Frank W. Stevens, attorney at law, in a letter dated March 11, 1975.

Tony (Francisco) Perez of Treasure Island told me that he once had a fish camp on the

West End of Galveston Island before he moved to Treasure Island. The land was used to graze cattle but space could also be rented from Mr. Baterillo who was manager of the West Bay Fishing Club. Tony rented an old trailer house and began teaching his children how to fish. In those days, no one had spare cash and they wanted the fun of just being together. Tony and his children built a barge from 2'x2'x12' Styrofoam, topped with plywood. Then they put a small outboard engine on it and began to have the time of their lives. One day a big amberjack got hooked on one of the fishing poles with the extra heavy leaders. Tony laughed as he told about that fish pulling the barge all over the place. They had the greatest times with that barge, finding it easy to gig flounder, seine for mud minnows and to use a cast net for bait. Tony said that you could buy a Treasure Island Canal lot on Cold Pass, or one on dry land for the same price of only $4,000. He snatched up the offer.

Chunn's Pier[20] in Cold Pass was a favorite place to go by boat to fish for flounder and to place crab traps on the shallow banks. It lies near what was Little Pass. The last time Little Pass sanded in, the state of Texas declared the land to be owned by the property owners on either side of the former pass and then divided the land down the middle.

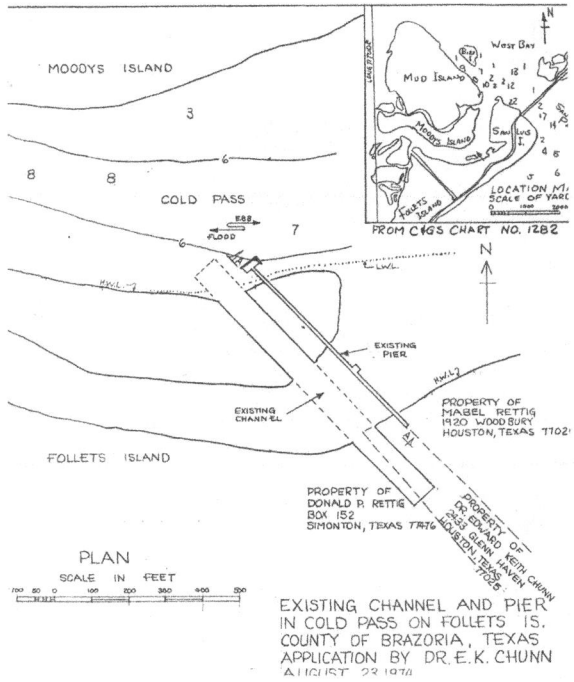

MOODYS ISLAND

COLD PASS

FROM C&GS CHART NO. 1282

EXISTING PIER

EXISTING CHANNEL

FOLLETS ISLAND

PROPERTY OF MABEL RETTIG 1920 WOODBURY HOUSTON, TEXAS 77021

PROPERTY OF DONALD P. RETTIG BOX 152 SIMONTON, TEXAS 77476

PROPERTY OF DR. EDWARD GLENN, KEITH CHUNN HOUSTON, TEXAS 77025

PLAN
SCALE IN FEET

EXISTING CHANNEL AND PIER IN COLD PASS ON FOLLETS IS. COUNTY OF BRAZORIA, TEXAS APPLICATION BY DR. E.K. CHUNN AUGUST 23, 1974

The photograph below shows permit houses along Titlum-Tatlum Bayou.[21]

225

Permit Houses[22]

The addition of permit houses became a debated issue. The following is based upon letters dated on July 8, 1974 and July 18, 1974, from Harry Bowles to the General Land Office in Austin, Texas. Also included is the response to Harry Bowles' letters from the General Land Office (GLO), Gene W. Clark, who worked in Coastal Supervision, Sales, and the Leasing & Mining Division.

Title 86 was enacted by the 63rd Texas Legislature, but was not funded. A great concern of Treasure Island involved the permit houses in the geographical area encompassing San Luis Pass, which included Cold Pass, Christmas Bay, Titlum-Tatlum Bayou, Churchill Bayou, Moody's Island, Mud Island, Guyton Cut (Mud Cut), Bastrop Bay, and inlets and coves in the general area. Another concern was wildlife preservation and the extremely fragile estuaries.

Response letter:

Refers to the Coastal Public Lands Management Act August 27, 1973. Prior to that date, the GLO photographed the coastal area twice from an altitude of 1,000' and numbered each cabin located on public lands. The inventory revealed approximately 1,100 structures on public lands, and they had received 535 applications for continued use. At this time, the GLO issued 304 permits for a one-year period, with the authority to renew the permits in the hands of the School Land Board. They also had 70 permits in suspense due to their proximity to Mud Island.

Letter to the GLO, Bob Armstrong, Commissioner, July 17, 1977

It is more than lack of sewage facilities, circumventing payment of county & school taxes, etc. Most of these small islands, spoil banks, etc., are only a few hundred yards square. Just the construction of a very few cabins can discourage the nesting of birds. One fire, to rid the area of mosquitoes, can destroy every egg & young bird on an island. When a few squatters build cabins in this small area, they do in fact feel as if they own the property and will do their utmost to keep intruders away from the general area. You have in effect approximately 1,100 squatters controlling the entire coastal area of Texas to their benefit, exclusive of the enjoyment of the majority of the public.
Quote from Harry Bowles, 1975
September 29, 1976,

Local resident, Harry Bowles cared deeply about the wildlife on San Luis. His land could have been known as the Gulf Coast Wildlife Preservation Society. Harry envisioned a wildlife preserve located at present day Flounder Flats. This wonderful project was never approved. Harry Bowles tried very hard to make this happen, but it just didn't work at the time.

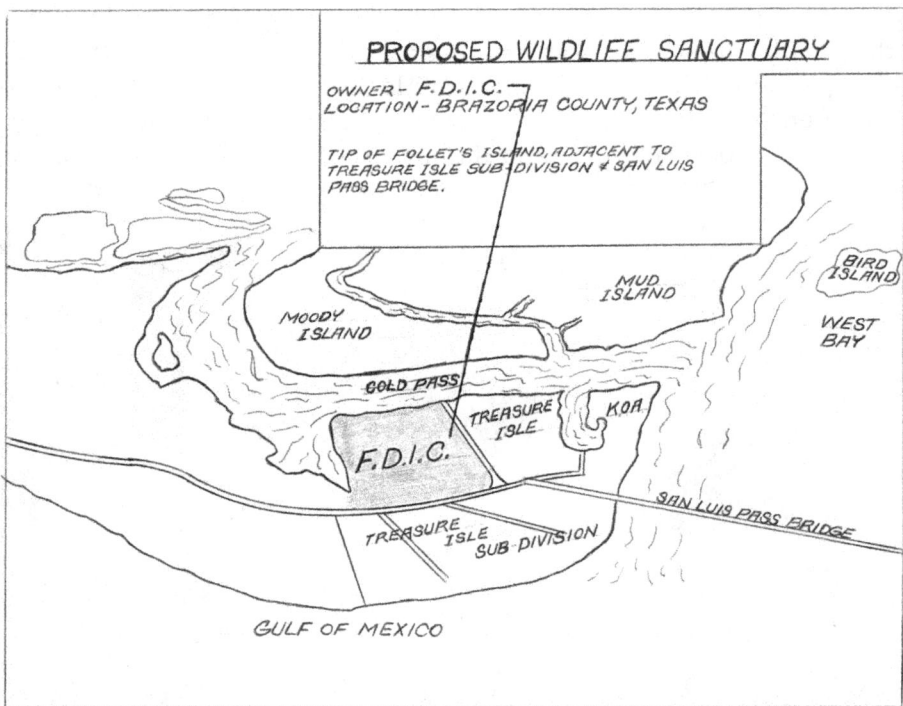

Proposed Wildlife Sanctuary[23]

Birds were not the only animals endangered by the growing traffic of people. Before fishing limits went into effect, daily bags were huge. A photo from 1977 shows Wally Gafner with an eleven pound trout. Wally, Robert Hyatt, and Evelyn Austermiller were often a fishing trio. I always wondered how they could have so many trout and reds on a stringer. There was no limit until 1977 for redfish (red drum) and until 1978 for speckled trout (spotted sea trout).

Jobs were scarce on the island and many people created their own line of work on or off the island. Realtor Shirley Gafner, a part-time resident, owned her own real estate company for many years. Treasure Island kitchen tables served as an office. If property was to be bought or sold, Shirley was the person to call, although Willard Nutt, Jim Fulmore and Mickie McCunn were brokers and also sold real estate. Willard Nutt, a full time resident, was forced to close his business as it is against the by-laws to advertise and run a business from a home. Jim Fulmore, a full time resident worked under Shirley Gafner.

The war against weather resumed with Claudette, July24-27, 1979. The tropical storm made landfall near Galveston, then turned a loop just after landfall, stalling over Southeast Texas for two days. At Nederland, the pressure bottomed out at 29.46". Winds gusted to sixty miles per hour. Chocolate Bayou had tides as high as five feet. A deluge of rain ensued, causing amounts greater than ten inches within forty miles of the coast from Matagorda Bay to Sabine Pass. Totals reached

Fishing Limits
Wally Gafner, Robert Hyatt, Evelyn Austermiller

forty-five inches at Alvin, forty-two inches of which fell in twenty-four hours, establishing a new U. S. rainfall record!

This caused widespread and nearly unprecedented flooding across the area and most streams didn't return to their banks until July 30th. Fifteen thousand homes and hundreds of businesses were flooded out. The rice crop was beaten into the soil by the heavy rain. Six counties in Southeast Texas were declared major disaster areas by President Jimmy Carter. About a year later, on August 10, 1980, Hurricane Allen formed 1,100 miles east of Barbados. On August 1, it moved westward through the Atlantic and became a hurricane on the 3rd when it was about 120 miles east of Barbados. The storm became the strongest hurricane ever recorded in the Caribbean on August 7, with sustained winds of 185 miles per hour and even higher wind gusts and a pressure of 899 millibars (26.55 inches). It began to weaken as it entered the Gulf of Mexico on the 8th and moved west-northwest. Dry air intruded upon the storm system, causing its decline. As it slowed to a crawl off Brownsville, dry dust air continued to be entrained and it continued weakening. Hurricane Allen made landfall as a Category 3 hurricane near Port Mansfield on August 10th. Port Mansfield reported wind gusts of 138 m.p.h. with storm surges of twelve feet. Five-foot surges were reported as far away as Galveston Island.

Severe beach erosion took place as far away as Port Arthur, completely destroying Texas Highway 87 between High Island and Sabine Pass on the 9th. The pressure at Brownsville fell to 28.62". Winds gusted to ninety-two mph at Corpus Christi. Buildings in Brownsville flooded in up to four feet of water. By one count, Padre Island was cut through in sixty-eight places. Tornadoes damaged twenty-five homes in Penita and injured three in San Antonio. About 300,000 people evacuated. Seven died in Texas and seventeen in Louisiana. Most of the casualties in Louisiana resulted from the crash of a helicopter evacuating from an offshore platform. Damages totaled $1 billion. On a good note, rains from Hurricane Allen relieved a serious drought in Southern Texas.

Fires were rare, but the DeMouche home burned to the ground when Hurricane Allen came on shore on August 10, 1980. This was one of the first homes built in Section II and was at the end of China Clipper.

Another fire started one night about midnight, destroying the homes of Al Kerr of Houston and James Pearson of Tomball. Lawrence Shipley's home was badly damaged home, receiving interior and exterior damage to the north wall. Two other homes were in danger, being downwind, but received no damage. The fire occurred in 1979 or 1980.

Being so far from a proper fire station, if a home caught on fire, we had little chance to properly put it out. We did have fire hydrants in place and a portable pump that we could put in the canals for some period of time.

When another home mysteriously burned, great concern was expressed by Surfside Fire Department. An arsonist was suspected and, after the Fire Department resolved to catch the culprit, the fires stopped.

About this time, residents had their first streetlights. The stars were so much brighter before the streetlights were installed. On very dark nights before streetlights, if we were close enough to the power lines, we would see the transformer boxes glowing green and crackling in the night air as a result of salty ocean air heavily accumulating on them. Occasionally, one of the boxes would trip and scare the dickens out of us!

After coming out of the bankruptcy in 1981 the concrete bulkheads were neglected and in need of repair. There were many washouts and the canals were in jeopardy. A committee was formed to photograph and document all areas. Nearly every lot had a problem. There were huge underground cables which held the concrete sidewalls in place. Many were exposed with holes. One could watch the tides wash in and out. Repairs became a community effort, and each homeowner paid for his or her portion.

Water was still a major problem for Treasure Island residents. The well water was orange with rust, making washing white clothes nearly impossible. No one even considered drinking the water. On August 7, 1982, a committee was formed consisting of Amelia (Mickie) McCunn, Bill Elder, Al Warrington, Harry Bowles, Wally Gafner and Jane Bright. They appointed H. J. (Jack) McCunn, Consulting Geologist, as chairman to do an informal report on the water situation. Jack, with his assistants, Wally Gafner, resident, and Bill Austermiller, our security guard and maintenance supervisor, prepared the study. According to McCunn's report, five water well tests were drilled in the Subdivision. Three were at the same site as existing water well system. Two were located at Highway 332 and China Clipper. Of the five tests, only two wells were producing at the time of his study. There are two main aquifers in the Treasure Island area known as the upper and lower Chicot sandstone. The upper Chicot was producing at the time of the study at Treasure Island, providing water for KOA, Peregrine Apartment complex, Sy's Bait stand, and Rooster Collins's bait stand. These were shallow wells of approximately 300 feet. The lower Chicot produced water at Dr. Chunn's at a depth of approximately 600 feet. In July 1982, there

Ground Water and Equipment Barn[24]

were 126 water connections present, as surveyed by Wally Gafner and Jack McCunn. The small storage tank of 6,000 gallons was old and rusty. One alternative was to bring water across the San Luis Pass-Vacek Bridge from Galveston Island, but this proved too expensive and unrealistic.

A Ground Water and Water System Report was written for the TIMUD Board on August 7, 1982 by Dr. H. J. McCunn, (Consulting Geologist,) and Wm. (Bill) Austermiller, (Security and Maintenance). As a result of this report, a new storage tank was approved, and construction began. A 1,000-barrel tank was chosen which held 42,000 gallons. Construction of the new building was financed by H.J. (Jack) McCunn. Keeping in the spirit of San Luis, many of the neighbors got together and donated their time to raising the building as the islanders united to improve their home.

Chapter 9
Great Fishing & Hunting

Dr. Cliff Atwood red snapper

Hunter Reed's redfish

Bob Franklin - 9 pound 3 ounce flounder caught in October 2003.

Mickie McCunn with tarpon caught in San Luis Pass.

Robert Luke at 2003 San Luis Pass Tournament.

Richard Roe with 66 lb. warsaw grouper at 2005 San Luis Pass tournament.

Ronnie Reed the day after Hurricane Alicia in 1983.

Morning duck hunt at Treasure Island

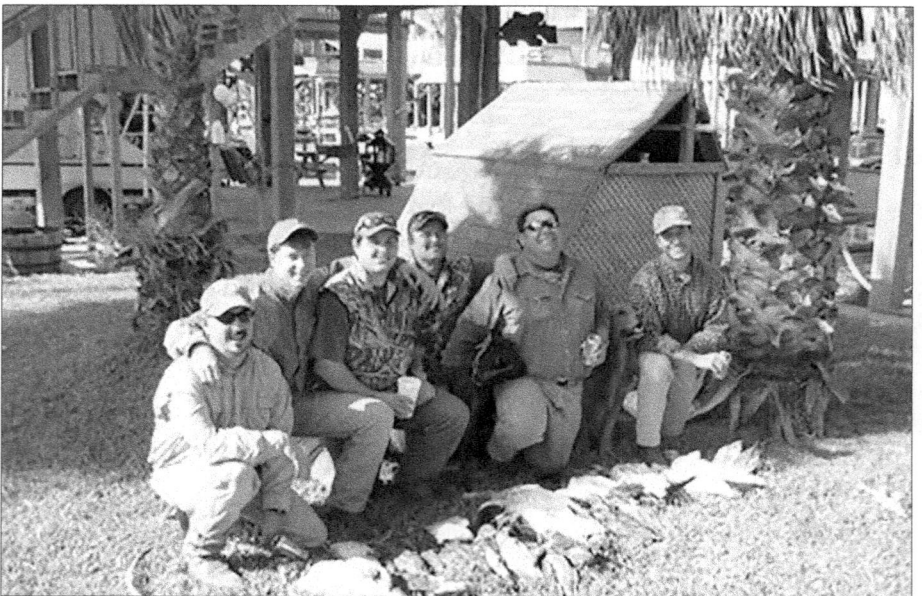

2005 duck hunt with Chuck Garrison, Matt Dennis, Brad Marsh, John Gann, Mike Ilenos, Ragen Stienke *Photo Gifted by John Gann*

Mark Hamilton, "The Wade Fisherman," with 30" speckled trout caught in July 2005 in San Luis Pass.

Isobel Herrod's 7 pound flouder with sister Jacqueline.

Eileen Wagner's Stringer

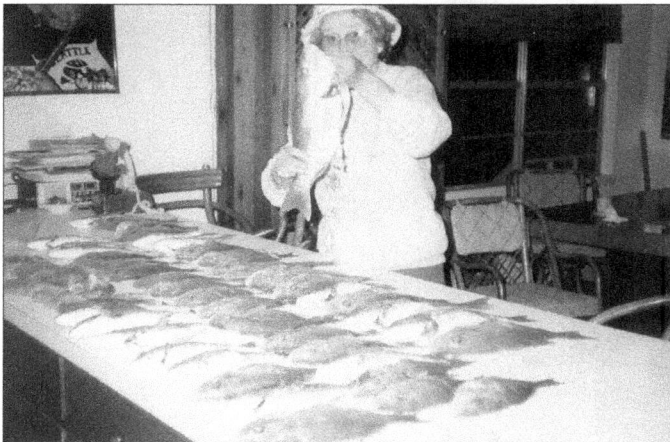

Marie Benitz with red snapper in 1991.

Ivan Boyd carries his son Zach and his morning catch from the surf.

Tony Lopez on July 22, 2004 at West Galveston Bay.

Jack and Hans Wagner

Chapter 10
Living Well

During the 1980s Treasure Island was well known throughout the region. Social and cultural development were in full swing through artwork and barbeques and San Luis even served a mystery film as a location for the feature film, *Fugitive Among Us*. From 1980 to 2008, there were eleven tropical depressions or hurricanes. Several caused severe erosion and damage. The community, once again, showed itself to be resilient; a determined group of board members and committee-men and women who would not be dissuaded, but rather strengthened through times of testing.

Lester Kamin, owner of the San Luis Pass Fishing Pier purchased Section 4 in 1983. He platted and mapped it. The area was never record-ed by the county after it was de-annexed. It was to have ten lots and five boat slips. Erosion took its toll before a bulkhead was built in 1992, when it was re-platted.

The reader will recall George (Buck) Hornback, the shrimper who owned the floating bait camp on Christmas Bay, and his wife Hazel.[2] If no one was at the bait camp, there was a coffee can in which to leave

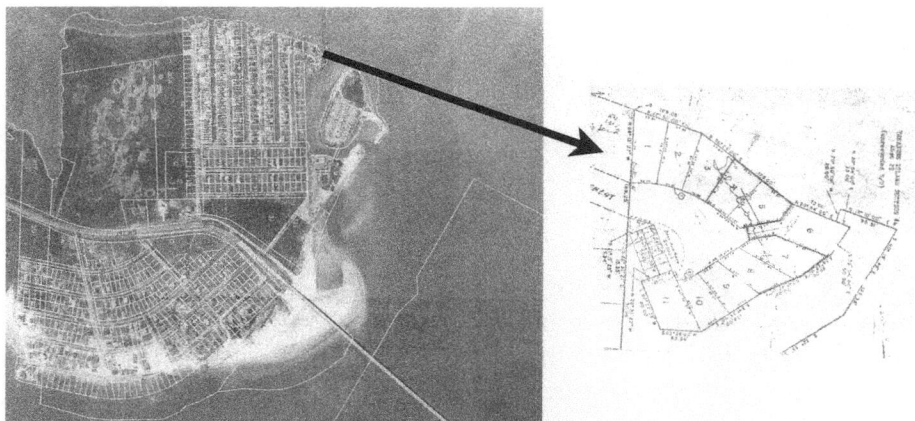

Lester Kamin File Sec IV[1]

237

Floating Bait Camp

Grandma at "Under-the-Bridge" party.[3]

Buck & Hazel[4]

one's money and help yourself to the bait. We would go by boat to their house on Bastrop Bayou for their annual crab, shrimp, and gumbo feast, "Under the Bridge." Buck would have twenty each forty-eight-quart coolers of cooked shrimp, twenty each forty-eight-quart coolers of cooked blue crabs, not to mention the stone crab claw coolers.

This was an amazing amount of seafood! "I-magin" was Buckaroo's famous reply to everything. Grandma stirred this gumbo pot with a two-by-four foot piece of wood, which she always laid back down on the ground. It took seventeen pounds of bacon to start her rue. In 1983, Hurricane Alicia left the floating bait camp high and dry. This was the end of a wonderful era.

Hurricane Alicia came ashore as a Category 3 Hurricane with the eye of the storm passing directly over San Luis Pass. With winds up to 127 miles per hour, gusts sustained at 115 miles per hour and a storm surge of water 12.1 feet, Alicia pummeled the island. The debris left on the southeast corner of the second floor wall of Lester Kamin's home measured twelve feet. More than 2,000 dwellings were destroyed between Surfside and Galveston, Texas. Seventeen people perished in the southeast Texas region.

The storm pushed up to five feet of sand inland and left several homes in front of the natural vegetation line. The Texas General Land Office red-tagged the homes and prohibited the repair or rebuilding of these homes, but not everyone complied. The San Luis Fishing Pier was destroyed again, and the buried car bodies were exposed. Damage was significant at Treasure Island. The "Davis" home, one block east of Gulf Beach Drive, which was built on pure sand, was totally destroyed. One dormer and doorknobs was all that remained.[5]

If a phone call had not been received from the author's father, Senator Max E. Benitz in Washington State advising us to contact FEMA (Federal Emergency Management Agency) immediately for assistance, we would have never known about the County Post Disaster meeting being held in Galveston. Mickie McCunn, Hortense Kamin, and the author went to Galveston where they were reluctantly allowed into the meeting. Mickie McCunn was president of the Treasure Island Municipal Utility District (TIMUD). Mickie was told San Luis was not "Incorporated" and did not qualify for FEMA support. Thankfully, she had all the proper documents with her to get into the meeting. We received monies from FEMA to clear the debris, and a permit from the Corps of Engineers to dredge the canals. Al Warrington later joined the group and helped finish the project.

A damaged house.

Wrecked shrimp boat at bridge.[6]

Mary Cannon said a Timex watch was found under the rafters of Bobby Lee's home, still running. Good watch!

Aid from the Red Cross quickly followed the disaster. A shrimp boat broke anchor and damaged the Vacek Bridge. Regretfully, residents were just about to finish paying for the cost of the bridge, and Galveston was going to remove the tolls. This was quite a setback as the tolls have continued ever since.

A four-by-eight foot piece of plywood stuck in the roof of a home like a toothpick. As the storm had completely covered our streets with sand, President Mickie McCunn hired a surveyor to relocate them. Just as they were cleared,

Hurricane Alicia took a heavy toll on the Bluewater Highway leading to the damaged bridge. The blacktop was picked up and moved sideways![7]

240

The left side of Paula Carroll's roof blew off and went through Brian Korshak's roof. It took a year for her son, Tom Carroll, to rebuild his mother's home.

another storm blew the sand right back over them again. Some houses were just simply "gone." The newly built condominiums were swept from their pilings. The remainder of the cement residue was finally removed from the beach after Hurricane Ike in 2008.

Though torn from their platforms, the condominiums were made of concrete and thus survived the storm. The twelve-foot wall of water picked them up and laid them on the ground with little harm to the structure. They were moved west on Follett's Island near Sy's Bait Camp and now have been relocated to Surfside.

Before the storm, San Luis Pass hugged the shoreline of San Luis Island. The position and depth of San Luis Pass' deep channel moves from the Galveston side to the San Luis Island side at will.

After the storm, the Kampground of America footbridge was

Sand on the roads.
Photos by Eileen M. Benitz Wagner

New Condo was gone with just the footings left after Hurricane Alicia.[9]

spared, but a great deal of land was lost. The Kampground of America buildings were severely damaged, leaving the property empty for a number of years. TIMUD had the opportunity to buy the property and buildings for $700,000, but declined. In February 1989, Fred Placke sold this property to Texas Parks and Wildlife. In turn, Texas Parks and Wildlife leased the land and building to Brazoria County where it now serves as a public RV Park.

A few permanent residents lived in trailer houses located at the KOA Park. During Hurricane Alicia in 1983, a couple from Sweden who had not evacuated sought safety in the KOA ladies bathroom. Sitting at sea level, they must have had a terrible experience riding out the storm, listening to the pounding surf, howling wind and the rising tide. The trailer houses ended up in our third canal, and Trotter's Lagoon opened at the east end to San Luis Pass.

Adding to the difficult weather, there were two hard freezes during winter 1982 into spring of 1983, and again in the winter of 1983. Freezes killed what remained of the landscaping after Hurricane Alicia. Christmas Bay froze on the edges, resulting in a huge fish kill. Large trout lay dead, floating in the canals. Many years passed before normal quantities of fish returned.

As the young community struggled to become a strong resort subdivision, committees were formed to bring everyone together. As chairman of the Beautification Committee, the author employed her cousin, Clifton Benitz in Kansas. He sandblasted redwood planks to create the

A shrimp boat broke anchor and drifted ashore near Surfside, where it sat for many months.[10]

San Luis Pass shows deep channel on Treasure Island side.[11]

following design for the new entrance signs. After extensive research, flagpoles were purchased and placed at each entrance. The final step was to locate palm trees and oleanders for our boulevards and streets.

The Treasure Island flags have a story of their own. The United States flag was flown over the United States Capital at the request of the author's father, Washington State Senator Max. E. Benitz, and the Texas flag was flown over the Texas Senate Building at the request of Congressman Ron Paul. Hurricane Alicia shredded the two flags and braided them together so tightly that no human hands could untie them.

Hurricane Alicia did considerable damage and construction had to begin again. Construction for the first store and bait camp built on the island since the 1840s began in early 1983 by Tom Bright. Janice Ramey and Tom Bright were always a pleasure to see when we stopped by. It was great having our own store. Our only other choice before Hurricane Alicia was to go to the Kampground of America, which had a retail store and gasoline for sale that they never reopened. Tom Bright and Johnny Calzada were always great hosts for a Saturday night par-

New Entrance Signs[12]

ty. Tom's son, Don Bright, is currently the owner and manager of the store.

The storms made the community strong and brought everyone together as neighbors who not only looked out for each other but enjoyed being together. I gave a party for the entire neighborhood in 1985. It was named "Beast Feast," because everything that we cooked was caught fresh from the sea or from our hunting lease. Serving began at 4:30 p.m. and finished with the last entrée at 8:30 p.m. Obviously this was a feast! The menu was elk, deer and long horned steer, as well as bear,

Memories of Eileen Benitz Wagner

Jack McCunn retrieved the braided flags. Later while visiting him, he gave them to me. It was my mother, Marie Benitz, who had said, "Give me those flags. We need to save those flags." I did save those flags. They are mounted on acid free linen in a shadow box frame as a reminder of the strength of nature's force. The cost to have this done was just under $1,000. Photographer J. Stern Ueckert of The *Houston Chronicle*, snapped this photo just as the flags began to shred, during Hurricane Alicia's approach. Ueckert named his photo "Alicia's Fury." Ueckert was the official photographer for the cook-off some time later. When he saw the picture framed and hanging on my beach house wall he said "I took that photo." I quickly took it off the wall and asked him to sign it.

244

Tom Bright and Johnny Calzada[13]

Flags during Hurricane Alicia.[14]

wild goose, wild duck, ring-necked pheasant and quail. Also served were salmon, halibut, speckled trout, flounder, shrimp, stuffed shrimp, oysters, king fish, blue crab, and stone crabs, creating a total of twenty-six entrées with all the condiments for each dish. Some of the guests ate so much they had to go home and rest before the cooking was finished and served.

Many nights we would fish together until morning. The chlorophyll-florescence found in plankton would be so thick that we could write our name in the water with the tip of the fishing pole. It is awesome to be near the surf and watch the waves crashing to shore full of florescence.

Residents would soon have to remember that the beauty of the sea is worth its temper as another storm hit.

Lester Kamin owned most of the Point in Section IV. When the Kampground of America was de-annexed, this section was not 're-incorporated' in the master plat of Treasure Island. The residents do pay taxes, but by law, are not required to pay maintenance fees. Everyone does pay

Section IV[17]

fees though. After tremendous erosion, this section was re-platted.

June 26th, 1986: Bonnie made landfall along the upper coast on the 26th. Jefferson County Airport had gusts of wind up to seventy-five mph, while Sabine Pass reported gusts to ninety-seven mph at the Coast Guard station near Sea Rim State Park. Debris littered the streets of Port Arthur and Beaumont. High winds ripped roofs off numerous homes and businesses. Tractor-trailer rigs were flipped over. Highway 87 was closed, due to fallen power poles, early on the 26th. Several aircraft were damaged at area airports. Winds in Sam Rayburn Reservoir caused $1 million in damage to boats and marinas.[16]

Notice the deep channels of San Luis Pass in this 1988 GLO Aerial photograph.[17] This configuration is subject to change at the whim of Mother Nature.

From the early years of Treasure Island, the meetings of the TIMUD board and the Civic Association were held in someone's home. In In 1988, Jim Deaton built the first community building at 146 Fathom Drive on land donated by Al Warrington. The facility saw an addition in May 2003 to accommodate growth. Almost every weekend, everyone would get together and cook food ranging from shrimp boil, crab boil, crawfish boil, and fried fish, some to the most elegant of prepara-

The 1988 GLO Photo

tions. It was normal for guests to begin to arrive at 3 p.m. or 4 p.m. in the afternoon and have thirty guests for dinner. What a fun day it was when the *Houston Chronicle*, July 27, 1988 featured the talents of Treasure Island![19] This was a Sunday feature story. We had so many excellent cooks, and the food was fabulous! This particular event was a "community" event.

In scope and power, Tropical Storm Allison stole the show early in

Feature story in the *Houston Chronicle* on Weekend Potluck.[18]

the season, producing over thirty inches of rain and severe flooding in extreme southeast Texas. Damage from Allison totaled $500 million, also putting it on the list of the nation's most damaging storms. Hurricane Chantal hit High Island, on the Bolivar Peninsula on the extreme eastern edge of Galveston County on August 1, 1989. It was an unusual storm as the strongest winds were on its western semi-circle. Hurricane Jerry crossed the east end of Galveston Island on October 15th through the 16th. Hurricanes Chantal and Jerry combined created damages totaling $170 million. Eleven died during Allison, thirteen during Chantal, and three during Jerry. - NOAA

Our claim to fame in 1991 was the movie *Fugitive Among Us*. Using the Zalenski home, the movie had scenes filmed at Jolly Roger Drive and Gulf Beach Drive on Treasure Island. It was directed by Lili Fini Zanuck. The story was about two small town Texas policemen, going undercover to catch a major drug runner and ending up getting drawn into the drug culture.

The ever-shrinking shoreline, along which Gulf Drive runs, is next to impossible to stop. In 1991, Ramona Darden, then president of the TIMUD, ordered emergency repairs to the shore following Hurricanes Michelle and Tropical Storm Allison. Heavy rocks were placed on the Gulf side of Treasure Island, as seen on Gulf Beach Drive, to try to stop the erosion. Next, hay bales were placed along the frontage of San Luis Pass. Needless to say, that did not work.

This photograph gives the reader an idea of the damage acquired from storms and erosion. Efforts to save Gulf Drive still present a challenge today.

Fresh Water

On January 10, 1992, San Luis finally had fresh water that drained from Lake Houston and flowed to Galveston. From Galveston, the water lines then went west down the Island to the Vacek Bridge and

The barriers made from hay bales proved as ineffective as the car bodies, though they were much safer for the environment.[19]

onward to Treasure Island. Alfred C. Warrington, IV, known to most of us as Al, was responsible for getting all permits and approvals from the state of Texas to bring fresh drinking water to our community. Harold Pfeiffer and Tom Carroll designed the hardware to attach to the San Luis Pass bridge to bring water from Galveston. Tom built all of the brackets and supplied the pipe for the project. Finally, no more rusty water.

Lots number four and five in Section IV became available for purchase in 1992. The author persuad-

Memories of Eileen Benitz Wagner

I decided to gift the land to Treasure Island Municipal District to be a park in honor of my mother, Marie Benitz, for all of Treasure Island residents to enjoy. In 1995, the gift was accepted, but the officers of the TIMUD board sold the property for quite a hefty profit without even considered using the gift for the community. Too bad!

Even though the park I envisioned never took shape, the island is full of other interesting features. The *Dolphin on its Tail* and *Nessie*—short for Loch Ness Monster—were Jim Fulmore's artistic works that brought pleasure to thousands of tourists along *Bluewater Highway*. Fulmore created these masterpieces in May 1996.[23] The bodies were driftwood with concrete used to form the head, teeth, and scales, etc. Time and storms took their toll, and the artwork is no longer with us.

Park envisioned by Eileen Wagner in memory of her mother, Marie Benitz.[20]

Artwork on Blue Water Highway.[21]

Clowning Around[24]
Photo by Eileen Benitz Wagner

ed Houston Lighting & Power to run transmission lines underground. It was my dream to build a home there, but as tensions grew with an unruly neighbor and personal health problems.

Various talents of the residents help comprise our way of life into unique adventures. Treasure Island has its very own "Clown," Miss Billie Redinger, who entertains for all the community picnics.

Wade fisherman Reggie Corley can read the surf faster than anyone. If he says the fish are there, they're there! If not, he moves on until the time is right. One night Reggie took the author's two grandsons, Max and Zach and myself to the surf, just under the Vacek Bridge at about midnight. The moon was so full that headlights were not needed. He had a small seine with which to make half circles from the bank and brought back huge white shrimp with each pull. A forty-gallon cooler was

Max C. Boyd shows off his shrimp catch.
Photo by Eileen Benitz Wagner

filled to the top in thirty minutes! If a shrimp gets caught on land with no water it will bury itself in the sand until the next wave comes. Then it will resurface and go back to sea. What a treat to watch![25]

Though the pipes from Galveston helped conquer the difficulty in gaining fresh water, a water-waste treatment plant threatened the health of the island. The following quote by neighbor Patricia C. Newsom recalls:

In the middle 1990's a waste water treatment plant (WWTP) was proposed by TI Municipal Utility District (TIMUD) to the property owners. One of the TIMUD directors said that he knew the developer who had purchased the Louis Pauls property. The developer would deed several acres of his property to the subdivision upon which the district would place the proposed WWTP. In consideration for the donation of the land and resurfacing TI's roads into his project, the developer would connect to the district's waste water treatment plant and the potable waterlines. There was no other cost to this developer to hookup to Treasure Island utilities. After two years of protesting by a majority of the property owners at numerous utility district meetings, which included environmental damage to our bay system should the plant fail, the property owners voted to change the utility district board members. Unknown to the property owners, the Executive Director of the Texas Natural Resource Conservation Commission had already recommended the denial of the current application for a WWTP permit. An Administrative hearing by the state of Texas, Docket No. 582-97-1392, TNRCC Docket No. 97-0724-MWD, postponed the issuance of

Occasionally a Blue Norther and a low tide combination will draw all the water out of our canals, and this very thing happened on December 30, 1997. It was quite a sight to see! View of Canal A & B.[22]

the necessary permit. Then, after several meetings of the new TIMUD directors, the application for a WWTP permit was withdrawn......... the project failed.

The original plan was for the developer, who happened to be only a "trustee," to develop 30 one acre residential lots. In my research at the county, if you have water and sewage hookups, you only need ⅓ acre for a residential lot. After the waste water treatment plant was built, the developer would go back and subdivide the original 30 one acre lots to 90 one-third acre residential lots. The profits would have been huge.

If TIMUD had been successful, the property owners would have been in debt for between 2 to 3 million dollars for the relocation and renovations of an old out-of-date plant that would be purchased from Brazoria County for the cost of $1. The cost for laying sewer lines had not even been discussed.

The trustee and his unnamed developers/investors would be rich and TI property owners would have a multi-million dollar debt hanging around their necks. Hurricane Ike passed though our neighborhood in September 2008. Little Pass tried to reopen its natural route, which is located in the area where the waste water treatment plant would have been located. The storm blew out the beach, sand dunes, part of the county highway and, if constructed, the waste water treatment plant...No land - no plant and a huge environmental disaster surrounding an entire community of private homes which would suddenly become uninhabitable.

Though this disaster was avoided, it was not long before Tropical Storm Frances also added its mark onto the map.

September 10th-14th, 1998: On the 7th, an area of disturbed weather formed in the Central Gulf of Mexico. It was complex, with a broad area of low pressure, induced by a nearby upper low to the west of the circulation. Strong easterly winds had barely relaxed after Charley, which had just made landfall in Texas, before re-developing. Air Force aircraft investigated the system on the 8th, and a tropical depression was found 220 miles southeast of Corpus Christi. It moved

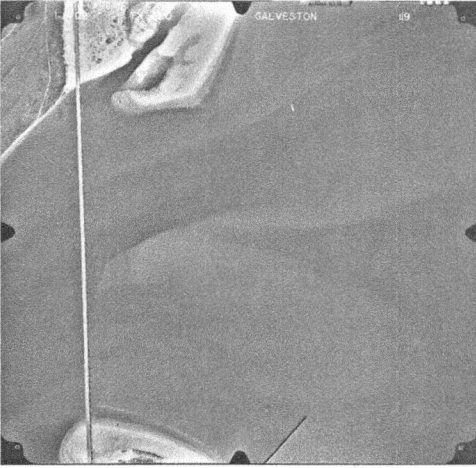

GLO Aerial - August 8, 2002[23]

very little over the next twenty-four hours, slowly strengthening into Hurricane Frances by the 9th. Strong winds along the Louisiana and Texas increased, resulting in a large area of coastal flooding. The system strengthened and moved north as feeder bands moved inland. The deluge caused a large area of ten inches or more of rain across south Louisiana and east Texas. The highest rainfall in Texas was 17 inches at Matagorda Colorado Locks. San Luis pier was damaged.

NOAA(History of Texas Hurricanes-David Roth)

The island changes every time a storm hits. This aerial photo shows Galveston's west end and San Luis Pass, as well as the tip of Treasure Island on August 8, 2002. The main channel of San Luis Pass had shifted more toward the Galveston side. A cross reference of a photo taken in 1954, shows a land mass on the Galveston side which looks as if a smiling face is shaped in the sand. The 2002 aerial shows a similar face about to appear. History seems to be repeating itself in this photo, reminding us all of San Luis's past.

Chapter 11
Hurricanes, Erosion - Resort Community's Survival

The history of San Luis has been marked by a pattern of development by mankind and destruction by nature. Shipwrecks and pier demolition were amongst the troubles left by five hurricanes from 1980 to 1989. This constant battle to build and rebuild has shown the true colors of its residents as either proud and courageous or dumb and defiant!

Over the years in San Luis Pass, there have been at least thirty-one known recordings of sunken ships. The following information has been provided to the author by Steve Hoyt, marine archaeologist for the Texas Historical Commission. This information is protected under the Texas Public Information Act and may only be accessed through inquiry. The report given to me covers waters within a one-mile radius of the mouth of San Luis Pass.

Although not listed, we also know that the *Lafitte* sank in the pass after the ship was overloaded. In addition, a letter by Joseph Boswell Follett notes eleven schooners, including his own *Lucille* that sank during the Storm of 1900.

In 1987, several friends and I found a portion of a wrecked ship's hull, half-buried in the sand near the Vacek Bridge. A few days later, marine archaeologists from Texas A&M University came to document the main support beam. The archaeologists informed us that the boat could not be from the 1800s, since not all of the iron pegs were hand hewn. The mystery vessel must be from the early 1900s. We speculated that we had found a victim of the great storm.

Several months later, on February 1, 1991, I experienced what it was like to be on a sinking vessel. My mother and I were guests of a friend for a red snapper fishing excursion into the Gulf of Mexico. Our yacht, the *Meaner Marie*, hit the jetties at Galveston, ripping the entire forward port side open. Here's how The *Houston Chronicle* article began the next morning:

$1 million yacht sinks; all six on board are safe.
February 1, 1991, an exceptionally warm day, three men and three women set
course from the Galveston Yacht Basin in a 57 foot Yacht to Red Snapper fish.
With a fine day of fishing and all ice chests full to the top, the yacht headed for
port.

My late mother, Mrs. Marie Benitz, and I recall the story well. As we returned to port we neared the Galveston jetties at dusk, still feeling very warm with quiet seas. I went topside to chat with the owner and the captain. About that time, I noticed a grey line in the water. I asked the captain, "What was that gray line we just crossed?" The next moment we came to an instant stop from twenty-two knots! I will never forget watching all the instruments and wiring harnesses go flying through the air. I was holding onto the rail and remember how the muscles in my chest came away from my rib cage.

The captain yelled for me to go below and see if anyone was hurt. As I entered the lounge, I saw an extremely heavy picnic table had tipped over, and my mother trapped beneath.

"What happened?" She asked, before admitting, "I think my legs are broken."

I yelled to the captain that we had a huge gaping hole in the forward port side, and water was coming in very fast. I told him to call the Coast Guard and to tell me where the life jackets were. He came down from above and started handing out life jackets. I grabbed one for mother, knowing that she did not swim, but the rotting strap fell apart as I latched it. I did the best that I could to secure mother's life jacket and then ran back top side. The captain had gone forward outside the cabin decking to get the hard dingy. He yelled for me to get him a knife, because the straps were rusted in place, preventing him from freeing the dingy. We had hit the tip of the granite jetties and were stuck on the rocks. The captain then went back to the helm and put the engines in reverse. We looked like a fireboat the way the water was spewing so high. As we were beginning to break loose from the rocks, the yacht tilted into steep list. Water lapped near the salon in the cabins. One of the rubber life rafts inflated, but the other failed. Each life raft could hold only three people. I shouted that we needed to get off, and now!

The captain got off first in the hard dingy. His girlfriend was next. The situation had grown serious by then, and I asked my mother to slide down the aft of the yacht into the one good rubber raft. She was so afraid that she refused. So the paying male guest slid down the aft into the rubber raft and asked that mom come next. Oh no, she would still not do it! So I slid down and into the raft and then mother slid into my arms. We took on water in the raft, and we were now sitting about six inches out of the water. The owner, who also could not swim, was still on board. I yelled for him to throw some flares down to me. He found a box on deck and tossed it into the lifeboat. Then he slid down the side into the hard dingy with the captain. I shouted for everyone to try to get the two lifeboats together. The yacht lay close to her side and would go down soon, leaving us stranded with one oar for each boat.

As we drew close to each other, I called for someone to light one of the flares. When one of the men opened the flare and tossed the cap into the water, I almost choked, realizing that he had thrown away the striker. The second flare did not work at all. I opened the box the owner had tossed to me, discovering that it was a socket set, not a flare. By then it was nearly dark. We had drifted into the middle of the ship channel, and a shrimp boat was headed straight toward us!

"For sure, I think we are going to be killed now!"

The yacht started popping with sparks as the batteries and electrical went under water. The entire sequence of events had happened in twelve minutes. The ship sank from view. The paying guest had called a Mayday. A helicopter and a Coast Guard rescue boat were sent for us. After we were retrieved, truly looking like a group straight from the *Gilligan's Island* series, we were taken to Galveston's world famous John Sealy Hospital. Despite the catastrophe, everyone checked out un-

Author's photo of a Shell Cloud, taken from her front porch in San Luis.

scathed.

A storm hit that night, and *Meaner Marie* was never seen again. Weather often changes as quickly as a ship can sink. Billowing clouds can roll in, providing a spectacular show.

As the past two centuries stand witness, weather at San Luis Pass is very unpredictable and can bring severe destruction.[3] On many occasions, we can watch a storm front suddenly arrive with wind gusts of cold air driving the rain sideways. The temperature can drop thirty to forty degrees in seconds. It can get scary, really fast! Funnels form quickly, dropping from the clouds!

Fog can also move into the area very quickly, sometimes making it impossible to see your hand in front of your face. I recall one evening in the mid-1980s when Johnny Calzada and Dr. Cliff Atwood were fishing in the Bay that the fog suddenly really socked in. We all rushed to the end of the canals with our car headlights on, honking our horns, hoping to guide them out of danger. With no radios on board, they became so turned around that they completely lost their way. About 3 a.m., the fog lifted slightly and the two men safely found Treasure Island.

The blue-black clouds of a cold front streak down from the north, creating what is popularly known as a "Norther." The land mass of South Central Texas above us to the North consists of thousands of miles of flat prairie with no hills or mountains. In short, there are no

The Sky is Falling[1]

Brazoria County Emergency Management[2]

natural barriers between us and the Arctic Circle to slow down the speed of an Arctic weather front. It's 'Katy bar the door,' when a front chooses to move south.

During July 8-17, 2003, NOAA Weather reported Hurricane Claudette, as a Category 1 hurricane. It came ashore at Port O'Conner, Texas with sustained winds of 85 miles per hour. Though this was not a direct hit for Treasure Island, we received high water on both the bay side as well as the Gulf of Mexico. Debris is always a huge problem following a storm. Rattlesnakes also present a hazard, because they are washed out of their normal habitat and usually climb onto the stairs of our homes to seek protection from the rising water. Small animals and varmints are similarly displaced. The coyotes swim quite well though, and it does not take long time for them to return.

GLO 2003 Aerial Photo July 27, 2003[3]

258

The hurricane destroyed San Luis Pass Fishing Pier again. The decking ended up traveling north to the San Luis Pass Park parking lot. The damaged pier house and restaurant were removed and rebuilt. A temporary office was brought in to accommodate patrons and fishermen. The next big storm washed the trailer house office out to sea in March of 2007. At this point, the damaged remaining portions of the pier house were removed. Erosion to the septic tank and a lack of fresh water finally closed the pier house and restaurant for the last time. Crews were brought to remove the final pilings from San Luis Pass during the summer of 2010, and the ocean was returned to the same state as when San Luis Island was discovered. The road to the pier is covered with sand, and its path now stands empty.

As noted earlier, during the mid-1960s over two hundred car bodies were placed from the location of the present day County Park, to the South end of San Luis Pass. Many of these buried north of the San Luis Pass Fishing Pier became exposed after Claudette. The storms also take a toll on the frontage road, creating a constant struggle to keep Gulf Beach Drive passable. In recent years, more environmental-friendly attempts have been employed against the erosion problem.

The September 1998 tropical storm Frances washed away the hay bale erosion protection project constructed on our beaches. During discussions with FEMA, TI resident Patricia C Newsom, mitigated the hay bale project to a new type of shoreline stabilization program referred to as geotextile tubes. Ge-

Pier House/Office is gone.[4]

Gertrude Toro with car bodies.
Photo by Eileen Benitz Wagner

otextile tubes are made of permeable fabric filled with a sand/water slush. Ms Newsom made application for this new program to Brazoria County and received the "first permit" issued in the State of Texas to place geotextile tubes on our beaches. With her help, the Office of Emergency Management in Galveston secured their permit to place geotextile tubes on their beaches - over 7 miles on Port Bolivar and several miles on West Galveston Island. Many of TI beach side home-owners were very supportive of this project, while other concerned home-owners in Treasure Island, including Dr. H.J. McCunn, a geologist, did not approve of the tube project. As hurricane Claudette came on shore in July of 2003, the storm waters carried debris, including sharp objects, which pierced and deflated the geotextile tubes. This was a short term and very expensive project, and sadly, little was left of the geotextile tubes project after hurricane Claudette.[5]

Barnacle-covered logs and debris shredded the tubes before they could stop the onslaught of the tidal surge from the storm. Below are

Geotubes Before and After the Storm[6]

260

Erosion at the Hal Hudson/ Guiberson home.[7]

photographs of the geotubes, showing them before and after the storm.

I believe this photo just about says it all as to the fact that what Mother Nature wants, she takes! However, Mother Nature is not always cruel. She often gives beautiful days and colorful sunsets. On Christmas Eve, 2004, she sent a complete surprise.[12] A rare "White Christmas," with record totals of snowfall and cold temperatures, was brought to the Texas Gulf Coast and Rio Grande Valley across deep

In our traditional island spirit, we celebrated our snowy shores with a snowman and Shiner Beer.[8]

South Texas on Friday, December 24th, 2004. Saturday's Christmas Day total in Galveston was the largest snowfall recorded in the area since precise record keeping began in 1947. Corpus Christi, with 4.4 inches, broke the old record of 4.3 inches set on February 14, 1895. Victoria, with eleven inches, had its first White Christmas since 1918!

Snow Totals	
Brazoria:	13 inches
Ganado	12"
Victoria	11"
Beelville	10"
Bay City	8-10"
El Campo	7"
Rockport	6"
Hebbronville	5"
Galveston	4"
McAllen	3.5"
Pearland	2"
Brownsville	1.5"
Missouri City	1"
Anahuac	Less than 1/2"

Source: National Weather Service

The excitement spread throughout the coast, which received various amounts of snow. Detailed records reflect the different depths.

The snow quickly melted, leaving fond memories and photographs that residents still pull off the shelf and share.

The erosion and storms reshaped the island. This General Land Office aerial photo from 2007, shows that Galveston Island's west end had became "blunt," again, resembling the maps from the early 1900s. The deep channel of San Luis Pass currently runs all the way toward the Galveston side.

Canal "A" looking South and West[9]

Texas General Land Office 2007 Aerial Photo

Though the storms are normally to blame for destroying buildings, the toll booth of Vacek bridge met a far different fate.[18] A car collided with the toll booth one summer afternoon in July, 2008, destroying the structure. Can one even imagine being the toll collector inside, when it was struck with such force it that had to be completely demolished and rebuilt? I captured the final demolition of the booth nearly forty-two years after it was built.

During the summer of 2008, we prepared for *four hurricanes!* On July 23rd, Hurricane Dolly spared the three "in the ocean" homes on Treasure Island's Gulf Beach Drive standing, as shown in the following picture. On August 3rd, Hurricane Edouard developed as an Atlantic tropical storm in the northeastern Gulf of Mexico. It made landfall on

Toll Booth Destruction[10]

August 5th, east northeast of Treasure Island near Port Arthur where it was downgraded to a strong tropical storm. Then on September 1st, Hurricane Gustav made a morning landfall near Grand Isle, Louisiana, too far away to pose a serious threat to Treasure Island.

The next hurricane was not so kind. On September 13th, Hurricane Ike hit Galveston around midnight. Ike came on shore as a Category 2 hurricane, with winds of 110 miles per hour. Located at Latitude 28.60 and Longitude 94.40 with pressure measured at 952, it made a direct hit on the Bolivar Peninsula just east of Galveston. The flood level reached was considered a Category 4. The water began to rise two days prior to Ike's landing. Once on shore, the waves added to the huge rise in water. It had been just twenty-five years since Hurricane Alicia came on shore as a direct hit at San Luis Pass.

Even the seventeen foot tall Galveston Seawall could not stop Ike's high waters from the back bay. Individual shops at Galveston's famed Strand district had as much as eight feet of water standing on their floors. Treasure Island could not find a waterline, but it was estimated to be between nine and a half to twelve feet. An upside down boat on "Bluewater Highway" at the entrance of Treasure Island was from Louisiana! San Luis Island was on the left side of the eye of Ike. The winds are from NW to SE caused an Ekman Current. "Steady winds blowing on the sea surface produce a thin, horizontal boundary layer, the *Ekman layer*.[11] The "Norther" cold front the following day added to the push of debris to the South, which may explain why two hundred boats ended up in Mexico, including the author's.

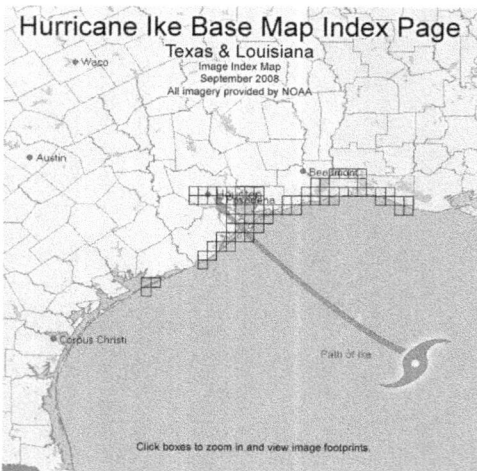

Map of Hurricane Ike's path.[12]

When Gulf Beach Drive was platted a full row of lots were seaward of the street, where many homes were built along the oceanfront. One by one, they are disappearing. One was lost to a fire, the others taken by storms. Recently, we had only three homes still standing along Gulf Beach Drive, two of which stand on piers which are immersed. Hurricane Ike left only two still standing. On the upside, Hurricane Ike solved the problem of being in front of the vegetation line, at least for

Ocean side of Gulf Beach Drive with three houses standing.[13]

one homeowner.

Another landmark which was swept away was the second set of entrance signs of TIMUD. Our first TIMUD entrance signs had been a community effort in 1983. Its art design was created by long-time resident Brian Korshack, and the sand blasted Redwood Planks street signs were prepared by Evean Benitz of St. Joseph, Missouri.

When a car accident took out the Bayside sign, as Chairman of the "sign committee," (a committee of one) the author had designed a new entrance sign to add to the charm of Treasure Island. Construction had just completed when the hurricane came on shore.

The sign from the Gulf of Mexico side found its way to Padre Island, where a group of Texas A&M students discovered the treasure of their lives. Sure enough, it was the new Treasure Island entrance sign! These young students were kind enough to return the wayward sign. We say "Thank you!"

Of the two hundred and twenty homes at Treasure Island, only two were completely washed away. Though every life was spared, there was great loss of infrastructure. The "Bluewater Highway" had been fourteen miles long, stretching from Surfside to the San Luis Pass-Va-

Erosion Gulf Beach Drive
Photo by Eileen Benitz Wagner

cek Bridge. Approximately four miles of the road was washed away. Estimates for reconstruction ran as much as $100 million.

The only way to get to Treasure Island from Brazoria County was to drive what became known as the "Pig Trail," along the beach, then through the marsh and maybe back on a little bit of blacktop in places.

With the power poles laying on the ground and the utility cables exposed, electricity took two months to be restored. Right-of-ways were relocated and makeshift roads reestablished. Richard Gaido worked for Galveston Center Point Energy which was one of the first utility companies to assess the damage at Treasure Island on October 4, 2008. Many homes along the Gulf Coast barely escaped collapse. Some were leaning at angles so severe that one wondered how they still stood, while others were gone altogether.

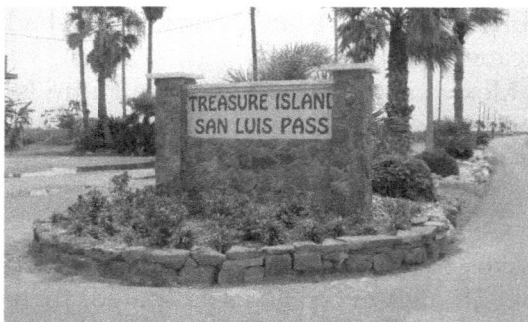

New Entrance Signs
Design by Eileen Benitz Wagner

The "bridge" that carried the motor homes and

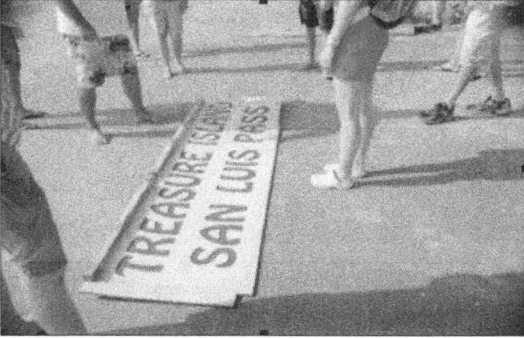

Padre Island and our sign.[14]

campers to the County Park at San Luis Pass was ripped apart and slammed into my neighbor's home.[25] The timbers were around eight inches by thirty inches and twenty feet long. The amount of debris was huge. Anyone could clearly see that it would take house moving equipment to remove or demolish the bridge.

The equipment barn and pump house were destroyed. No utilities of any type were available. Jim Coursey, manager of Treasure Island Resort Community, and Bill Jones, security guard, spent endless hours and months working on the clean up and restoration.

Hurricane Alicia in 1983 had cut an opening in Trotter's Lagoon to San Luis Pass. The sand nearly refilled the lagoon by November 16, 2008, resembling its natural state before the dredge work of 1971. Note the mud that left the canals with the outgoing tide and exit of Hurricane Ike!

Bliewater Highway destroyed again and telephone cables exposed again.
Photo by Eileen Benitz Wagner

267

Brazoria County Park bridge stuck under a house.
Photo by Eileen M. Benitz Wagner

Texas General Land photo Ike mud coming from canals.

Little Pass is nearly cut back open in this Texas General Land Office Aerial of Ike.

Little pass maybe photo by Eileen

Here, a photo of what Little Pass must have looked like when it flowed freely. We had an unusually high tide, a north wind and a full moon on May 6, 2007. For certain, if "Bluewater Highway" were not there, Little Pass would have opened again.

An aerial photo displaying the tremendous amount of erosion at San Luis Island. The erosion has devoured the entire front row of lots on Gulf Beach Drive. Two other factors contributing to this erosion are the jetties at Surfside and the redirecting of the Mouth of the Brazos River. Both have caused the currents to change their path, resulting in erosion of the shoreline, as well as San Luis Island.

History repeats itself, reminding us of past events. One hundred and seventy years after John Bradbury Follett built his first home on Galveston's West End, the Pointe West Beach Resort broke ground in 2005, launching a spectacular resort at San Luis Pass. Pointe West offers a zero line swimming pool, fine dining, exquisite condos and stand-alone single-family homes.

2006 Aerial Erosion - Brazoria County Tax Office

Point West Galveston Island, Texas[15]

Make No Mistake !

San Luis Pass

Has

Very dangerous currents

The Tidal Water moves very fast and with strong undertows.

Many lives have been lost at San Luis Pass.

Be Careful, if the water begins to move, get out!

Eileen M Benitz Wagner

Whether it's a relaxing resort, a simple pier, or a large gumbo shared by neighbors, the spirit of San Luis Island can be summarized by one photo.[16]

This image just about says it all: A cork screw wine opener hanging from a deer antler, a fishing line, and a leisurely Blue Heron, characteristically standing on one leg, overlooking calm seas. Always remember that a bright shining new day waits at San Luis Pass.[17]

Known Sunken Ships Off San Luis

Ship: *Laura R. Burnham* **Official Number:** 15962
Date Lost: November 10, 1883 **Vessel Type:** Sailing Ship, Merchant
Sailing Rig: bark **Flag:** USA
Length: Unknown **Beam:** Unknown **Tons:** 673.0
Cargo: Coal **Cause of Loss:** Unknown
Source: *National Archives (NARA), RG 26, USCG, #89, Table of Casualty Reports from Life Saving Stations, 1876-1914, Annual Reports, US Life Saving Service San Luis Station, west end Galveston Is., 3.5 miles SW of station. Owned Boston, Mass by Nickerson, 673"*

Ship: *Jennie S. Butler* **Official Number:** Unknown
Date Lost: March 22, 1900 **Vessel Type:** Sailing Ship, Merchant
Sailing Rig: Schooner **Flag:** USA
Length: Unknown **Beam:** Unknown **Tons:** 943
Cargo: Coal **Cause of Loss:** Unknown
Source: *Lonsdale, Adrian L. and Kaplan, H.R., Guide to Sunken Ships in American Waters, 1964. p. 95. 29 03.2, 95 07.1. Schooner, 943 tons. Wrecked March 22, 1900 with cargo of coal.*

Ship: *Joe M.* **Official Number:** Unknown
Date Lost: March 9, 1960 **Vessel Type:** Unknown
Sailing Rig: Unknown **Flag:** USA
Length: Unknown **Beam:** Unknown **Tons:** 67
Cargo: Unknown **Cause of Loss:** Foundered
Source: *Berman, Bruce D. Encyclopedia of American Shipwrecks. The Mariners Press Nc., 1972. p. 175*

Ship: *Columbia* **Official Number:** Unknown
Date Lost: April 5, 1862 **Vessel Type:** Sailing Ship, Merchant
Sailing Rig: Schooner **Flag:** Confederacy
Length: Unknown **Beam:** Unknown **Tons:** Unknown
Cargo: Cotton **Cause of Loss:** Hostile Action
Source: *Shomette, Donald C., Shipwrecks of the Civil War, An Encyclopedia of Union and Confederate Losses. Donic Ltc. Washington D.C. San Luis Pass, schooner captured and destroyed by Union forces. Cargo of cotton.*

Ship: *Rattler* **Official Number:** 56328
Date Lost: November 15, 1874 **Vessel Type:** Sailing Ship, Merchant
Sailing Rig: Schooner **Flag:** USA
Length: Unknown **Beam:** Unknown **Tons:** 14
Cargo: Lumber **Cause of Loss:** Grounded
Source: *National Archives (NARA), Records of the US Custom Service, RG 39, Wreck Report, P. 2, November 15 1874. Cargo of lumber. Anchor chain parted at night and she drifted ashore. Total loss.*

Ship: *Reindeer* **Official Number:** Unknown
Date Lost: October 3, 1861 **Vessel Type:** Sailing Ship. Merchant
Sailing Rig: Schooner **Flag:** Confederacy
Length: Unknown **Beam:** Unknown **Tons:** 4
Cargo: Salt **Cause of Loss:** Hostile Action
Source: *Shomette, Donald C., Shipwrecks of the Civil War, An Encyclopedia of Union and Confederate Losses. Donic Ltc. Washington D.C. San Luis Pass, schooner captured and sunk by Union forces. 4 tons, cargo of salt.*

Ship: *Rosina* **Official Number:** Unknown
Date Lost: April 13, 1864 **Vessel Type:** Sailing Ship, Merchant
Sailing Rig: Sloop **Flag:** Confederacy
Length: Unknown **Beam:** Unknown **Tons:** Unknown
Cargo: Unknown **Cause of Loss:** Hostile Action
Source: *Shomette, Donald C., Shipwrecks of the Civil War, An Encyclopedia of Union and Confederate Losses. Donic Ltc. Washington D.C. San Luis Pass, burned by Union forces, blockade runner, sloop.*

Ship: *Flight* **Official Number:** Unknown
Date Lost: 1837 **Vessel Type:** Sailing Ship, Merchant
Sailing Rig: Brig **Flag:** USA
Length: Unknown **Beam:** Unknown **Tons:** Unknown
Cargo: Unknown **Cause of Loss:** Grounded
Source: *Rosenberg Library, S.M. Williams Collection. Letters: 23-1487 Balt. 6 Jan 1837; 23-1492 Quintana March 14 1837 (Sarah Williams) Brig Flight, Bought by Samuel M. Williams in Baltimore, sailing Baltimore to Galveston, 1837, Delayed by ice in Baltimore.*

Ship: *Saint Mary* **Official Number:** 23664
Date Lost: November 15, 1874 **Vessel Type:** Sailing Ship, Merchant
Sailing Rig: Schooner **Flag:** USA
Length: Unknown **Beam:** Unknown **Tons:** 28
Cargo: Lumber **Cause of Loss:** Storm
Source: *National Archives (NARA), Records of the US Custom Service, RG 39, Wreck Report, P. 1, October 31 1874. Cargo of lumber. Leaking and run aground. Cargo total loss. Vessel may have been salvaged.*

Ship: *Unknown* **Official Number:** Unknown
Date Lost: 1865 **Vessel Type:** Unknown
Sailing Rig: Schooner **Flag:** Unknown
Length: Unknown **Beam:** Unknown **Tons:** Unknown
Cargo: Unknown **Cause of Loss:** Unknown
Source: *Creamer and Alderdice. East of San Luis Pass*

Ship: *Lady of the Lake*   **Official Number:** Unknown
Date Lost: 1840   **Vessel Type:** Sailing Ship, Merchant
Sailing Rig: Schooner   **Flag:** Republic of Texas
Length: Unknown   **Beam:** Unknown   **Tons:** Unknown
Cargo: Unknown   **Cause of Loss:** Unknown
Source: *Texas Treasury papers, pp 367 & 368. Edited by S.V. Connor, Texas State Library. Wrecked west end of Galveston Island.*

Ship: *Ella Elliot*   **Official Number:** Unknown
Date Lost: August 21, 1886   **Vessel Type:** Sailing Ship, Merchant
Sailing Rig: Schooner   **Flag:** USA
Length: 37   **Beam:** 11   **Tons:** 442
Cargo: Unknown   **Cause of Loss:** Unknown
Source: *National Archives (NARA), RG 26, USCG, *89, Table of Casualty Reports from Life Saving Stations, 1876-1914, Annual Reports, US Life Saving Service. 442 tons, sailing Rockport Maine to Galveston with ice. 8 person aboard, all saved.*

Ship: *Zenobia*   **Official Number:** Unknown
Date Lost: 1882   **Vessel Type:** Sailing Ship, Merchant
Sailing Rig: Schooner   **Flag:** USA
Length: Unknown   **Beam:** Unknown   **Tons:** 79
Cargo: Lumber   **Cause of Loss:** Unknown
Source: *National Archives (NARA), RG 26, USCG, *89, Table of Casualty Reports from Life Saving Stations, 1876-1914, Annual Reports, US Life Saving Service. 79 tons, sailing Pascagoula to St Marys, TX with lumber. 6 person aboard, all saved.*

Ship: *Amelia*   **Official Number:** Unknown
Date Lost: 1899   **Vessel Type:** Sailing Ship, Merchant
Sailing Rig: Schooner   **Flag:** USA
Length: Unknown   **Beam:** Unknown   **Tons:** 18
Cargo: General Cargo   **Cause of Loss:** Unknown
Source: *National Archives (NARA), RG 26, USCG, *89, Table of Casualty Reports from Life Saving Stations, 1876-1914, Annual Reports, US Life Saving Service. Sailing Velaso to Galveston with general cargo, total loss, 7 persons aboard, all saved.*

Ship: *Flora S.*   **Official Number:** 120274
Date Lost: July 20, 1896   **Vessel Type:** Sailing Ship, Merchant
Sailing Rig: Schooner   **Flag:** USA
Length: 58   **Beam:** 14   **Tons:** 22
Cargo: General Cargo   **Cause of Loss:** Unknown
Source: *National Archives (NARA), RG 26, USCG, #89, Table of Casualty Reports from Life Saving Stations, 1876-1914, Annual Reports, US Life Saving Service. Sailing Galveston to Brazos River with general cargo. 2 persons aboard, both safe.*

Ship: *Josie*   **Official Number:** Unknown
Date Lost: April 14, 1893   **Vessel Type:** Unknown
Sailing Rig: Sloop   **Flag:** USA
Length: Unknown   **Beam:** Unknown   **Tons:** Unknown
Cargo: Unknown   **Cause of Loss:** Unknown
Source: *National Archives (NARA), RG 26, USCG, #89, Table of Casualty Reports from Life Saving Stations, 1876-1914, Annual Reports, US Life Saving Service. Sailing Brazos River to Galveston. Value of vessel $150, total loss. 2 persons aboard, both saved.*

Ship: *Kleeburg*   **Official Number:** Unknown
Date Lost: **Vessel Type:** Sailing Ship, Merchant
Sailing Rig: Schooner   **Flag:** USA
Length: Unknown   **Beam:** Unknown   **Tons:** Unknown
Cargo: Possibly treasure.   **Cause of Loss:** Unknown
Source: *Townsend, Tom. Texas Treasure Coast. Eakin Press, Burnet, TX. Wrecked off San Luis Pass; reporte to have carried treasure.*

Ship: *Arkansas*   **Official Number:** 274669
Date Lost: 1977   **Vessel Type:** Fishing Vessel
Sailing Rig: None   **Flag:** USA
Length: 61.6   **Beam:** 18.4   **Tons:** 64
Cargo: None   **Cause of Loss:** Ran Aground
Source: *Automated Wreck and Obstruction Information System (AWOIS), Wreck #320, LNM 11/77, F/V 61 ft, aground and breaking up 2 mi SW San Luis Pass. Owner Liberty Fish and Oyster Company, P.O. Box 267, Galveston, TX.*

Information from Steve Hoyt Marine Archeologist, Texas Historical Commission.

Recorded Hurricanes and Storms

1818	Hurricane
1837	Racer's Storm
1854	Hurricane
1895	Snowfall Valentine's Day February 14, 1895
1899	Galveston Bay Freezes Over
1899	Flood at Velasco, Texas
1900	1900 Storm
1909	Storm
1915	Disastrous Hurricane and Flood
1932	Hurricane
1961	Hurricane Carla
1965	Storm destroys portions of Vacek Bridge
1968	Storm Candy
1979	Tropical Depression Claudette
1983	Hurricane Alicia
1986	Hurricane Bonnie
1989	Hurricane Chantal
1998	Tropical Storm Frances
2003	Hurricane Claudette
2004	Snowfall Christmas Eve
2008	Hurricane Dolly
	Hurricane Edouard
	Hurricane Gustaz
	Hurricane Ike

Chapter One Endnotes

1. BCHM Accession Number 1983.052.0001 1910 Book – "Hammond's Handy Atlas of the World."

2. Hayes Galveston

3. Galveston, Tex. Nov 16, 1896, RESPECTFULLY FORWARDED WITH REPORT OF THIS DATE, A.M.Miller, Major, Corps of Eng'rs U.S.A, RESPECTFULLY SUBMITTED TO MAJOR A.M. MILLER, CORPS OF ENGINEERS, U.S.A. WITH MY LETTER OF AUG. 7TH 1896, WM GOODSON, 1ST LIEUTENANT, CORPS OF ENGINEERS U.S.A., Galveston Corp of Engineers.

4. Jamie Murray, Brazoria County Historical Museum.

5. *Handbook of Texas Online*, s.v.", Http://www.tsha.utexas.edu/handbook/online/articles/CC/fca6.html)accessed May 8,2007). *The Handbook of Texas Online* is a project of the Texas Site Historical Association (http://www.tshaonline.org).Copyright ©, The Texas Historical Association, 1997-2002, Last Updated: January 18, 2008

6. Only one other hurricane has ever struck during November in 1839, according to the National Ocean and Atmospheric Administration.

7. http://www.press.uchicago.edu/Images/Chicago/hnocmap12.gif1200x793-9xels

8. Carlos de Sigtlenza y Go'ngora, Dolph Briscoe Center for American History University of Texas at Austin

9. The Western Coast of Louisiana and The Coast of New Leon By Tho. Jefferys Geographer to his Majesty. London for Robert Sayer 20th Feb. 1775, Public Domain.

10. Spanish Map, Island of St Louis With Permission, David Rumsey Map Collection www.davidrumsey.com.

11.http://tides.sfasu.edu:2006/cgi-bin/getimage.exe?CISROOT-Newton&CISOP-TR-2719 (9/30/2007) *The Handbook of Texas Online* is a project of the Texas Site Historical Association, (http://www.tshaonline.org) Copyright ©, The Texas Historical Association, 1997-2002 Last Updated: January 18, 2008

12. Blaine Kern Artists, New Orleans, La., exclusive for Eileen M. Wagner

13. Texas State Archives Map Number 0424 Publisher: Tanner, H.S., Philadelphia, 1840. Engraved by John and William W. Warr, Philadelphia.Cartographer: Austin, Stephen F.Scale: 11/2 inches = 35 miles Size: 74 cm x 60 cm Type of map: gen Format: col/elp   Language: e Related Map/s: 409a-409c, Courtesy of Texas State Library and Archives Commission.

14 http://www.tsha.utexas.edu/handbook/online/articles/view/AA/fau12.html   (accessed April 30, 2007)*The Handbook of Texas Online* is a project of the Texas Site Historical Association, (http://www.tshaonline.org) Copyright ©, The Texas Historical Association, 1997-2002 Last Updated: January 18, 2008

15. Traced by W.L. Darnell *James Franklin and Stephen Perry Papers*, 1785-1942 Dolph Briscoe Center for American History University of Texas at Austin, Helm, Mary S. and Wightman, Elias R. *Scraps of Early Texas History*. Austin, Published by the author, 1884. Appendix, compiled from the writing and field notes of E. R. Wightman, first surveyor of the colony of Col. Stephen F. Austin: 137-195.

16. Traced by W.L. *Darnell James Franklin and Stephen Perry Papers*, 1785-1942 Dolph Briscoe Center for American History University of Texas at Austin, Helm, Mary S. and Wightman, Elias R. *Scraps of Early Texas History*. Austin, Published by the author, 1884. Appendix, compiled from the writing and field notes of E. R. Wightman, first surveyor of the colony of Col. Stephen F. Austin: 137-195.

17. El C. Jose Gomez De La Cortina Coronel del batallion del Comercia y Gobernado del Distrito Permission Cengage Learning, Robert E. Lester, Permissions Program Manager, Gale, Cengage Learning, April 24, 2009.

18. Made by order of the Mexican Government, By Alexander Thompson of the Mexican Navy in 1828, By David Burr, Map purchased by Eileen Wagner.

19. Stephen F. Austin's third colony establishment. Brazoria County Historical Museum Collection Map of the original town of VELASCO, TEXAS From an original tracing made in 1889E.D.D., Feb 27, 1934: Diazotype white print Accession Number 1997. 028c.0001

20. Her account is contained in *Reminiscences, 1816-1903.* Her personal papers collections can be obtained from The Virginia Historical Society, Call Number 21487.

21. http://mappinghistory.uoregon.edu/english/US/assets/US_15.1/map09.jpg"Copyright © University of Oregon, Mapping History Project. All Rights Reserved."

22. Santa Ana Gift from Judy Bielstein, Issac Hoskins grandfather John Henry married Andrew Glass Follett's daughter Lydia Wilson Follett.

23. Brazoria County Surveyors Field Notes. Acquired May 1. 2006.

24. Cruger & Moore, editor. *Telegraph and Texas Register* (Houston, Tex.), Vol. 2, No. 41, Ed. 1, Wednesday, October 11, 1837, Newspaper, October 11, 1837; digital images, (http://texashistory.unt.edu/ark:/67531/metapth47954/ : accessed September 06, 2012), University of North Texas Libraries, The Portal to Texas History, http://texashistory.unt.edu; crediting Dolph Briscoe Center for American History, Austin, Texas. (who was the holder of the scrip, after having acquired it from Thomas Toby), the application was made at New Orleans on August 10, 1836. Samuel May Williams, entrepreneur and associate of Stephen F. Austin was born in Providence, Rhode Island, Oct. 4 1795 and died September 13, 1856. He was very active in the impresario years and throughout his life. He left a wealth of history in the Galveston Area.

25. Borden & Moore, editor. *Telegraph and Texas Register* (Houston, Tex.), Vol. 2, No. 15, Ed. 1, Tuesday, May 2, 1837, Newspaper, May 2, 1837; digital images, (http://texashistory.unt.edu/ark:/67531/metapth47928/ : accessed April 15, 2014), University of North Texas Libraries, The Portal to Texas History, http://texashistory.unt.edu; crediting Dolph Briscoe Center for American History, Austin, Texas.

26. Dr. Cary Mock is a graduate of the University of Oregon (1994) and is currently an associate professor at the University of South Carolina in their Department of Geography. As a synoptic and paleoclimatologist, Dr. Mock's research links atmospheric patterns with climate variations (El Nino/Artic Oscillation in particular), and recently received a grant from the National Science Foundation to study climatic extremes during the 19th century. Featured in many professional publications, it is our pleasure to have Dr. Cary Mock join the Southwest Pennsylvania Chapter of the American Meteorology Society on Friday, November 3, 2006 in EST 110 at 2 PM.

27. Stan Blazyk is a weather expert and the author of *A Century of Galveston Weather: 1900-1999 People and the Elements on a Barrier Island.*

28. Vice President/Founder Hurricane Consulting Inc., Past President – The Houston Chapter of the American Meteorological Society• Founder and Former Chairperson – The DuPont Hurricane Roundtable & it's Coastal Severe Weather Alert Team, Chairperson – The National Hurricane Conference's Private Industry Committee, Awarded the National Hurricane Conference's "Outstanding Achievement Award," awarded the National Weather Service's Southern Region "Special Service Award," Awarded the DuPont "Safety Gold Cross," Awarded the DuPont AG-Products Chem Safety-Health-Environmental (SHE) Excellence Award, Member – The American Association for the Advancement of Science, Associate Member – The American Meteorological Society, Member – National Weather Association, Member – Texas Gulf Coast Emergency Management Association, Member – Emergency Management Association of Texas• Member – Galveston County Historical Commission.

29. Undocumented map from the vertical files, Brazoria County Historical Museum.

30. *Pleasant Places A Goodly Heritage* by Anne Ayers Lide McCurdy, Eakin Publications, 1982.

31. *James Franklin and Stephen Samuel Perry Papers*, 1785 – 1942, Dolph Briscoe Center for American History University of Texas at Austin.

32. James Franklin and Stephen Samuel Perry Papers, 1785 – 1942, Dolph Briscoe Center for American History University of Texas at Austin.

33. *Recollections of Stephen F. Austin*, by George L. Hammeken, San Luis, February 28th, 1844 as it is recorded in *The Southwestern Historical Quarterly*, University of Texas Center for American History, and the University of Texas at Austin.

34. Kennedy, William. Texas: *The Rise, Progress, and Prospects of the Republic of Texas.* In Two Volumes. London: R. Hastings, 1841

35. Texas and the Texans Or. Advance of the Anglo-Americans to the South-West; including a History By Henry Stuart Foote. 2 vols. Philadelphia: Cowperthwait, 1841; rpt

36. Plat - Brazoria County Court House.

37. A little more than a century later, in 1943, the United States War Department reported San Luis Island to be 300 acres. *Brazoria County Abstract, Undated Analysis* Brazoria County Historical Museum

38. James Franklin and Stephen Samuel Perry Papers, 1785 – 1942, Dolph Briscoe Cen-

ter for American History University of Texas at Austin.

39. Courtesy of the Rosenberg Library, Galveston, Texas.

40. Brazos Courier. (Brazoria, Tex.), Vol. 2, No. 10, Ed. 1, Tuesday, April 21, 1840, Newspaper, April 21, 1840; (http:// texashistory.unt.edu/ark:/67531/metapth80155/ : accessed July 17, 2015), University of North Texas Libraries, The Portal to Texas History, http://texashistory.unt.edu; crediting Dolph Briscoe Center for American History, Austin, Texas.

Chapter Two Endnotes

1. Dolph Briscoe Center for American History, University of Texas at Austin.

2. *The Daily News*, 1842-2002 April 11, 2002.

3. San Luis City Plat on Map 423. Walker, J. & C. The Coast of Texas, From Documents Furnished by W. Kennedy,Esq., H, M, Consul at Galveston-Information file, San Luis, Brazoria County Historical Museum.

4. Dolph Brisco Center for American History, University of Texas at Austin.

5. San Luis City Plat on Map 423. Walker, J. & C. The Coast of Texas, From Documents Furnished by W. Kennedy,Esq., H, M, Consul at Galveston-Information file, San Luis, Brazoria County Historical Museum.

6. Courtesy of the Rosenberg Library, Galveston, Texas

7. San Luis City Plat on Map 423. Walker, J. & C. The Coast of Texas, From Documents Furnished by W. Kennedy,Esq., H, M, Consul at Galveston-Information File, San Luis, Brazoria County Historical Museum.

8. San Luis City Plat on Map 423. Walker, J. & C. The Coast of Texas, From Documents Furnished by W. Kennedy,Esq., H, M, Consul at Galveston-Information File, San Luis, Brazoria County Historical Museum.

9. Memories and newspaper clipping are contributed by Mrs. Georgia Shannon of Velasco.

10. *San Luis Advocate*, Tuesday March 23, 1841 Dolph Briscoe Center for American History at Austin.

11. *San Luis Advocate*, Monday, September 14, 1840, Volume 1 –No 3 Dolph Briscoe Center for American History, University of Texas at Austin.

12. San Luis City Plat on Map 423. Walker, J. & C. The Coast of Texas, From Documents Furnished by W. Kennedy,Esq., H, M, Consul at Galveston-Information file, San Luis, Brazoria County Historical Museum.

13. San Luis Advocate, Tuesday March 23, 1841 Dolph Briscoe Center for American History, University of Texas at Austin.

14. San Luis Advocate, Aug 20, 1840, Dolph Briscoe Center for American History University of Texas at Austin.

15. *San Luis Advocate*, Aug 20, 1840, Dolph Briscoe Center for American History, Uni-

versity of Texas at Austin.

16. *San Luis Advocate*, Aug 20, 1840, Dolph Briscoe Center for American History, University of Texas at Austin.

17. *San Luis Advocate*, Aug 20, 1840, Dolph Briscoe Center for American History University of Texas at Austin.

18. *San Luis Advocate*, Aug 20, 1840, Dolph Briscoe Center for American History University of Texas at Austin.

19. *San Luis Advocate*, Aug 20, 1840, Dolph Briscoe Center for American History, University of Texas at Austin.

20. *San Luis Advocate*, Aug 20, 1840, Dolph Briscoe Center for American History, University of Texas at Austin.

21. Map by John Arrowsmith, 1790-1873, Map of Texas compiled from Surveys recorded in the Land Office of Texas, and other Official Surveys, Soho Square, London, 1841 Hand-colored copperplate engraving Courtesy of the Texas General Land Office.

22. *San Luis Advocate*, San Luis, Texas, March 16, 1841 Dolph Briscoe Center for American History, University of Texas at Austin.

23. *San Luis Advocate*, San Luis, Texas, March 16, 1841 Dolph Briscoe Center for American History, University of Texas at Austin.

24. Galveston County Corp. Of Engineers.

25. Early Surfside Landmarks : Prepared by AA Callihan Route 3, #231 Hudgins Dr. Village of Oyster Creek, Freeport Texas 77541 (photo by Jack Greenberg Studio, Lake Jackson, Texas) Furnished to me by Kathy Shaw 7/19/07.

26. The original canal would become part of "The Great Connection" from Florida to Brownsville, texas and what is known today as the Intracoastal Waterway.

27. Silhouette of Mary Austin Holley/Guitar Courtesy Transylvania University Library, Lexington, KY.

28. A Civil War-era map by Confederate engineer Tipton Walker (1864) depicted the Canal that provided shipping access between the Brazos River and West Bay. The Canal became a strategic asset to Confederate Texas, which relied on the cotton being transported through the Canal by blockade runners. The originals of the maps from which this figure is compiled are in the collections of the National Archives.

29. The following are two handwritten letters by Mary Austin Holley, which are now stored at the Dolph Brisco Center for American History, University of Texas at Austin.

30. *San Luis Advocate*, San Luis, Texas, March 16, 1841 Dolph Briscoe Center for American History, University of Texas at Austin.

Chapter Three Endnotes

1. *San Luis Advocate*, Dolph Briscoe Center for American History University of Texas at Austin.

2. Gifted to the author by Sybil Andrus 1795-1846.

3. To ensure that the ferry was responsibly operated, Congress passed an act, approved January 14, 1843th Congress., R.S. 1843 Repub. Tex. Law 19. Reprinted in 2 *H.P.N. Gammel, The Laws of Texas 1822-1897*, at 839 (Austin, Gammel Book Co. 1898).

4. The United Kingdom Hydrographic Office came into being in August 1795, because the Admiralty had lost eight ships between 1793 and 1795, due to running aground. Great Britain. Admiralty. The Coast of Texas from documents furnished by W. Kennedy Esq. H.M. Consulate Galveston. Brazoria County Historical Museum

5. The progress on the canal inspired an even grander vision. The Interstate Inland Waterway League, now the Gulf Intracoastal Canal Association, was founded in 1905 by Clarence St. Elmo Holland and others. This was to be an 18,000-mile water transportation system running from the Great Lakes through the Mississippi, to Texas and Louisiana. By 1841, the system was extended to Corpus Christi, and by 1949 it already had been enlarged. *History of the Gulf Intracoastal Waterway*, Volumes 83-89 of Navigation history NWS, Lynn M. Alperin, National Waterways Study (U.S.) Galveston Corp of Engineers

6. *The Texas Times*, Galveston Texas, Nov 16, 1842, Dolph Briscoe Center for American History

7. Courtesy of the Rosenberg Library, Galveston, Texas

8. Civil War - War of the Rebellion for Follett's as mail carriers

9. http://www.senate.state.tx.us/CHBook/Facts.htm (accessedMay 6, 2007)

10. James Franklin and Stephen Samuel Perry Papers, 1785 – 1942

11. James Franklin and Stephen Samuel Perry Papers, 1785 – 1942, Dolph Briscoe Center for American History University of Texas at Austin.

12. San Luis City Plat on Map 423. Walker, J. & C. The Coast of Texas, From Documents Furnished by W. Kennedy,Esq., H, M, Consul at Galveston-Brazoria County Historical Museum

13 . An 188 report of the U.S. Army Corp of Engineers regarding that channel of water, refers to Little Pass as Follett's Pass.

14. *Pleasant Places a Goodly Heritage* by Anne Ayers Lide McCurdy. Eakin Publications, 1942 Page 32

15. Hayes/Galveston in Two Volumes

16. San Luis City Plat on Map 423. Walker, J. & C. The Coast of Texas, From Documents Furnished by W. Kennedy,Esq., H, M, Consul at Galveston-Brazoria County Historical MuseumBrazoria County Historical Museum Map is owned by Eileen Wagner, Sketch 1, No. 4 Preliminary Chart of San Luis Pass, Texas, From a Trigonometrical Survey under the direction of A. D. Bache, Superintendent of the Survey of the Coast of the United States, Triangulation by James S. Williams Assistant, Topography by J. M. Wampler Sub-Asst, Hydrography by the Party under the command of H. S. Stellwagen Lieutenant U. S. Navy Published in 1853.

Chapter Four Endnotes

1. Map is owned by Eileen Wagner; Sketch 1, No 4; Preliminary Chart of San Luis Pass, Texas; From a Trigonometrical Survey under the direction of A.D. BACHE, Superintendent of the SURVEY OF THE COAST OF THE UNITED STATES; Triangulation by James S. Williams Assistant; Topograsphy by J.M. Wampler Sub-Asst; Hydrography by the Party under the command of H.S. STELLWAGEN Lieutenant U.S. Navy Published in 1853

2. United States Congressional Serial Set ANNUAL Report of the National Board of Health, 437 .

3.David Roth, National Weather Service, Meteorologist–Forecaster, NWS/ HPC Forecast Operations Branch.

4. Courtesy of Rosenberg Library, Galveston Texas.

5. *Pleasant Placed A Goodly Heritage*, Anne Lide McCurdy, Copyright 1982 By Eakin Publications.

6. Alexander Glass Follett, Compiled in 1974 by Lewis Hall Follett, age 83 and edited by Mrs. Addie Hudgins Follett, age 98.

7. Stephen F. Austin Abstract 29, Brazoria County Tax Office.

8. Gross Appraisal, Dated April 9, 1943, file: Bombing and machine gun target range, Galveston Army Air Force Base, Subgroup G-4-Property Acquisition records of the Galveston District Office. Record Group 77-. Records of the Corps of Engineers, in the SW Region (Fort Worth) National Archives and Records Administration.

Chapter Five Endnotes

1. *The Official Atlas of the Civil War* by U.S. WAR DEPT., George B Davis, Leslie J. Perry, Joseph W. Kirkley, Calvin D. Cowles (Compiler) Creator, Jeremy Francis 1818-1883, A map of the coast of Texas and its defenses, drawn under the direction of Captain Tipton Walker, Chief of Topographical Bureau of Texas, New Mexico and Arizona, by P. Helferich, Assistant Engineer (hand-drawn and colored).

2. Following letters: *The Official Atlas of the Civil War* by U.S. WAR DEPT., George B Davis, Leslie J. Perry, Joseph W. Kirkley, Calvin D. Cowles (Compiler) Creator, Jeremy Francis 1818-1883, A map of the coast of Texas and its defenses, drawn under the direction of Captain Tipton Walker, Chief of Topographical Bureau of Texas, New Mexico and Arizona, by P. Helferich, Assistant Engineer (hand-drawn and colored).

3. www.texas-settlement.org/markers/brazoria/97.html.

4. Alexander Glass Follett. Compiled in 1974 by Lewis Hall Follett, age 83, and edited by Mrs. Addie Hudgins Follett age 98.

5 The *New York Times*, Published October 26, 1863 Copyright © The *New York Times* Public Domain Per NY Times 3/23/09 Blockade Runners in the Gulf Coast.

6. Blockade Runners Brazoria County Historical Museum Vertical Information Files, Acadia folder.

7. This 1870 Map of Texas counties; Accession Number 1988.096c.0003 Brazoria County Historical Museum Sept. 09, 2008 2:10 PM CDTS. Augustus Mitchell "County Map of Texas." Phila. 1870. Colored 10 ½ X 13 ¼ published in *Mitchell's New General Atlas* in Philadelphia in 1870. Pg 143.

8. Brazoria County Historical Museum Collection Accession 1986.015p.0029.

9. Curator Michael Bailey has provided from Brazoria County Historical Museum Archives Collection, a photo of the painting of the Hiawatha by Don Hutson. (1986.003c.0001).

10. Brazoria County Historical Museum 2002.016p0005.

11. *Clippings From a Scrapbook* by J. P. Underwood, East Columbia, Texas possibly in 1916 Underwood Family Papers, 1834-1924, Herzstein Library, San Jacinto Museum of History.

12. *1899 Spofford's New Cabinet Cyclopaedia*, Published by the Gebbie Publishing Co., Ltd, 1899 in Portfolia of Maps of *Spofford's New Cabinet Cyclopaedia* updated/by 09/14/2006 09:13 AM Brazoria County Historical Museum.

13. John Phillips to Sayers, July 6, 1899/ Records of Joseph Draper Sayers, Texas Office of the Governor, archives and information Services Division. Texas State Library and Archives Commission.

14. *Pleasant Places A Goodley Heritage*, Anne Ayers Lide McCurdy, Eakin Publications 1982 43, 44.

15. *Pleasant Places A Goodley Heritage*, Anne Ayers Lide McCurdy, Eakin Publications 1982.

16. Seining The Pass USCG-Gallaway, Courtesy of the United States Coast Guard.

17. Gift from Judy Willy Bielstein.

18 Roth, David. *Texas Hurricane History*. National Weather Service, Lake Charles, LA, 2010.

19. Brazoria County Abstract, 2006.26C Map stored at Brazoria County Historical Museum.

20. Courtesy of the Gallaway Collection USCG, Courtesy of the United States Coast Guard.

21. Information gifted by Timothy Dring: CDR,USNR (Retired) Robbinsville, NJ.

22. Annual Report of the United States Life-Saving Service Published by Gov. Print. Off., 1911 Page 31.

23. Information gifted by Timothy Dring: Commander, United States Naval Reserve (Retired) Robbinsville, NJ.

24. 1985.040p0001 ~ Photographic Print Brazoria County Historical Museum.

25. Courtesy Brazoria County Historical Museum 2004.005p.004.

26. Roth, David. *Texas Hurricane History*. National Weather Service.

27. With permission, Gary Cartwright, *Galveston, A History of The Island*, 209, April 14, 2009.

28. Progressive Military Map of the United States Department of Texas 1916-1918, Brazoria County Historical Museum.

29. *Freeport Facts* map, Brazoria County Historical Museum, Library information files, filed under Brazoria County Maps.

30. With Permission: Bertha McKee Dobie, *The Legends of the Salt Marshes (San Luis Pass, Brazoria County)*. *Legends of Texas*, J. Frank Dobie, ed. Publications of the Texas Folklore Society, no. 3. Dallas: Southern Methodist University Press, 1924, 143.

31. Hennell Stevens Brazoria County historical MUSEUM 1996.003P0001 Oct.28, 1832 - July 9, 1895.

32. Frank W. Stevens photo Gift from Eleanor Steven Vaughn, Feb. 27, 1859 - Dec. 30, 1928.

33. Frank K. Stevens photo Gift from Eleanor Steven Vaughn; Sept. 24, 1885 - Jan 1, 1975.

34. Brazoria County Historical Museum 1983.006.0003.

Chapter Six Endnotes

1. Forts of Texas- Wikipedia: Text is available under the Creative Commons Attribution-ShareAlike license; additional terms may apply. By using this site, you agree to the terms of use and Privacy Policy. Wikipedia(R) is a registered trademark of the Wikimedia Foundation, Inc. a non-profit organization.

2. *Guns of Quintana* by Garvin Germany and Michael J. Bailey.

3 . *Guns of Quintana* by Garvin Germany and Michael J. Bailey.

4. National Oceanic And Atmospheric Administration.

5. Galveston Bay & Approaches No 1282; August 22, 1936 Audobon Society; K-6-1292c; General Land Office File.

6. Photo's gifted from Steve Roberts.

7. National Oceanic And Atmospheric Administration.

8. 2007.010c001 ~ Map Brazoria County Historical Museum Collection.

9. Robert L. Wright, The *West Columbia Light*, 6/2/09.

10. The *Houston Press*, August 19, 1940; Houston Chronicle Publishing Company Reprinted with permission All rights reserved.

11. Eleanor Stevens Vaughn 1916 - 2015.

12. The *Brazosport Facts*, January 30, 1972, reported a portion of a beached wale about five miles Northeast of the jetties on Surfside. Sharks had already eaten about half before it washed ashore. Texas A&M researchers found forty-one sperm whales in Octo-

ber of 1996 (*Physeter macrocephalus*) living off the Mississippi Delta. They also noted ten whale groups.

13. *The Facts*, Clute, Texas All Rights reserved "The Facts," Brazoria County newspaper.

14. National Oceanic And Atmospheric Administration.

15. Gross Appraisal, Dated April 9, 1943, file: Bombing and machine gun target range, Galveston Army Air Force Base, Subgroup G-4-Property Acquisition records of the Galveston District Office. Record Group 77-. Records of the Corps of Engineers, in the SW Region (Fort Worth) National Archives and Records Administration.

16. Gross Appraisal, Dated April 9, 1943, file: Bombing and machine gun target range, Galveston Army Air Force Base, Subgroup G-4-Property Acquisition records of the Galveston District Office. Record Group 77-. Records of the Corps of Engineers, in the SW Region (Fort Worth) National Archives and Records Administration.

17. Gross Appraisal, Dated April 9, 1943, file: Bombing and machine gun target range, Galveston Army Air Force Base, Subgroup G-4-Property Acquisition records of the Galveston District Office. Record Group 77-. Records of the Corps of Engineers, in the SW Region (Fort Worth) National Archives and Records Administration.

18. Gross Appraisal, Dated April 9, 1943, file: Bombing and machine gun target range, Galveston Army Air Force Base, Subgroup G-4-Property Acquisition records of the Galveston District Office. Record Group 77-. Records of the Corps of Engineers, in the SW Region (Fort Worth) National Archives and Records Administration.

19. Gross Appraisal, Dated April 9, 1943, file: Bombing and machine gun target range, Galveston Army Air Force Base, Subgroup G-4-Property Acquisition records of the Galveston District Office. Record Group 77-. Records of the Corps of Engineers, in the SW Region (Fort Worth) National Archives and Records Administration.

20. National Oceanic And Atmospheric Administration.

21. Texas General Land Office.

22. National Oceanic And Atmospheric Administration.

23. Fishing Camp at San Luis, glossy photo from The Facts Newspaper, Brazoria County Museum cropped and enlarged by computer. Reprinted with permission, The Facts, clute, Texas, All rights reserved, September 2, 1952.

24. National Oceanic And Atmospheric Administration.

25. National Oceanic And Atmospheric Administration.

26. National Oceanic And Atmospheric Administration

27. Texas General Land Office.

28. Brochure gifted by Keith Chunn.

29. Brochure gifted by Keith Chunn.

30. *Island News*, Aug. 21. 1954 Reprinted with Permission, The Facts, Clute, Texas All Rights reserved.

31. *Island News*, Aug. 21. 1954 Reprinted with Permission, *The Facts*, Clute, Texas All Rights reserved.

32. Gifted from Keith Chunn.

33. *Island News*, Aug. 21. 1954 Reprinted with Permission, *The Facts*, Clute, Texas All Rights reserved   Brazoria County Historical Museum.

34. National Oceanic And Atmospheric Administration.

35. Aerials provided by Nat Hickey, Mikro, Inc., Freeport Texas   Photographer Bill Schlig.

36. Aerials provided by Nat Hickey, Mikro, Inc., Freeport Texas   Photographer Bill Schlig.

37. Aerials provided by Nat Hickey, Mikro, Inc., Freeport Texas   Photographer Bill Schlig.

Chapter Seven Endnotes

1. Aerials provided by Nat Hickey, Mikro, Inc., Freeport Texas Photographer Bill Schlig 5/30/1968.

2. Brazoria County Court House.

3. *The Freeport Facts/ Brazoria County Museum.

4. In 2008, Hurricane Ike completely demolished it. The pilings were removed with no remaining sign of such a wonderful recreation spot so many people for 45 years.

5. Aerials provided by Nat Hickey, Mikro, Inc., Freeport Texas Photographer Bill Schlig.

6. U. S. Army Engineer Permit No. 5803 for San Luis Corporation, Lamar Golding: April 12, 1963.

7. With permission Army Corp of Engineers Galveston Texas.

8. Welcome Wilson, Sr. Collection.

9. Welcome Wilson, Sr. Collection.

10. Welcome Wilson, Sr. Collection.

11. Welcome Wilson, Sr. Collection.

12. Welcome Wilson, Sr. Collection.

13. Brazoria County Historical Museum Library Information Files, San Luis folder (enclosure in history report Treasure Island by Kathy Nutt).

14. Welcome Wilson, Sr. Collection.

15. Ken Nutt Collection.

16. Ken Nutt Collection.

17. Photo Gifted to me by Doug Lowry.

18. Keith Chunn, Jr., Collection.

19. *The Freeport Facts*, Oct 8, 1942.

20 . Welcome Wilson, Sr. Collection.

21. Mary Cannon Photo.

22. Photo gifted by Gaylen Purett, San Luis Pass Fishing Pier 5/12/2005.

23. Aerials provided by Nat Hickey, Mikro, Inc., Freeport Texas Photographer Bill Schlig Aerial 2758.

24. Welcome Wilson, Sr. Collection.

25. Platt Section II Treasure Island Resort community Brazoria County Court House.

26. Welcome Wilson, Sr. Collection.

27. Mary Cannon Photo.

28. Aerials provided by Nat Hickey, Mikro, Inc., Freeport Texas Photographer Bill Schlig.

29. Aerials provided by Nat Hickey, Mikro, Inc., Freeport Texas Photographer Bill Schlig.

30. Aerials provided by Nat Hickey, Mikro, Inc., Freeport Texas Photographer Bill Schlig.

31. Aerials provided by Nat Hickey, Mikro, Inc., Freeport Texas Photographer Bill Schlig.

32. Aerials provided by Nat Hickey, Mikro, Inc., Freeport Texas Photographer Bill Schlig.

33. Aerials provided by Nat Hickey, Mikro, Inc., Freeport Texas Photographer Bill Schlig.

34. Aerials provided by Nat Hickey, Mikro, Inc., Freeport Texas Photographer Bill Schlig.

35. Aerials provided by Nat Hickey, Mikro, Inc., Freeport Texas Photographer Bill Schlig.

36. Welcome Wilson, Sr. Collection.

37. Aerials provided by Nat Hickey, Mikro, Inc., Freeport Texas Photographer Bill Schlig..

38. E-mail response to me from Sam Guiberson, second owner August 22, 2004.

39. Mary Cannon Photo.

40. Author's conversation with Red Miller, June 27, 2005.

41. Paula Carroll Photo.

42. Texas General Land Office, Austin Photo 2004.

43. The *Brazosport Facts* (newspaper), Brazoria County Historical Museum.

44. Sandscripts, Welcome Wilson Sr. Collection.

45. Sandscripts, Welcome Wilson Sr. Collection.

46. Brazoria County Historical Museum, Original from The *Freeport Facts* Newspaper.

47. Photo taken by Lt. Col. Bill Cannon.

48. Aerials provided by Nat Hickey, Mikro, Inc., Freeport Texas Photographer Bill Schlig.

49. Welcome Wilson, Sr. Collection.

50. Welcome Wilson, Sr. Collection.

51. Welcome Wilson, Sr. Collection.

52. Welcome Wilson, Sr. Collection.

53. Welcome Wilson, Sr. Collection.

54. Harry Bowles files.

55. At present, he serves his second term as Chairman of the University of Houston Board of Regents.

Chapter Eight Endnotes

1. Brazoria County Court House.

2. Photo gifted to me by Judge Robert Lowry July 2004.

3. Aerials provided by Nat Hickey, Mikro, Inc., Freeport Texas Photographer Bill Schlig Aerial Negative 4080 5/30/1968.

4. This tract was recorded in Vol. 855, Pg. 340 and dated the 3rd day of April, 1967. Brazoria County Court House.

5. Aerials provided by Nat Hickey, Mikro, Inc., Freeport Texas Photographer Bill Schlig Neg 4085 5/30/1968.

6. Aerial provided by Nat Hickey, Mikro, Inc., Freeport Texas Photographer Bill Schlig 4002 5/30/1968.

7. Mickie McCunn Collection.

8. Aerials provided by Nat Hickey, Mikro, Inc., Freeport Texas Photographer Bill Schlig No.4019 5/30/1968.

9. Aerials provided by Nat Hickey, Mikro, Inc., Freeport Texas Photographer Bill Schlig 4020; 5/30/1968.

10. Photo by Eileen Benitz Wagner.

11. Mary Cannon Photo.

12. Brazoria County Historical Museum collection 2007.010c001.

13. Welcome Wilson, Sr., Collection March 8, 1971.

14. Fred Placke quote, August 10, 2004.

15. Welcome Wilson, Sr., Collection.

16. Mary Cannon Collection.

17. Mary Cannon Collection.

18. Mary Cannon Collection.

19. Keith Chunn, Jr. Collection.

20. Keith Chunn, Jr. Collection.

21. Paula Carroll Collection.

22. Cindy Boyd Photography.
23. Harry Bowles file Wildlife Sanctuary.

24. Mickie McCunn Collection.

Chapter Ten Endnotes

1. Lester Kamin File Sec IV1.

2. Mary Cannon Photo.

3. Gumbo photo by Eileen M.Benitz Wagner.

4. Photo by Eileen M. Benitz Wagner.

5. Photo by Eileen M. Benitz Wagner

6. *The Facts* Newspaper Michael Booty Photographer; Citing Approval 9/10/2012 Brazoria County Historical Museum.

7. Photo by Eileen M Benitz Wagner.

8 . Photo By Eileen M Benitz Wagner.

9. Photo by Eileen M. Brnitz Wagner

10. Mary Wagner Photo.

11. Paula Carroll Photo.

12. Photo by Eileen M. Benitz Wagner.

13. Johnny Calzada Photo.

14. Photographer J. Stern Ueckert of The Houston Chronicle with approval.

15. Section IV Eileen Wagner file.

16. 1988 Texas General Land Office File Photo.

17. Eileen M Benitz Wagner file.

18. Copyright 1988 Houston Chronicle Publishing Company. Reprinted with permission. All rights reserved.

19. Community photos saving Gulf Beach Drive.

20. Photo by Eileen M. Benitz Wagner.

21. Jim Fulmore photo.

22. Photo by Eileen M. Benitz Wagner.

23. Texas General Land Office, Austin Aerial Aug 8, 2002.

Chapter Eleven Endnotes

1. Photo by Eileen M. Benitz Wagner.

2 Brazoria County Emergency Management Collection located at the Brazoria County Historical Museum.A Brazoria County Historical Museum Photo Group Accession No 2012.017p.

3. Texas General Land Office, Austin 2003 Aerial Photo.

4. Photo by Eileen Benitz Wagner.

5. Several years later, a representative of the engineering firm who designed the project told Ms. Newsom that the geotextile tube project located in TI was a "pilot project."

6. Photo by H. J. McCunn.

7. Texas General Land Office, 2004 Aerial Photo.

8. Linda Strickland photo.

9. Caron Dobbs photo.

10. Eileen M. Benitz Wagner photo.

11. By this, I mean a layer that is at most a few-hundred meters thick, which is thin compared with the depth of the water in the deep ocean." The "Norther" cold front the following day added to the push of debris to the South, which may explain why 200 boats ended up in Mexico, including mine.

12.http://oceanworld.tamu.edu/resources/ocng_textbook/chapter09/chapter09_02. htm Accessed September 26, 2008 NOAA.

13. Photo By Eileen M. Benitz Wagner.

14. Internet photo.

15. Cindy Boyd Photography.

16. Cindy Boyd Photography.

17. Photo by Eileen M. Benitz Wagner.

Index

Author Bio

Eileen M Benitz Wagner has devoted her business career to product design, manufacturing, and national sales for the wholesale floral, nursery and mass merchant markets throughout the United States. As an owner of a small business, each category demands unlimited attention.

The late 1990s took her to the agricultural field and the growing of newly planted wine grapes. During this period she traveled to the wine grape regions of France, Canada, Chile, Argentina and Australia seeking additional information to improve her product.

A founding member of the International Pirates, (a charity entertainment group from across America) that began in the middle 1980s, she sang and danced to warm the hearts of elderly, special needs children, Shrine Burn Hospital patients and all she met as a Lady Pirate. "It is giving something back. We say it is putting a little color in black and white worlds when nothing but pain is in sight."

Her love of history and having lived at Treasure Island, San Luis Pass, Texas since 1981 became her passion to save this portion of Texas history which has never been written.

She lives in The Woodlands, Texas near her family. One daughter lives in Dallas and the other lives in Spring, Texas.